Trevor Brown.

Rigorously researched and written with both clarity and passion, Bethany Sollereder's new book makes a highly creative contribution to a significant and much neglected debate. It will be a vital resource for researchers and students alike.
— Christopher Southgate, Professor of Christian Theodicy,
University of Exeter, UK

A thoughtful, original and important exploration of an important theological topic. Dr Sollereder opens up some of the most challenging questions arising from Darwin's theory of evolution, and offers fresh insights and perspectives to her readers.
— Alister McGrath, Andreas Idreos Professor of
Science and Religion, University of Oxford, UK

In this engaging book Sollereder is "joining a conversation" on evolutionary theodicy that has now spanned a decade or more. She does so with aplomb, with new insights, coherence, courage, and with lively and intelligent interactions with her peers. Spanning a wide theological horizon, Sollereder delves deep into the issues of divine action, the goodness and freedom of creation, the problems of evolutionary suffering, God's temporality, kenosis, passability and above all God's love for all of creation. Hers is an account that sees humanity as uniquely capable of love, as uniquely transcending the natural inclinations of the evolutionary process, and God as having loving and saving intentions for all creatures.
— Nicola Hoggard Creegan, co-director, New Zealand Christians in
Science and author of *Animal Suffering and the Problem of Evil*

This is a ground-breaking study which faces fearlessly the implications of believing that God creates through the process of evolution, with the consequent suffering caused to animals. Rejecting any explanations which rely on a single-point, historic fall of the universe the author develops a highly original alternative account, taking seriously the meaning of the love of a creator God, that all theologians will need to take a view on. At times provocative, always clear, expert, readable and interesting, this is essential reading for all who want to continue writing theodicies in the modern era of biological science.
— Paul S. Fiddes, Professor of Systematic Theology,
University of Oxford, UK

Instead of providing food for doubt, Sollereder argues that evolutionary science leads us in the opposite direction, towards a richer and more inspiring account of a loving, ever-present God. This book doesn't indulge in the platitudes that so often beset this area, but instead grapples with the problems with sobriety and realism. For all those who have worried, like Darwin, that the world is simply too cruel for religious optimism, Sollereder provides a robust alternative. This book will surely become the go-to resource for this most intractable of all theological problems.

– Mark Harris, Senior Lecturer in Science and Religion,
University of Edinburgh, UK

God, Evolution, and Animal Suffering

After the publication of *On the Origin of Species* in 1859, theologians were faced with the dilemma of God creating through evolution. Suddenly, pain, suffering, untimely death, and extinction appeared to be the very tools of creation, and not a result of the sin of humanity. Despite this paradigm shift, the question of non-human suffering has been largely overlooked within theodicy debates, overwhelmed by the extreme human suffering of the twentieth century. This book redresses this imbalance by offering a rigorous academic treatment of the questions surrounding God and the suffering of non-human animals.

Combining theological, philosophical, and biblical perspectives, this book explores the relationship between God and Creation within Christian theology. First, it dismantles the popular theological view that roots violence and suffering in the animal kingdom in the fall of humanity. Then, through an exploration of the nature of love, it affirms that there are multiple reasons to suggest that God and creation can both be "good," even with the presence of violence and suffering.

This is an innovative exploration of an under-examined subject that encompasses issues of theology, science, morality, and human-animal interactions. As such, it will be of keen interest to scholars and academics of religion and science, the philosophy of religion, theodicy, and biblical studies.

Bethany N. Sollereder is a Postdoctoral Research Fellow at the University of Oxford, UK in the Faculty of Theology and Religion. She is a fellow of the International Society for Science and Religion and of the Royal Society of Arts. She has written for a number of journals and magazines, including *Zygon*, *Theology & Science*, and *The Christian Century* and she is a regular contributor to the BioLogos website.

Routledge Science and Religion Series

Series editors:
Michael S. Burdett,
Wycliffe Hall, University of Oxford, UK

Mark Harris,
University of Edinburgh, UK

Science and religion have often been thought to be at loggerheads but much contemporary work in this flourishing interdisciplinary field suggests this is far from the case. The Science and Religion Series presents exciting new work to advance interdisciplinary study, research, and debate across key themes in science and religion. Contemporary issues in philosophy and theology are debated, as are prevailing cultural assumptions. The series enables leading international authors from a range of different disciplinary perspectives to apply the insights of the various sciences, theology, philosophy, and history in order to look at the relations between the different disciplines and the connections that can be made between them. These accessible, stimulating new contributions to key topics across science and religion will appeal particularly to individual academics and researchers, graduates, postgraduates, and upper-undergraduate students.

Science and the Truthfulness of Beauty
How the Personal Perspective Discovers Creation
Robert Gilbert

Against Methodology in Science and Religion
Recent Debates on Rationality and Theology
Josh Reeves

Interreligious Perspectives on Mind, Genes and the Self
Emerging Technologies and Human Identity
Edited by Joseph Tham, Chris Durante and Alberto García Gómez

God, Evolution, and Animal Suffering
Theodicy without a Fall
Bethany N. Sollereder

For more information and a full list of titles in the series, please visit: www.routledge.com/religion/series/ASCIREL

God, Evolution, and Animal Suffering

Theodicy without a Fall

Bethany N. Sollereder

LONDON AND NEW YORK

First published 2019
by Routledge
2 Park Square, Milton Park, Abingdon, Oxon OX14 4RN

and by Routledge
52 Vanderbilt Avenue, New York, NY 10017

Routledge is an imprint of the Taylor & Francis Group, an informa business

British Library Cataloguing-in-Publication Data
A catalogue record for this book is available from the British Library

Library of Congress Cataloging-in-Publication Data
Names: Sollereder, Bethany N., author.
Title: God, evolution, and animal suffering : theodicy without a fall /
    Bethany N. Sollereder.
Description: Abingdon, Oxon ; New York, NY : Routledge is an imprint
    of the Taylor & Francis Group, an Informa Business, 2019. | Series:
    Routledge science and religion series | Includes bibliographical
    references and index.
Identifiers: LCCN 2018039398 (print) | LCCN 2018045323 (ebook) |
    ISBN 9780429466519 (e-book) | ISBN 9780429881862 (PDF) | ISBN
    9780429881855 (ePub) | ISBN 9780429881848 (Mobi) |
    ISBN 9781138608474 (hardback : alk. paper)
Subjects: LCSH: Creationism. | Evolution (Biology)—Religious
    aspects—Christianity. | God (Christianity—Goodness. | Pain—Religious
    aspects—Christianity. | Suffering—Religious aspects—Christianity. |
    Violence—Religious aspects—Christianity. | Animal welfare—
    Religious aspects—Christianity.
Classification: LCC BT695 (ebook) | LCC BT695 .S65 2019 (print) |
    DDC 231/.8—dc23
LC record available at https://lccn.loc.gov/2018039398

ISBN: 978-1-138-60847-4 (hbk)
ISBN: 978-0-429-46651-9 (ebk)

Typeset in Times New Roman
by Apex CoVantage, LLC

This work is dedicated in loving memory of
Gail Laidlaw Stevenson (1936–2018)
"It is all about the journey."

Contents

Acknowledgements

I first started thinking about animal suffering and evolution in 2007 and have pursued the topic through a Master's degree and a PhD. Working on this topic has spanned two continents, four cities, and eight houses. This is by way of apologising for not being able to acknowledge all the people who have contributed to the making of this book – there is not room to name you all, but know that I am so very grateful.

I want to thank Christopher Southgate, whose superb supervision and continued friendship have kept this project alive. My thanks to the examiners of the PhD out of which this project grew: Niels Gregersen and David Tollerton. I want to thank those who have read and commented on the full manuscript: Loren Wilkinson, Paul Fiddes, and Sarah Williams. My grateful thanks go to Becca Hawkins for help with transcribing Hebrew in the second chapter. I am also extremely grateful to my "patrons," those whose support in friendship and housing have enabled me in so many ways to continue my work: Christy Hildebrand, Melodie Storey, Margaret Brunette, and Diana Gee. My thanks also to Laura Cummings for proofreading.

To the faith communities that have provided a patient audience, allowing me to try out various arguments, especially Kitsilano Christian Community Church, Isca Church in Exeter, and St Mary Magdalen's in Oxford. My thanks go to the work colleagues and fellow academics here in Oxford, particularly the TWCF crowd, the community at Regent's Park College, and Alister McGrath.

My heartfelt thanks also goes to my students who have so often been my teachers. Your passion and interest and impossible questions are what keep me motivated.

I am grateful to Joshua Wells for his help in walking through the editorial process, as well as to the two Science and Religion series editors Mark Harris and Michael Burdett, for comments on the manuscript. I am also grateful for the comments of the three anonymous peer reviewers, whose comments helped expand the scope of the work. Any remaining problems are entirely my fault.

I am grateful to my family, mom, dad, and the whole extended Sollereder clan, for their unstinting support in my odd endeavours across the pond. I am grateful also to the Salladin clan for creating a second home in England for me.

Finally, I have dedicated this book to Gail Stevenson, who inspired and supported so much of the heart that went into this book. She always stressed the importance of the journey, and gently taught by her example to wait in the questions rather than rush in with answers. Rest in peace, and rise in glory.

1   Leaving the courtroom

Every night thousands of non-human animals meet a grisly end. They are pierced, stung, strangled, and torn apart piece by piece. In our day of ecological crisis, we might expect this description to be yet another human atrocity acted upon the non-human world, whether of deforestation or the cruelties of intense farming practices. But the suffering I am describing has no human involvement at all and precedes human existence by hundreds of millions of years.

In order to survive, creatures compete for limited resources. Those who cannot draw enough energy from the sun, or lack the means of converting light energy into sustenance, must consume one another. Every reader of these words has committed themselves to this exchange: killing and eating other living beings (whether plant or animal) in order to survive.

Charles Darwin's insight was that it is precisely the competitive nature of creatures fighting for limited resources that brings about evolutionary change. In Darwin's own celebrated words:

> Thus, from the war of nature, from famine and death, the most exalted object which we are capable of conceiving, namely, the production of the higher animals, directly follows. There is grandeur in this view of life, with its several powers, having been originally breathed into a few forms or into one; and that, whilst this planet has gone cycling on according to the fixed law of gravity, from so simple a beginning endless forms most beautiful and most wonderful have been, and are being, evolved.[1]

Natural selection operates by allowing the victors in the war of nature to live long enough to reproduce and pass on their inherited advantages, while those who lose the competition die without progeny – taking their disadvantages with them. From a systemic view, this seems a neat and tidy affair. At the level of the individual, it is a never-ending struggle: a constant battle against starvation and predation, parasite and disease. Where is God's goodness in such a system? Could a loving God really use such bloodstained methods to create? If God is omnipotent, why did God not simply create creatures "according to their kinds," rather than allow a natural process to painfully and wastefully chisel diverse species out of an initial form? For the theologian, two major problems exist when faced with non-human suffering in evolutionary process.

First, the strongest Christian explanations for suffering – freewill and soul-making approaches – do not apply easily to the non-human world.[2] The world was full of violence and suffering long before there were humans around to sin; long before a human "fall" could have corrupted non-human behaviour.[3] Nor, as far as most scholars are concerned, are non-human animals spiritually formed and improved through the suffering they encounter.[4] They cannot draw near to God in consequence of suffering, and do not (so far as we know) have the conscious decision to respond to suffering in the complex and redemptive ways that a human might. Non-human animal pain in evolutionary process is excluded from the strongest Christian theodicies.

Second, creation through evolution is problematic when considered in light of God's nature. One of the primary claims of Christian believers is that the invisible God is most fully revealed in the person of Jesus Christ.[5] "God is love," writes John, "God's love was revealed among us in this way: God sent his only Son into the world so that we might live through him."[6] The nature of God's love is revealed in Jesus. Jesus defended the weak and powerless, healed the sick, calmed the violent storm, and defeated death. Evolution, by contrast, sets creatures against each other and privileges the strong, the violent, and the healthy. I do not mean to overstate the case: evolution also contains altruism, symbiosis, and cooperation of various kinds, but even these alliances between creatures must compete against other alliances for ever-scarce resources.[7] Though evolutionary theory has developed a great deal since Darwin's day – with the addition of genetics in the 1940's up to the current work on the Extended Evolutionary Synthesis with its multiple sources of inherited variation – none of the changes have seriously displaced the major role of competition and death in evolutionary process.[8] The process, in turn, jars uncomfortably against the nature of God revealed in Jesus Christ. It does so most pointedly when the suffering of individuals is considered. How is God's love expressed in the intense suffering of a young fawn, brought down by a predator or, worse still, accidentally burnt alive in a forest fire?[9] The question arises: "Is the project of creation worth the risk of even one innocent creature who suffers and dies in agony?"

In this book, I plan to explore the disjunction between the God of love and creation through the violence, suffering, and untimely deaths imposed upon so many creatures in the course of evolutionary history. I want to argue that evolution is the process by which God has created the world, and that the violence and suffering inherent in the process can be both contextualised and redeemed in light of the creative suffering of God. However, this book will not be a typical theodicy, where I lay out several specific reasons that account for the suffering we see in nature. Instead, it is far more of an exploration of the God-world relationship in which the suffering of animals is a coherent part of the created landscape. I will spend far less time talking about specific instances of suffering and their justification, and far more time talking about the nature of love, the risk of creation, the ongoing work of God, and the promise of redemption.

The nature of this work

Is this book a "theodicy" or a "defence"? In the debate about these terms, it is usually agreed that a theodicy intends to give specific purposes why God allows evil,[10] while a defence sets the less ambitious goal of simply trying to show that genuine evil and God's existence are not logically incompatible. Peter van Inwagen explains, "the difference between a defense and a theodicy lies not in their content but in their purposes. A theodicy is a story that is told as the real truth of the matter; a defense is a story that, according to the teller, may or may not be true" but which entails either logical consistency or epistemic possibility.[11] Will this be a defence or a theodicy? It is not an easy question to answer, because my approach does not fit comfortably into either category.

I *do* attempt to say true things about God's relationship to the created world, and God's relationship to the suffering that occurs amongst non-human creatures. As such, my work may deserve to be called a theodicy. However, when I think and write about God, I am fully aware that I cannot comprehend the reality of God. Even the basic physical realities of the world are far more complex than any one human could hope to understand. Add to this the mystery of suffering and I could happily agree with Darwin's statement, "I feel most deeply that the whole subject is too profound for the human intellect. A dog might as well speculate on the mind of Newton."[12] So although I may try to say true things, and give actual reasons stemming from my understanding of Scripture, Christian tradition, reason, and experience for why God might allow suffering and use death in creating, I cannot insist that my description of these things is certainly true. Does my hesitancy about certainty make this work a defence? I hesitate at that term too.

Defences, by and large, are written to convince the sceptics of theism that the Christian faith is possibly true. The visual metaphor of the defence is the courthouse. In van Inwagen's words, the one offering a defence produces "reasonable doubts by presenting to juries stories that entail their clients' innocence."[13] It is up to the defence lawyer – the apologist – to deconstruct the accusations set against the divine defendant and to secure a verdict of "not guilty" from the panel of unbiased, sceptical jurors.

I do not intend to pursue such a project. I do not intend to stay in the courtroom making cases, but to head out into the fields and forests, to observe and to join a conversation of other thinkers and writers who wonder about what sort of God we find in an evolutionary world. I think this difference in setting and tone is one of the major distinctions between the philosophical work of theodicy and the theological work of theodicy. The difference will be more fully examined in Chapter 3. Perhaps the safest course would be to describe this book as an exploration of theology relating to suffering and creation, rather than a traditional theodicy or defence.[14] I will use the term "theodicy," but I am less interested in giving ten good reasons God allows suffering than I am in understanding how our models of the relationship between God and creation are challenged and changed by a steady gaze at evolution's suffering past. The goal is not to tie up all the intellectual loose ends that suffering in the world presents us, but to find theological language that helps one feel grounded in light of the challenge of an evolutionary creation.

Perhaps a visual image is the easiest way to portray the spirit of this project.

Imagine the practice of theology as the work of a cartographer drawing a large map of the world. The theologian attempts to accurately represent the world we live in, drawing the contours and contexts of our wandering explorations of reality. The task is especially challenging because the theologian even tries to represent the dynamic (and often invisible) work of God: as difficult as drawing the unpredictable and ever-changing winds. Out of the mapping endeavour come various theological systems that hold coherence and help find a path through numerous philosophical and existential quagmires. I am not searching for water-tight reasons, so much as trying to trace a weight-bearing path.

My guiding question throughout the book will be: "How could a good and loving God create through an evolutionary process that involves so much suffering, death, extinction, and violence?" I do not offer logically incontrovertible reasons for why God allows suffering, but I invite the reader to join an exploration of theological models that, in the words of fellow-explorer Christopher Southgate, "arise out of protest and end in mystery."[15]

Why should we walk this path? My own inspiration for writing comes from those I have seen struggle with the concept of evolution. People who are ready to accept the scientific evidence for the long history of the world and the slow change of organisms that inhabit it baulk at the method of change. Indeed, Darwin himself wrote, "What a book a Devil's chaplain might write on the clumsy, wasteful, blundering low & horridly cruel works of nature!"[16] To accept an evolutionary history forces a re-evaluation of the world we inhabit, and perhaps of our notions of God as well. The world familiar in its benevolence and loveliness becomes suddenly alien in its ubiquitous pain and violence. The disorientation this causes can be profound. I hope this book will allow some approaches that can reorient a theology that includes evolution.

But this is not just a book for those new to evolution. It is for all those who do not know how the violence and suffering of the world can be held together with the love and goodness of God. Traditional theology once drew a familiar map.[17] It stated that God created a perfect and peaceable world. Then humans (particularly Adam and Eve) ruined the whole perfect scene with their sin, and now we live in a profoundly broken world characterised by the previously unknown elements of violence, death, and suffering. But using the fall as an explanation is, I will argue, no longer a plausible way forward. Evolutionary evidence suggests that the world was only free from death and competition when it was also free from life. The complexity, interrelatedness, and beauty of life are directly related to the ever-present violence, death, and extinction of numberless creatures. In an evolutionary world, there is a new ecology of exchange amongst organisms, a new set of connections between creatures and God, and a new role for death. A new theological map is needed, with new pathways. And new maps may require new definitions and new terms as well. To those we now turn.

Natural evil

The first and most important definition is of the central term "natural evil." Natural evil is normally defined over and against moral evil, which is harm caused by free moral agents choosing evil.[18] We might simplify the distinction as between "wicked" and "harmful." However, the term "natural evil" can tend to slide between these two meanings because of the traditional narrative of the fall. The fall narrative, which will be discussed at much greater length in later chapters (particularly 2 and 3), tells of a perfect creation where there was nothing that was either wicked or harmful – no evil in either sense. From that perfection there was a "fall" due to sin. In that fall event, due to the entrance of moral wickedness, there was, in the words of Michael Lloyd, "a hiatus on the line from the way God intended things to the way things are now, a fall away from God's creational purposes."[19] In this narrative the harms of predation and lightning strikes, of parasites and hurricanes, were never intended by God to be part of world history. Thus, natural evil (harm) represents moral *evil* (wicked) since natural evil (harm) only came about due to sin. So John Calvin could say:

> All the evils of the present life, which experience proves to be innumerable, have proceeded from the same fountain. The inclemency of the air, frost, thunders, unseasonable rains, drought, hail, and whatever is disorderly in the world, are the fruits of sin. Nor is there any other primary cause of diseases.[20]

In Calvin, natural evil was due to, and part of, moral evil. Calling it natural *evil*, then, was singularly appropriate.

However, for thinkers such as Christopher Southgate, Niels Gregersen, John Polkinghorne, Arthur Peacocke, Daryl Domning, Monika Hellwig and others, these same realities of violence and natural disaster are not evil.[21] Disvalues and harms are part of God's "very good" world, although they cause death and suffering.[22] The difference between the terms "natural evil" and "disvalue" is one of origins. If evolutionary violence emerged due to a force opposing God or has moral content, then natural evil is the appropriate term. If violence and other harmful realities are an intrinsic and necessary part of God's good creation, then disvalues is the more precise term. Southgate calls this difference of perspective a "key fault-line" in the debate of evolutionary theodicy.[23] However, this distinction of terms is not universally observed. Many authors use the term natural evil to refer to both harm and evil while others use the terms natural evil and disvalue interchangeably. Since I am arguing against the fallenness of the natural world (though not of humans), I will join those who use the term "disvalue" to discuss the suffering in the deep time of evolutionary history. When quoting those who do not make such a distinction, I will simply try to make the difference clear whenever possible.

"Fallenness"

Fallenness is another ambiguous term. The entire notion of a "fall" fosters a belief that there was initially a height achieved from which a fall was possible. If there was no original and perfect height from which to fall, this terminology does not make much sense. Life floated, swam, and crawled along history's timeline, ever diversifying and multiplying. While I hesitate to invoke the notion of progress (as if the world were always becoming a better place), life has clearly become immeasurably more complex, more skilled, and more interdependent than it was when it started. Life forms have also grown in their capacity to suffer. Intelligence and affective abilities are part of the ever-increasing complexity, and these add to the problem of theodicy. Yet, I maintain that the world is "unfallen," that the suffering experienced in evolutionary process was within the boundaries of God's creative intent. How can I refrain from calling the world "fallen" when creatures use their skills and abilities to harm one another, and to pursue desires that are so different from the peaceable and loving nature of God? Ultimately, it is because the harms are not antithetical to God's purposes. The harms suffered by creatures are not beyond the scope of redemption, and the very same desires that motivate creatures to harm one another also serve as the foundations, the raw ingredients, of love.

Drawing on the work of Andrew Elphinstone,[24] I will argue that love is a particular divine act in the person that transmutes the basic evolutionary desires into the desires of divine love. Insofar as this is true, the basic evolutionary desires are necessary to fulfil part of creation's ultimate aim. Aggressive, protectionist, and selfish desires are ingredients every bit as potent in the brewing of love as desires that are altruistic or self-giving. I do not think that one moves from selfishness to altruism to love on a single line, as if love were merely being better at altruism. Love is a transformation of the spectrum of desires entirely. As such, all evolutionary desires, whether the lion seeking the death of the gazelle, or orcas desiring violent play with baby seals, are part and parcel of God's intention to form a loving creation. Until there is the capacity to transform natural desires into love, the existence of these desires is not a sign of fallenness. In this approach, the love-echoing desires expressed in evolutionary altruism and cooperation are not "better" than the violent and selfish desires. Both are necessary and both need to be transformed. Despite the great amounts of suffering caused by the desires of disvalue, the non-human world is not fallen. It is simply immature.

"Flourishing" and "Selving"

How are disvalues to be judged? A standard cannot be found for what constitutes a disvalue unless we have a concept of what is considered good. Throughout this book, I will use the key concepts of "flourishing" and "selving" as measures for evaluating harms and disvalues at the level of the individual. Flourishing refers to the overall well-being of an individual creature, similar to the biblical notion of "shalom." Flourishing is not just basic health, but includes relational well-being. A flourishing creature is in proper relationship to other members of its own species, members of other species, to environmental conditions, to God, and to the stage of life it is in. This relational component might lead to some counterintuitive results, such as after a full life and in light of the new creation, a creature's best flourishing at a particular moment may be to die.

Closely linked to flourishing – and an aid to clarifying what is meant by flourishing at any given moment – is the concept of "selving." Gerard Manley Hopkins coined the term, and it has been used in theodicy most extensively by Southgate. Consider Hopkins's poem "As kingfishers catch fire":

> As kingfishers catch fire, dragonflies draw flame;
> As tumbled over rim in roundy wells
> Stones ring; like each tucked string tells, each hung bell's
> Bow swung finds tongue to fling out broad its name;
> Each mortal thing does one thing and the same:
> Deals out that being indoors each one dwells;
> Selves – goes itself; *myself* it speaks and spells,
> Crying *Whát I dó is me: for that I came.*
>
> I say móre: the just man justices;
> Keeps gráce: thát keeps all his goings graces;
> Acts in God's eye what in God's eye he is –
> Chríst – for Christ plays in ten thousand places,
> Lovely in limbs, and lovely in eyes not his
> To the Father through the features of men's faces.[25]

In Hopkins's thought, each creature "selves" as it acts "*myself*" through deeds of its own characteristic expression. The diving kingfisher or the darting dragonfly alight in the dawn rays are simply doing what kingfishers and dragonflies do, but in doing so they are acting in God's eyes what in God's eyes they are. Southgate links Trinitarian creativity to this self-proclaiming, self-creating creaturely behaviour. He writes:

> When a living creature 'selves' in the sense of Hopkins's kingfishers, behaving in its most characteristic way, and flourishing in doing so, it is conforming to the pattern offered by the divine Logos, the pattern of that type of selfhood imagined by the divine Word, and begotten in the Spirit out of the perfect self-abandoning love of the Father.[26]

A creature "selves" when it behaves in "its most characteristic way." I do not follow Southgate's approach entirely when it comes to the idea that the gift of God is the pattern of the species. At best, the concept of species-level characteristics are always an approximation. In a species, there will be shared characteristics, yet there are also characteristics unique to each individual. Thus, selving is some combination of acting in the received common inheritance and innovating on that gift. Through innovation, new characteristic behaviours can be established. In these innovations, creatures can develop new ways of being in the world that are not under divine control. Rather, they are actions arising out of the desires of the creature combined with the opportunities of the environment. So, perhaps it would be better to speak of the gift of community and genetic inheritance that creatures are born into which confer regular ways of being, rather than a sense of Platonic "pattern" to which creatures are meant to conform.

The South Georgia pintail, for example, is a plain-looking brown duck that lives across several islands near Antarctica. Exposed to the harsh temperatures and confronted with the scarcity of usual food sources, the pintail has developed a survival technique unique amongst the dabbling ducks: it will make a feast of any large animal remains it can access, plunging its whole head into the carcass in a way typical of vultures or petrels.[27] For the pintail, scavenging meat has become part of its process of selving and of its flourishing, yet this uncommon behaviour likely would have begun when a bold and hungry individual seized upon an uncommon opportunity.[28] For that individual, the process of selving took it beyond the normal pattern of its species, into a self-transcendence that is also part of flourishing.[29] That carnivorous way of being in the world has now become the species norm, but it emerged out of the individual using its agency to explore new ways of being. Flourishing, then, has a fluid definition depending on the particularities of the individual, its environment, inter- and intra-species relationships, and stage of life. Most of the time, however, a common-sense definition of flourishing will serve the reader well: a creature diminished by parasites and disease, or killed in early life, does not flourish. A creature that lives a long life and is successful in terms of procuring food, safety, and offspring has flourished.

It is a problem that each creature's flourishing often depends on the death and lack of flourishing of many other creatures. The lion flourishes at the expense of the antelope. The parasite flourishes at the expense of the host. Yet, within the providence of God, I hope to suggest that the loss of flourishing of many creatures is not inconsistent with the love of God, and that the love of God is constantly at work to bring redemption in each and every instance of suffering.

The path

The path I will explore begins with the Bible. Does my position, of upholding the unfallen goodness of the natural world, contradict the teachings of Scripture? The second chapter will try to answer this question. This chapter stands apart from the later chapters that form one long argument about the nature of the world and divine action. The argument in this chapter is simple: the biblical witness does not require the assumption that disvalues such as suffering and death entered the world due to human or Satanic sin. Since the Reformation the most popular place to pin the argument that disvalue is due to sin is in the curse narrative of Genesis 3, and later in Romans 8. For readers who take the Bible seriously as a necessary source of theological knowledge, it is important to know that the Bible does not forbid the sort of argument I will make in the later chapters. Therefore, the task of Chapter 2 is not to understand what the Bible says about evolutionary suffering, but to show that the Bible does not unambiguously teach a cosmic fall narrative.

First, I argue against the various views that teach that a cosmic fall is found in the Bible. Then I explore the theme of the curse that winds its way through Genesis 3–9, and I seek to show that the curse laid on the land in Genesis 3 was not immutable, but rather was lifted after the flood narrative. The Hebrew Bible knows nothing of the fallenness of the natural world apart from direct human action. I go on to address the key passage of Romans 8 that might seem to strongly imply that the natural world is inherently fallen, and argue that even here, what is on offer is not the cosmic fall of Milton or Calvin, but a frustration of creation along the lines of a symphony performance being disrupted by one section of instruments being out of tune. Even if the rest are in tune, their performance is ruined.

The third chapter begins the exploration of theological and philosophical positions in theodicy. I will use the organisational structure of Southgate and Robinson's "Good-Harm Analyses" to show how philosophical and then theological thinkers have outlined and tried to solve the problem of non-human animal suffering before me. There are significant differences between the philosophical and theological debates in presuppositions, methods, and audience. Analytic philosophy approaches argue that there are always outweighing goods to be found that account for natural disvalues: goods of property-consequence, developmental, or constitutive types.[30] Many of these approaches seek to show either that the harms experienced by non-human animals are necessary for some other essential and greater good, or that there is simply no alternative to the present state of affairs in light of the values God desires in creation. Ultimately, these approaches conclude with compound defences: strategies that combine more than one good-harm analysis into a whole that is intended to be stronger than any one consideration.

I then draw out the differences between philosophical and theological theodicy: differences in audience and purpose. The contrast between the "courtroom" and the "exploration" has already been set out earlier, and is drawn out in reference to the literature, with a particular focus on philosophical work that bridges the divide. I contrast theological approaches that "solve" the problem of suffering by either redefining God or denying creation's integrity, to the approaches that embrace the tension of Love's creative suffering.

The last part of the third chapter explores the theological offerings that have been put forward. Fall narratives, kenotic approaches, freedom-based solutions, divine creative co-suffering, and redemption are explored, culminating in wide-scope cosmological narratives that wrap suffering into a seamless theological narrative. The chapter as a whole provides a panorama of recent work, and should be useful to those who are learning about the debates in theodicy for the first time. But there is yet another reason to spend a good long time listening to the conversation that has been happening. That has to do with the fact that this project is not a courtroom presentation with one approach that is meant to triumph over all the others. Readers may (and no doubt will) disagree with my approaches, and so the time spent in exploring other paths will provide options for people who do not take my view.

Chapter 4 begins the proper development of my own theodical approaches. I begin with divine love and the nature of freedom. Instead of starting with an example of suffering, and then asking: "How could this possibly be worth it?" I begin instead by asking, "how does love create?" Based on a Thomist definition of love, read through the lens of W. H. Vanstone's classic work *Love's Endeavour, Love's Expense*, I argue that love's essential nature is non-controlling, particular, vulnerable to suffering, and responsive to the needs of the beloved. As such, the path of God's love for creation leads to a world marked by radical freedom and careful divine interaction. Traditional accounts of freewill have been heavily anthropocentric, and I attempt to work out what freedom for the non-human world entails in light of the two desires of love: the desire for the good of the beloved and the desire for union with the beloved. God's love leaves room for creatures to develop towards their own good, the good of the ecosystem they participate in, and in the ultimate history of the world. I explore further the sense that this freedom is part of the narrative of suffering in a world without considering the effects of fallenness. Creatures can explore violent and harmful ways of being in the world that don't reflect God's loving nature, yet still rest within the overall purposes of God's intentions of creation. Still, freedom is not sufficient to account for suffering if considered alone. If love is the reason God created through a process marked by radical risk and freedom, there remains the question of how God will respond to and heal the pains suffered by those who are the losers in evolution's processes.

In Chapter 5, I will carry forward the basic conclusions of the particularity of love from Chapter 4 into an argument concerning divine action. In light of God's love, how is God at work in the world? Giving freedom is not enough. I propose a four-fold model of divine action that includes the gift of being, God's presence in suffering, divine lure towards the good, and divine participation in creation through embodiment and meaning-making. My work in this chapter departs from the regular "science and religion" focus on the mechanism of divine action ("how God acts") and turns instead towards the character and effect of divine action ("why God acts"). Yet, this chapter is limited to God's work here and now and stands incomplete without a sense of the final completion of creation.

The sixth chapter will explore the nature of the final work of God in redemption. I will argue that redemption is radically individual as well as communal, and that it combines the personal and universal narratives of history into a coherent and redemptive whole in such a way that each creature individually inhabits and participates in the good of the whole. The glories of redemption never occur "at the cost" of an individual, and the seemingly senseless events that have no coherence when they occur can be forged into meaningful events by the eschatological work of God. I use the image of a fractal mosaic (pictures where each pixel is itself a picture) to illustrate the reciprocal relations of redemption.

The overall goal is not to defend or justify God against attacks, but to paint a picture of God and the world that incorporates the suffering and the joy, the death and the life, the loss and the redemption that is revealed through investigation of the natural world and the Christian story. It is a theological reflection on scientific knowledge, a journey of *fides quearens intellectum*.[31]

Notes

1 Charles Darwin, *On the Origin of Species: By Means of Natural Selection, or the Preservation of Favoured Races in the Struggle for Life* (London: John Murray, 1859), 490.

2 Some have tried to apply elements of both to the non-human world. These perspectives will be explored in Chapter 2.

3 William Dembski attempts to maintain the link between human sin and non-human suffering by postulating a retroactive application of the effects of the fall on the pre-human creation. His views are critiqued in Chapter 3, 67–68.

4 There are exceptions to this, such as David Clough, but the majority of theologians do not think soul-making arguments can be properly applied to the non-human world.

5 Colossians 1:15.

6 1 John 4:8b–9. NRSV.

7 For more on altruism and cooperation in evolution, see Martin A. Nowak and Sarah Coakley, eds., *Evolution, Games, and God: The Principle of Cooperation* (Cambridge, MA: Harvard University Press, 2013).

8 For an accessible overview of current evolutionary theory, see Sy Garte, "New Ideas in Evolutionary Biology: From NDMS to EES," *Perspectives on Science and Christian Faith* 68:1 (March 2016): 3–11.

9 William Rowe famously challenged theism on what he considered the senseless suffering of a fawn caught in a forest fire. William L. Rowe, "The Problem of Evil and Some Varieties of Atheism," *American Philosophical Quarterly* 16:4 (October 1979): 335–341.

10 Richard Swinburne, *Providence and the Problem of Evil* (Oxford: Clarendon Press, 1996), 39; Alvin Plantinga, *God, Freedom and Evil* (Grand Rapids, MI: Eerdmans, 1977), 10–12, 27–28.

11 Peter van Inwagen, *The Problem of Evil: The Gifford Lectures Delivered in the University of St Andrews in 2003* (Oxford: Clarendon Press, 2006), 7. C.f. Plantinga, *God, Freedom and Evil*, 28. Michael Murray also proposes the category of "De Causa Dei" or the case made for a defendant in court to prove their innocence in light of charges made. *Nature Red in Tooth and Claw: Theism and the Problem of Animal Suffering* (Oxford: Oxford University Press, 2008), 40.

12 Charles Darwin to Asa Gray, "Letter 2814," 22 May 1860, The Darwin Correspondence Project. Online: www.darwinproject.ac.uk/letter/entry-2814.

13 van Inwagen, *The Problem of Evil*, 7.

14 Christopher Southgate describes his own excellent book on evolutionary suffering as "an exploration of models of the triune God in relation to creation and of what that means for humans. Above all it is an exploration in theodicy, posing the question, how can God be understood as good, just, and loving in a world full of suffering?" *The Groaning of Creation: God, Evolution, and the Problem of Suffering* (Louisville, KY: Westminster John Knox, 2008), x.

15 Southgate, *The Groaning of Creation*, 16.

16 Charles Darwin to J. Hooker, "Letter 1924", 13 July 1856, The Darwin Correspondence Project. Online: www.darwinproject.ac.uk/letter/entry-1924.

17 See Christopher Roedell, "The Beasts That Perish: The Problem of Evil and the Contemplation of the Animal Kingdom in English Thought, c. 1660–1839," (PhD Dissertation, Georgetown University, 2005), Chapter 2.

18 Murray, *Nature Red in Tooth & Claw*, 73.

19 Michael Lloyd. "Are Animals Fallen?" In *Animals on the Agenda*. Edited by Andrew Linzey and Dorothy Yamamoto, 147–160 155. London: SCM Press, 1998.

20 John Calvin, "Commentaries upon the First Book of Moses called Genesis (1554)," in *Calvin's Bible Commentaries: Genesis*, Part I, trans. J. King (London: Forgotten Books, 1847, 2007), 113.

21 Southgate, *Groaning of Creation*, 28–31; Arthur Peacocke, *Theology for a Scientific Age: Being and Becoming – Natural, Divine, and Human* (Minneapolis, MN: Fortress Press, 1993), 222; Daryl Domning and Monika Hellwig, *Original Selfishness: Original Sin and Evil in Light of Evolution* (Burlington, VT: Ashgate, 2006), 76.
22 See especially Southgate, *Groaning of Creation*, 2.
23 Christopher Southgate, "Re-Reading Genesis, John, and Job: A Christian Response to Darwinism," *Zygon* 46:2 (June 2011): 370–395, 378.
24 Andrew Elphinstone, *Freedom, Suffering & Love* (London: SCM Press, 1976).
25 Gerard Manley Hopkins, *Poems and Prose*, ed. Helen Gardner (London: Penguin, 1953, 1963), 51.
26 Southgate, *Groaning of Creation*, 63.
27 David F. Parmelee, *Bird Island in Antarctic Waters* (Minneapolis, MN: University of Minnesota Press, 1980), 69–81.
28 Jablonka and Lamb write of this sort of innovation: "A new behavior can be initiated by a lucky or curious individual who learns by trial and error, or by observing individuals of another population or species, and once acquired it may be transmitted to other members of the group through social learning. But what is learned and transmitted depends on the ability of an individual to select, generalize, and categorize information relevant to the behavior." See Eva Jablonka, Marion J. Lamb, and Anna Zeligowski, *Evolution in Four Dimensions: Genetic, Epigenetic, Behavioral, and Symbolic Variation in the History of Life*, revised ed. (Cambridge, MA: MIT Press, 2014), 169–170. A more recent and more well-studied phenomenon of this type (where genetic change was ruled out as a cause) was the spread of milk-thieving behaviour amongst great tit birds in the UK. Tits learned that glass milk bottles delivered to doorsteps contained a tasty treat if they could find a way to remove the tinfoil top. Various methods were found to succeed and the practice spread quickly across populations and even across avian species until the humans changed their behaviour and stopped delivering milk in foil-topped bottles.
29 Southgate's interest in "selving" also allows a unique view of fallenness: a creature is fallen when it does not embrace the divine invitation to transcendence and therefore remains what it is. In this notion of fallenness, it is potential that is lost rather than acquired characteristics.
30 See Christopher Southgate and Andrew Robinson, "Varieties of Theodicy: An Exploration of Responses to the Problem of Evil Based on a Typology of Good-Harm Analyses," in *Physics and Cosmology: Scientific Perspectives on the Problem of Natural Evil*, eds. Nancey Murphy, Robert J. Russell, and William R. Stoeger, S. J. (Vatican City and Berkeley, CA: Vatican Observatory, CTNS, 2007), 67–90.
31 St Anselm's phrase, usually translated "faith seeking understanding."

2   The Bible and The Fall

Introduction

Central to a Christian understanding of the world is the account of Scripture. The way the Bible is read is of central importance to any theodicy, or any description of the world whatsoever, within a Christian worldview. An exploration of theodicy and the natural world, then, cannot proceed without at least a glance at biblical concerns.

An exegetical exercise can have at least two aims. It can try to dismantle a reading that is commonly held, or it can try to establish the positive meaning of text. This chapter will only attempt the former, while leaving a few hints toward the latter aim. Genesis 1–9 has been extensively explored, and I can cover only a small fraction of what has been written about it. To speak positively about its meaning would necessitate an extensive study that is beyond the scope of this book to provide. However, it is still worth looking at the biblical material for the sake of dismantling popular readings that have more to do with cultural habits than with the text itself. In particular, I want to argue against the reading that finds a justification for the theology of a cosmic fall in the curse language of Genesis 3:17–19 – a universal curse on the natural order that has corrupted God's good world allowing the presence of death, suffering, competition, and violence amongst animals.

While almost no contemporary theologian endorses the notion that death and violence first entered the world through human sin because of the chronological issues involved,[1] a growing contingent of theologians point to the corrupting influence of Satan or some other shadowy spiritual reality as the origin of disvalues in nature.[2] This is particularly attractive within the U-shaped interpretation of the Christian meta-story as a journey of "creation-fall-redemption." In this chapter I aim to show that the fallenness of the natural world is not a concept that can be derived from the opening chapters of Genesis. Rather, apart from human sin and its direct effects, the world remains God's "very good" creation. It is not "fallen" in the sense of being wicked, corrupted, or unable to bring about God's good intentions, and the realities of death and suffering are not unambiguously condemned as irreconcilable with God's goodness.

A note on terminology: the term "fall" is elusive as there are several different meanings of "fall" that can be intended. I will explore in Chapter 3 how there are both event-based fall theories and mysterious fallenness theories.[3] "Event-based" fall theories usually refer to the "human fall" and the "satanic fall." The human fall, sometimes called the "relational fall," refers to the event that marks the entrance of sin into the world through human action.[4] The effect of the human fall is the severing of harmonious relationship between human persons and God, between one person and other people, and between humans and the non-human creation. However, apart from the direct result of sinful human action in the world, such as pollution or exploitation of natural resources, the human fall does not independently affect the wider cosmos but only humans and their relationships. In the same way, the satanic fall refers to the event of some of the heavenly host deciding to rebel against God, and becoming fallen angels. The satanic fall was primordial, meaning that it was in effect from the very origin of physical creation.[5]

Closely linked to these two fall events is the "cosmic fall."[6] The cosmic fall refers to the effects of sin on the wider cosmos, but independent of the direct action of the sinful party, either human or angelic. It defines the concept that when either humans or angels fell, the rest of the cosmos was pulled down from an original perfection or uncorrupted state, and made subject to natural evil. Yet, these evils are usually not related to the direct action of the agents in the way that demonic possession, for example, or human environmental degradation would be.[7] Instead, these natural evils – such as death, pain, predation, and suffering – entered the non-human creaturely experience as part of the punishment for human or angelic sin.

I think these are important to distinguish because although they are conceptually distinct they are often conflated. Most historical Christian thinkers accepted a primordial satanic fall, but did not think that a cosmic fall occurred because of .it.[8] Contemporary advocates of a satanic fall, including Gregory Boyd, Paul Griffiths, Michael Lloyd, and Stephen Webb, usually link the satanic with a cosmic fall. I accept both a satanic and a human fall,[9] but I do not think there ever was a cosmic fall: a conclusion I argue for in this chapter. If it can be shown that the non-human creation is considered uncorrupted at any point in real history by the Scriptural accounts, the primordial fall theories will face a serious challenge.

The cosmic fall in scripture

Historically, looking for natural evil in a cosmic fall due to human sin was *not* the default position of the early church, despite the possible reading of such thought in Paul's writings. Athanasius, for example, wrote:

> Nothing in creation had erred from the path of God's purpose for it, save only man. Sun, moon, heaven, stars, water, air, none of these had swerved from their order but, knowing the Word as their Maker and their King, remained as they were made. Men alone having rejected what is good, have invented nothings instead of the truth, and have ascribed the honor due to God and the knowledge concerning Him to demons and men in the form of stones.[10]

Likewise, when Augustine wrote about the curse in Genesis 3, he made a distinction between the bare existence of thorns growing in a field, and thorns growing in the fields "to" humans in a way that would afflict them. He wrote:

> Concerning thorns and thistles, we can give a more definite answer, because after the fall of man God said to him, speaking of the earth, Thorns and thistles shall it bring forth to you. But we should not jump to the conclusion that it was only then that these plants came forth from the earth. For it could be that, in view of the many advantages found in different kinds of seeds, these plants had a place on earth without afflicting man in any way. But since they were growing in the fields in which man was now laboring in punishment for his sin, it is reasonable to suppose that they became one of the means of punishing him. For they might have grown elsewhere, for the nourishment of birds and beasts, or even for the use of man.
>
> Now this interpretation does not contradict what is said in the words, Thorns and thistles shall it bring forth to you, if we understand that earth in producing them before the fall did not do so to afflict man but rather to provide proper nourishment for certain animals, since some animals find soft dry thistles a pleasant and nourishing food. But earth began to produce these to add to man's laborious lot only when he began to labor on the earth after his sin. I do not mean that these plants once grew in other places and only afterwards in the fields where man planted and harvested his crops. They were in the same place before and after: formerly not for man, afterwards for man.[11]

Augustine thought that it was only the subsequent state of affairs of thorns growing "to" humans that was due to the curse placed on the ground in Genesis 3:17–19. Augustine even allowed for orderly predation before the human fall, since "one animal is the nourishment for another," and he argued for orderly decomposers, thus presuming the existence of death.[12] In contrast, later in the history of interpretation emerged the now more recognisable interpretation of the curse on the ground as a cosmic fall, introducing death to the whole of the created order for the first time.

The history of how the doctrine of the cosmic fall has grown and developed from the scant text in Genesis and a few New Testament references to a defining understanding of the natural world in Western thought is long and interesting,[13] but the primary intention of this chapter is to investigate the Scriptural support for this notion. I hope to show the curse laid down in Genesis 3 is lifted after the flood narrative, and therefore any possible cosmic curse associated with the human fall was only temporary. The world, apart from humans, remains the "very good" creation of God.

Genesis 1: The very good creation

Why did pre-human animals suffer in the evolutionary process? Those theologians who hold to a primordial fall maintain that it is because the pre-human world was already corrupted or otherwise compromised. Thus, although God never intended their suffering, they were caught up in a cosmic struggle as unfortunate casualties. Thomas Oord, Gregory Boyd, and Stephen Webb, in particular, claim that hints of the primordial fall are found in Genesis 1.[14]

The Hebrew Scriptures begin with the world pictured as a watery depth. "The earth was a formless void and darkness covered the face of the deep (*tĕhôm*), while a wind from God swept over the face of the waters."[15] This deep, this *tĕhôm*, is common to the creation myths of other ancient Near Eastern (ANE) mythologies.[16] Instead of a creation described *ex nihilo*, the "formless and void" (*tōhû wābōhû*) nature of this watery world does not picture a lack of material existence, but rather describes a place that is uninhabitable, or unusable, like a desert wasteland.[17] The absolute origins of matter are not a primary concern for the author of Genesis.[18] Norman Habel writes: "Clearly *Erets* [the earth] exists, but as yet has not assumed its final shape or function and has not yet been filled with life forms."[19] The six ordering and creative days of Elohim's work will form it into a place that is useful and habitable for all creatures. At the end of the days of creative activity, Elohim surveys all that has been made and blesses it, and recognises its goodness, calling it in 1:31 "very good."

The questions raised by Oord and Boyd about the goodness of this completed creation revolve around whether the existence of the *tĕhôm* or the description of the world as *tōhû wābōhû* opens the exegetical possibility of reading in some sort of conflict, resistance, or corruption. I do not think the text offers such a possibility.

Thomas Oord's "Creation out of chaos"

Oord claims that a model of creation out of chaos, based on the *tĕhôm* of Genesis 1, is a better answer to the problem of natural evil then either kenotic or traditional notions of *creatio ex nihilo* allow.[20] Is it plausible to hold that the initial chaos of the *tĕhôm* overwhelmed God's possibility of creating a truly good and peaceable world? Did the chaotic nature of the world refuse cooperation with divine intention in such a way that natural evil was an inevitable result?

To begin answering these questions we must set Genesis 1 in its cultural context and evaluate its form. The chaos explored in this chapter is not the constructive chaos of complex systems known by today's scientific world, but the disordered forces of destruction that lived in the Ancient Near Eastern (ANE) imagination. Is the chapter an example of converted *Chaoskampf* literature – a struggle between the ordering God and chaos (or other possible spiritual forces) – or is it another genre of literature?

Hermann Gunkel was the first to suggest that the mention of *tĕhôm* was a veiled reference to the Babylonian goddess Tiamat, and thus hints at oppositional forces in the creative work.[21] Yet, when comparing Genesis to other ANE mythologies, Gunkel himself notes:

> The pagan myths tell of gods whose relationships in reproduction and battle give rise to the world. Gen 1, however, knows of a sole God, not begotten

and not begetting, at whose feet lies the world. There is no greater contrast, then, than between the colorful, fantastic mythology of these peoples and the intellectually clear, prosaic supernaturalism of Gen 1.[22]

Whatever might have been the source material in Genesis 1 of ANE mythological influence, commentators generally agree that there are no remains of oppositional forces in the current form of the text.[23]

Oord tries to garner support for his idea of creation out of chaos by attributing the idea of opposition to Jon D. Levenson. Oord writes "Levenson and other biblical authors argue that Genesis 1 suggests that even in the first moments of creation, God encounters other forces. These forces oppose, at least partially, God's creative will."[24] Yet, in the book Oord is drawing from, Levenson clearly states: "First, in Genesis there is no active opposition to God's creative labor. He works on inert matter. In fact, rather than *creatio ex nihilo*, 'creation without opposition' is the more accurate nutshell statement of the theology underlying our passage."[25] Oord could claim that he does not think the chaos *actively* – but only passively – opposes God (nearer, perhaps to Neil Messer's position), but it still leaves the contradiction between some sort of opposition in creation and Levenson's "creation without opposition" unresolved.

Instead of a struggle with evil chaos, what *is* seen in Genesis 1 is simply the existence of the chaos: unordered water that has no proper boundaries. God's creative work brings some order and limitations to this watery chaos so that the world can become habitable and useful. However, as Levenson points out, even though God is not opposed in any way by the chaos, "God has not annihilated the primordial chaos. He has only limited it. The same holds for the other uncreated reality, darkness. Light, which is God's first creation, does not banish darkness."[26] Instead, light and darkness alternate, as each is useful for different things. So too, the land and the seas alternate, and neither holds dominance over the other. The chaos, therefore, is not something that God *could not* subdue, but rather something that God *did not* entirely subdue.[27] The Genesis account does not leave room for Oord's idea that this chaos has in any way inhibited God's creative endeavour. Instead it claims that even the waters and the darkness form a necessary part of creation. The (literally) dark and dangerous elements of creation were left precisely because they were good and useful – fit for the purposes of God's very good creation.[28]

Satanic opposition?

What, then, of another possibility – the possibility that the problem was not a chaotic force that hindered God, but a malicious one that corrupted God's world? Various theologians have come to the conclusion that the world was corrupted with the fall of the angels. C. S. Lewis wrote:

> It seems to me . . . a reasonable supposition, that some mighty created power had already been at work for ill on the material universe, or the solar system,

or, at least, the planet Earth, before ever man came on the scene. . . . If there is such a power, as I myself believe, it may well have corrupted the animal creation before man appeared.[29]

Gregory Boyd is more specific when he writes:

God wasn't the only agent involved in the evolutionary process: Satan and other malevolent cosmic powers have also been involved. I will contend that the process of evolution may be seen as a sort of warfare between the life-affirming creativity of an all-good God, on the one hand, and the on-going corrupting influence of malevolent cosmic forces, on the other.[30]

Paul Griffiths agrees, but extends the corruption beyond the process of evolution to the very fabric of creation:

Among these [created] creatures are angels; (almost) simultaneously with creation (*in ictu*), some among these rebel against their creator and introduce thereby deep damage into the otherwise harmoniously beautiful space-time fabric of the cosmos. All creatures, material and immaterial, living and non-living, are damaged by this fall.[31]

While an angelic rebellion causing a cosmic fall solves the chronological problem of pre-human animal suffering, it raises two other serious questions: first, why is God's creation (including humans and all living creatures) called "very good" and continually attributed to God's work later in Scripture, if in fact it has been deeply corrupted all along? Second, how does one account for the lack of Scriptural evidence for such a view? Where is this story of nature's satanic corruption recounted in clear terms?

That the earth is considered God's good work, and continues to operate under God's sovereign dominion, is a common theme in the Bible:

"God saw everything that he had made, and indeed, it was very good."[32]

"The earth is the Lord's and all that is in it,
the world, and those who live in it;
for he has founded it on the seas,
and established it on the rivers."[33]

"O Lord, how manifold are your works!
In wisdom you have made them all;
the earth is full of your creatures."[34]

"In his hand are the depths of the earth;
the heights of the mountains are his also.
The sea is his, for he made it,
and the dry land, which his hands have formed."[35]

The whole of the divine dialogues in Job are an eloquent attribution of all the most problematic parts of creation to God's handiwork, from carnivorous birds and giant sea monsters to hail and whirlwinds.[36] If one set aside readings of Genesis 3 weighted by later tradition (or set aside the chapter itself for a moment), one would never arrive at the idea that the natural world was deeply corrupted by God's curse from the texts in the Hebrew Bible. Moreover, if there *had* been a profound corruption of the earth, if these aggressive elements of creation *were* against the divine will, why is it not mentioned? Gregory Boyd would protest that it is mentioned, that the struggle between God and oppositional forces is reflected in the Old Testament passages where God rebukes the hostile waters of the *tĕhôm* or fights sea monsters, such as Psalm 29:3–4; 18:15; 74:10–13; 89:9–10; 104:3–9; 106:9; Proverbs 8:27–29; Job 9:13; 38:6–11; Habakkuk 3:8–15.[37] Boyd acknowledges that this opposition is not present in Genesis 1,[38] but crops up throughout the Hebrew Bible. He goes on to elaborate that:

> The point of these passages is clearly to stress that Yahweh (and no other god) reigns supreme over the "proud" chaotic waters that threaten the foundation of the earth. Indeed, unlike Baal, Tiamat, Enki or any other Near Eastern hero who is said to have controlled the chaos, Yahweh's sovereignty is such that he can master these destructive forces by his mighty voice alone.[39]

But if God is utterly sovereign over these chaotic forces, then, what is the problem? If God "mastered these destructive forces," how can they also still be plaguing the creation? Boyd argues "A very real battle took place when God created the world, and is still taking place as Yahweh (not Baal or Marduk) preserves the world from chaos."[40] However, there is no biblical justification for the second clause of Boyd's claim. All the passages that Boyd references celebrate God's past and ultimate defeat of these chaotic elements. There is no mention of their ongoing harassment of creation. Quite the opposite, the past defeat of these mythological enemies is invoked as the reason that God should be able to save people from their current human enemies,[41] as is seen in Psalm 74:10–14:

> How long, O God, is the foe to scoff?
> Is the enemy to revile your name forever?
> Why do you hold back your hand;
> why do you keep your hand in your bosom?
>
> Yet God my King is from of old,
> working salvation in the earth.
> You divided the sea by your might;
> you broke the heads of the dragons in the waters.
> You crushed the heads of Leviathan;
> you gave him as food for the creatures of the wilderness.

The God able to crush Leviathan should surely not hold back against those who now scoff at God's name. Boyd suggests that the "foe" referred to in this Psalm is the evidence of the presence of these chaotic spiritual forces in creation,[42] but the actions of the foe (which include roaring within the holy place, setting up emblems, hacking the wooden trellis at the upper entrance with axes, and smashing the carved works with hatchets and hammers before setting the sanctuary on fire) rule out the possibility that it is spiritual forces that are here being considered: it is plainly referring to human soldiers.[43] The sea, the dragons in the waters, and the Leviathan appear only as *already defeated* enemies. They are not only defeated, but they fail to put up any kind of resistance to God's attack. Rebecca Watson notes, "it appears that although Leviathan and Rahab are sometimes portrayed as recipients of Yahweh's antagonism, the lack of resistance (or even acknowledged provocation or hostility) precludes speaking of a 'combat' proper."[44] There is no indication that there is any sort of an enduring struggle with them. Similarly, Boyd's claim that "these hymns express the authors' perception that the cosmos is besieged at a structural level with forces of evil that God himself must battle"[45] is simply not borne out by the biblical content. Everywhere the total victory of God over chaotic forces and creatures is announced, proclaimed, and celebrated. Where the chaotic forces or sea creatures do appear as currently existing, they are universally seen as one of God's good created creatures or well within the boundaries of God's current control.[46] In Genesis 1:21 the great sea creatures are simply creatures that Elohim created along with the rest. In Psalm 104:26 the Leviathan *that God formed* (the text emphatically reminds us) frolics in the sea. In Job 41:1–11 the Leviathan is pictured as God's servant, whom God can lead on a leash and play with like a pet bird.[47] The character of Satan is also noticeably absent in the creation stories. God, and God alone, is the Creator.[48]

Finally, Boyd (like Oord) points to the existence of the *tĕhôm* in Genesis as having "ominous overtones" or "indicating a lingering element of the *Chaoskampf* creation stories."[49] Increasingly, however, exegetes are moving away from even the initial identification of the *tĕhôm* with elements of chaos.[50] Whereas older exegetes regularly identified the *tĕhôm* with chaos,[51] Ellen van Wolde and Norman Habel both conclude that chaos is not the primary aspect of the pre-created waters[52] and David Tsumura's intensive exploration concludes "The Hebrew term *tĕhôm* is simply a reflection of the common Semitic term *tihām-* 'ocean,' and there is no relation between the Genesis account and the so-called *Chaoskampf* mythology."[53] More colloquially, William Brown writes

> But not to worry: the 'deep' (*tĕhôm*) and the 'waters' (*mayim*) lack the combative chaos that raged in *Enūma elish*, the Ba'al Epic, and for that matter Psalm 74:12–17. . . . Rather, the curtain of creation rises to reveal a benign primordial soup.[54]

While the Genesis account may have been written in response to Canaanite, Ugaritic, and Mesopotamian stories that contained such divine forces of watery chaos, an element of chaotic opposition in Genesis 1 is noticeable only by its absence.[55] Formless matter is present, but not oppositional chaotic forces.[56] Elsewhere, we are told "The Lord sits enthroned over the flood";[57] even the mighty flood waters are not a threat, but a foundation for enthronement.

The dome of Eden

Stephen Webb proposes that between Genesis 1:1 and 1:2 is a large chronological gap, and that the effect of the Satanic fall is indirectly attested to by the "chaotic" state of the world in 1:2.[58] Not only does all the evidence about the non-chaotic nature of the primordial seas, explored earlier, contradict Webb's thesis, but even he admits that the Gap Theory "is not widely accepted even among evangelical and fundamentalist theologians."[59] None of the other theologians who defend a satanic corruption of the world, even those like Boyd who are convinced that the Scriptures do tell of Satan's fall, reference this passage as a plausible source.[60] Michael Lloyd, who defends a cosmic fall caused by the satanic fall, made a careful study of the origins of the angelic fall, but never mentions Genesis 1:1–2.[61] Webb's use of this highly implausible argument to root his theory already puts his account into question.

Far more important to Webb's theory, however, is the idea that the "firmament" or "dome" created on the second day (Genesis 1:6–8) was a protective dome surrounding the Garden of Eden, excluding Satan's otherwise ubiquitous corrupting effect on creation. Inside the dome, according to Webb, was a world of peace and plenty, while outside it evolution took its course, leaving all the physical evidence of strife we see today. Webb therefore claims that his position accounts for the violence and suffering evidenced by the fossil record, while still maintaining a historical Eden where harmony and cooperation prevailed. Webb's exegesis is profoundly questionable when it comes to the construction of the firmament. It is perhaps best to quote him at length:

> The dome is an arching vault that covers the Earth, or at least one part of the Earth. I say one part of the Earth because it is not clear what cosmology the writer of Genesis is using. . . . On the one hand, if the sky or heaven is an immense vault that rests upon the Earth, then the Earth must be flat; otherwise, the dome could not encompass all of the Earth. The land left out of the dome would then have no sky. On the other hand, if the dome was not the sky but some kind of symbol of God's protective providence and if the Earth was not considered flat, then the Dome would cover only part of the Earth, and the earth that was left out of the Dome would indeed be waste and void. Even if the Genesis writer thought the Earth was flat, he still could have conceived of the Dome as covering only part of the Earth, with parts of the Earth left out at the fringes of the Dome.[62]

First, Webb does not address the ANE context that attests to a firmament covering the whole earth and separating it from the heavens, a concept that Wenham calls "a familiar theme in ancient cosmologies."[63] It is more plausible to assume that the author of Genesis 1 is adopting the common cosmological construction of the time (i.e. that the dome covers the whole earth) than to assume that he is radically innovating on it while giving so little indication that he is doing so.[64]

Second, there is absolutely no indication in the Genesis text that the dome only covered part of the earth, or that there were lands excluded from it. Not only is there not the slightest hint of lands existing outside the dome, but also the internal coherence of the text would be hugely compromised if that were the case. In Genesis 1:16–17 Elohim sets the heavenly lights – the sun, the moon, and the stars – "in the firmament," to give light to the earth. If the dome only covered part of the earth, so too would the light of the sun, moon, and stars. Since this is clearly not the case, Webb's thesis that the dome only covers part of the earth is highly implausible.

Third, Webb's case assumes that the dome that made Eden a paradise is inaccessible in present times.[65] Yet, David praises God for the existence of the firmament in Psalm 19:1, and recounts how day-by-day it "pours forth speech." If God had removed it after the fall, how can David conceive of it as still existent in his day?

Finally, the dome theory leaves serious theological questions. If God could so easily exclude Satan's corrupting influence from a part of the earth, why would God not choose to do the same for all the rest of the earth? Why allow creatures to suffer needlessly when it was obviously preventable? Webb's theory simply does not hold up on either biblical or philosophical grounds.

From the considerations explored in regard to Oord, Boyd, and Webb, I conclude that the identification of natural evil as the result of malicious corruption, including satanic or chaotic ANE entities, which opposed God's creative activity, simply cannot be maintained on exegetical grounds.[66]

Other fallenness scenarios

There are various other positions that advocate for a mysteriously fallen cosmos without specifying more carefully what is meant, or where the evil in the cosmos originates. I will explore the philosophical merits of these proposals further in Chapter 3, but it is worth noting the biblical difficulties now. The mysterious fallenness scenarios include Nicola Hoggard Creegan's "wheat and tares" analogy, Celia Deane-Drummond's "shadow sophia," and Neil Messer's Barthian "nothingness." Their approaches differ in important ways. Hoggard Creegan's approach, for example, is closer to the satanic opposition theory since it admits some sort of opposition against God's works in creation.[67] Deane-Drummond's approach is far more constitutive in nature: the goodness of creation necessarily creates shadows of evil, not as opposition, but as *privatio boni*.[68] Messer's approach is closer to Oord's position, as it holds that an active principle of chaos, or "nothingness" has threatened God's creation since before recorded history.[69] Violence and want are evidence of this non-being.

Yet, none of these positions can account for God calling the creation "very good" once it rests in completion at the end of Genesis 1. Nor can they account for the biblical tradition where God claims the violent aspects of creation as particular points of pride – particularly in the book of Job. I adopt a different paradigm, leaving aside the notion of fallenness. But first, we must explore the most important biblical texts that were developed into the fall story. I will argue that a fallen cosmos is not a required interpretation of the Scriptural witness.

Genesis 3–9: the curse

The case for the cosmic fall rests on the curse language in Genesis 3:14–19:

> The Lord God said to the serpent,
> 'Because you have done this,
> cursed are you among all animals
> and among all wild creatures;
> upon your belly you shall go,
> and dust you shall eat
> all the days of your life.
> I will put enmity between you and the woman,
> and between your offspring and hers;
> he will strike your head,
> and you will strike his heel.'
> To the woman he said,
> 'I will greatly increase your pangs in childbearing;
> in pain you shall bring forth children,
> yet your desire shall be for your husband,
> and he shall rule over you.'
> And to the man he said,
> 'Because you have listened to the voice of your wife,
> and have eaten of the tree
> about which I commanded you,
> "You shall not eat of it,"
> cursed is the ground because of you;
> in toil you shall eat of it all the days of your life;
> thorns and thistles it shall bring forth for you;
> and you shall eat the plants of the field.
> By the sweat of your face
> you shall eat bread
> until you return to the ground,
> for out of it you were taken;
> you are dust,
> and to dust you shall return.[70]

Genesis 3:16: the birth pain myth[71]

Before considering the main argument of the nature of the curse on the ground, I want to investigate the seemingly tangential question of pain in childbirth which will act as a prototype for the main argument I wish to make, namely, that a long tradition of one particular reading of these texts has influenced theology beyond the proper emphasis of the text.

The curse of increased pain for women in childbirth is a helpful way to look at one of the problems of the classic cosmic fall argument. In short, throughout the history of interpretation, the curse language was understood to reflect some sort of physiological change in women that caused childbirth to be especially painful.[72] Developmental anatomists, however, show that the pain in childbearing results from the large size of the human brain, and therefore of the human head, conflicting with hips that are ever-narrowing due to an upright walking position. Birth pains are not a result of the punishment of sin, but of conflicting anatomical endeavours. But does the text really claim that labour pains are a result of the curse on the woman?

The first thing to acknowledge is that modern English translations stand almost entirely against the interpretation I will try to make. Here is a brief scope of the English translations of Genesis 3:16a:

NRSV: "I will greatly increase your pangs in childbearing; in pain you shall bring forth children"

TNIV: "I will make your pains in childbearing very severe; with pain you will give birth to children."

NASB: "I will greatly multiply your pain in childbirth, in pain you will bring forth children;"

CEV: "You will suffer terribly when you give birth."

ESV: "I will surely multiply your pain in childbearing; in pain you shall bring forth children."

Early translations, either because they are more comfortable with the woodenness of the Hebrew text, or because they feel less need to interpret for their readers, translate the Hebrew more literally:

KJV: I will greatly multiply thy sorrow and thy conception; in sorrow thou shalt bring forth children.

Wycliffe: I shall multiply thy wretchednesses and thy conceivings; in sorrow thou shalt bear thy children.

The Hebrew phrase in question is:

הרבה ארבה עצבונך והרנך בעצב תלדי בנים

The first obvious difference between the early and the new translations is that the phrase *'iṣṣĕbônēk wĕhērōnēk* is treated as a hendiadys and is translated as a modified noun (pain in childbirth) in the modern translations and is left as a conjunctive phrase in the older versions. As Hebrew metre allows for both enhancing parallelism, which would suggest the use of a hendiadys here, and contrasting parallelism, which would favour a contrasting conjunctive phrase, there would be little reason to choose one reading over another, all other things being equal. However, the use of the word *'iṣṣābôn*, in the first part of the line and its root, *'eṣeb*, in the second is significant because, as Wenham points out "Neither the word used here for 'pain,' עצב [*'eṣeb*], nor the earlier one, עצבון [*'iṣṣābôn*], is the usual one for the pangs of childbirth."[73] Hebrew has several different ways of expressing specifically the pains of childbirth,[74] so why does the author use this particular word for pain? Nowhere else is this word or its derivatives used in the context of birth pains.[75] Indeed, the word *'iṣṣābôn* is exceedingly rare, occurring only three times – twice here in the curse formulation of Genesis 3 and once in Genesis 5 at the beginning of the flood narrative. We shall come to a full discussion of the implications of that in the next section. The word *'eṣeb*, which is far more common, usually refers to mental or emotional distress.[76] It can mean hard labour in a physical sense, but it never means physical pain. Indeed, the *Theological Dictionary of the Old Testament* (TDOT) makes a special case about the use of this word in Genesis 3:16:

> The traditional translations render both terms [עצב and עצבון] with words for physical pain. Since *ʻṣb* II refers more to mental than to physical pain, however, this traditional interpretation must be called into question. . . . In the nuanced biblical lexical field of pregnancy and birth (→הרה *hārâ*), that latter does not refer to the actual process of childbirth. . . . The second clause of v. 16 deals with the theme of "having children"; it does not necessarily refer to the process of childbirth itself, for → ל' *yālaḏ* can mean simply "have" or "produce" children and is used of both men and women. Having many children was a desirable and fundamental aspect of the labor-intensive agricultural society, albeit not without difficulties: parenting had its own special "pain." Thus, the meaning of *'eṣeḇ* in this text is ambiguous: it can mean "labor" and "work" and intensify that statement of the preceding clause; it can refer to the psychological stress of family life; or it can mean both. But it does not mean physical pain.[77]

These considerations move one away from interpreting the phrase *'iṣṣĕbônēk wĕhērōnēk* as a hendiadys meaning "birth pains" and towards separating the two words into being represented individually, as in: "your pains and your conceptions I shall greatly increase."

What difference does this make? The punishment laid on the woman is not an increase in physical labour pains as the modern translations imply, but rather a warning that the general circumstances surrounding the birth of a child will become extremely painful. Where childbirth ought to be a joyful occasion – bringing new life into a world of relational peace and harmony – now children are introduced into a world of pain and uncertainty. Yet, despite human sin, the promise of increased conceptions also gives hope of God's continued work with humans.[78] Life will continue, and people will still multiply and fill the earth. Thus, even in this larger textual passage of curse formula (though no curse is laid directly on the man or the woman, only on the snake and the ground), the promise and blessing of God continues.

In summary, the text does not conflict with the modern scientific understandings of birth pangs, simply because the text does not actually claim what the popular imagination has, because of modern translations, assumed it does.[79] Genesis 3 makes no claims at all about the origins of physical labour pains, but only of the sorrow-filled world into which children are born.

In a similar way, I will argue, the opening chapters of the Bible make no negative claim about the ontological nature of the created world. There is no cosmic fall in the Hebrew Scriptures. The curse laid in Chapter 3 is lifted in the Noahic flood episode, leaving the ground released from its curse.

Use of ʿēṣeb

Part of constructing the argument that Genesis 3 and Genesis 5–8 form one story about the laying down and the lifting of a single curse involves finding lexical links that draw the narratives together. I want to return for a moment to the repetition of those strange words in Genesis 3:16, ʿeṣeb and ʾiṣṣābôn. Why does the author use these two rare words in this passage? The word ʾiṣṣābôn, in that form, is used only three times in the entire Hebrew Bible. Twice it is used in the Genesis 3 curse formula, once of the man and once of the woman, creating a parallel between their judgements. The final time it appears is in Genesis 5:29, in the Noahic episode. Is there any other reason for the author to use this particular word for pain when other, perhaps clearer words, were available?

I want to suggest that the author's use of עצב, ʿeṣeb (root: ʿāṣab) in this context is due to a play on words being created with the phonetically similar word עזב, ʿāzab. Meaning "to forsake" or "to leave," this word has already shown up in the garden episode in 2:24 in which a man "*will leave* his father and mother in order to cleave to his wife." With ʿāzab used once in a positive sense of normal human relations, a play on the words with ʿāzab and ʿeṣeb in the context of the disruption of human relations, particularly between the husband and the wife, seems apt.

Elsewhere in the Hebrew Bible the two terms show up together, most notably in Isaiah 54:6a:

> For the Lord has called you
> like a wife forsaken and grieved in spirit
> כי־כאשה עזובה ועצובת רוח קראך יהוה

The description is of a woman who is both abandoned (ʿāzab) and in pain (ʿāṣab) of spirit. The prophet uses both these words together in the context of speaking of the marriage bond between Yahweh and Israel, and it seems to indicate that in the covenant context these words could have a close lexical link.[80] In 2 Samuel 5:21 and 2 Chronicles 24:18, these same Hebrew roots show up together again, although in these cases a slightly different word with the same root ʿāṣab is used, which means "idol."[81] The use of these two related words together, particularly as we find them once again in the context of covenantal themes, reinforces the possibility that the writer of Genesis used ʿeṣeb in order to evoke its similarity to ʿāzab, and having used ʿeṣeb, would then in turn use the rare but related word ʾiṣṣābôn. Word play of this sort is not unfamiliar to the author of the garden narrative. Indeed, wordplays run throughout this passage, the most obvious of which are the play between ʾādām, and ʾădāmâ, in 2:7 and 3:17 and the play between ʿārôm, and ʿārûm, in 2:25 and 3:1. While a link between ʿāzab and ʿeṣeb is by no means certain, it may explain why the very rare word *'iṣṣāḇôn* is used twice of the human pair in the context of their self-alienation from God and from each other, particularly in light of their marital and covenantal bonds.

Genesis 3, Noah, and *'ārar*

I have mentioned the word *'iṣṣāḇôn* only shows up in three places: twice in the curse formula of Genesis 3, and once just before the Noahic narrative in Genesis 5:29. Comparing Genesis 3:17 and 5:29 gives a clear picture of the similarities:

Gen 3:17 "And to the man he said, 'Because you have listened to the voice of your wife, and have eaten of the tree about which I commanded you, "You shall not eat of it," cursed (*'ărûrāh*) is the ground (*hā'ăḏāmâ*) because of you; in toil (*'iṣṣāḇôn*) you shall eat of it all the days of your life.'"

ולאדם אמר כי־שמעת לקול אשתך ותאכל מן־העץ אשר צויתיך לאמר לא תאכל ממנו ארורה
האדמה בעבורך בעצבון תאכלנה כל ימי חייך

Genesis 5:29 "He named him Noah (*nōaḥ*), saying, 'Out of the ground (*min-hā'ăḏāmâ*) that the Lord has cursed (*'ērĕrāh*) this one shall bring us relief (*yĕnaḥămēnû*) from our work and the toil (*ûmē'iṣṣĕḇôn*) of our hands'.'"

וַיִּקְרָא אֶת־שְׁמוֹ נֹחַ לֵאמֹר זֶה יְנַחֲמֵנוּ מִמַּעֲשֵׂנוּ וּמֵעִצְּבוֹן יָדֵינוּ מִן־הָאֲדָמָה אֲשֶׁר אֵרְרָהּ יְהוָה

The related themes between these two passages are clear: the ground, the curse, and the toil. Nowhere else do these three terms come together. In between these two narratives, in 4:1–16, is the account of Cain, who is cursed (*'ārar*) from the ground on account of his brother's blood, and so the theme of the curse weaves like a thread through the early Genesis narratives, linking the stories together.

When the reader arrives in Genesis 5:29, the curse has been laid down and the prophetic statement that Noah will relieve people of the toil of the curse has been received. In 5:29 there is a play on words: Noah (*nōaḥ*) "brings us relief" (*yĕnaḥămēnû*, from the root *nāḥam*). The flood narrative follows in which the world is uncreated and the chaos of the seas rules over the earth. But as the flood subsides (*qallû*), the earth re-emerges and God reaffirms the covenant with all living creatures in Chapter 9 and assures Noah that a similar destruction will never overtake the earth. Just before the new covenant is established, Noah builds an altar and offers a sacrifice:

Genesis 8:21, NRSV
And when the LORD smelt the pleasing odour, the LORD said in his heart, 'I will never again curse the ground because of humankind, for the inclination of the human heart is evil from youth; nor will I ever again destroy every living creature as I have done.'

וַיָּרַח יְהוָה אֶת־רֵיחַ הַנִּיחֹחַ וַיֹּאמֶר יְהוָה אֶל־לִבּוֹ לֹא־אֹסִף לְקַלֵּל עוֹד אֶת־הָאֲדָמָה בַּעֲבוּר הָאָדָם
כִּי יֵצֶר לֵב הָאָדָם רַע מִנְּעֻרָיו וְלֹא־אֹסִף עוֹד לְהַכּוֹת אֶת־כָּל־חַי כַּאֲשֶׁר עָשִׂיתִי

I mentioned earlier the play on words between Noah and the relief he was to bring. A similar play on words occurs here between Noah, the relief of Chapter 5, and God's response of finding the offering soothing. Noah (*nōaḥ*) is to "bring relief" (*nāḥam*) and offers a sacrifice that produced "the soothing aroma" (*rēaḥ hanîḥoaḥ*) to God's nostrils. These sacrifices are restful to God. As Gordon Wenham writes:

> Here however, it is also a deliberate pun on Noah's name. We might even paraphrase it, 'The LORD smelt the Noahic sacrifice.' Lamech called his son 'Noah' because he hoped he would bring him rest from the labor of his hands (5:29): here God implies that Noah's sacrifice has soothed him.[82]

God, being soothed by the sacrifice, relieves the people of the curse on the ground.[83] Lamech's hope for his son is fulfilled. "Now," writes Norman Habel, "with the revoking of this curse, nature will no longer suffer divine curses because of human sinfulness. . . . The natural order is declared safe from divine acts of judgment provoked by human deeds."[84] So far, the removal of the curse seems like a fairly easy argument to sustain: the curse narrative is a typical Hebraic *inclusio* encompassing creation and recreation.

A problem

There is however a problem. Look again at the lexical links that draw the passages together. The use of the word *'ārar* or "curse" in both 3:17 and 5:29 is of particular interest as a link, since *'ārar* is only otherwise used of Cain and of Canaan in the first 11 chapters of Genesis.[85] In Cain's case, there is a strong lexical current in favour of linking the curse in Chapter 4 with the curse in Chapters 3 and 5 since both *'ārar* and the ground, *'ădāmâ*, show up together: "And now you are cursed (*'ārûr*) from the ground (*min-ha'ădāmâ*), which has opened its mouth to receive your brother's blood from your hand."[86] The cursed ground extends its curse up to Cain.

By contrast, when Canaan is cursed in 9:25 after the flood, he is cursed independently of the ground on account of his own (or rather, his father's) evil action. This is the first time the word *'ārar* is used independently of the ground, *'ădāmâ*. Indeed, after 5:29 and the Noahic flood, the *'ārar* curse is never again used in conjunction with the ground, *'ădāmâ*,[87] indicating perhaps that in the new world order established after the flood people are cursed only by their own actions (most obviously laid out in Deuteronomy 27:15–26) and no longer on account of, or through, the ground as Adam and Cain had been – the same curse that Lamech recognised he toiled under. Again, this reinforces the case that the *'ārar* on the ground was lifted. Yet, a problem enters the argument when we look at 8:21 more closely. When the LORD proclaims that he will never again curse the ground, the same word, *'ārar*, is not used of the curse, but rather the much milder curse word *qālal*.

If there is a case to be made for the lifting of the Genesis 3 curse on the ground in Genesis 8:21, why did the author not use *'ārar* again but change to *qālal*?

Gordon Wenham argues – against my position – that the author changed words because the original curse on the ground was not lifted, but rather God only promised not to add to it.[88] "The flood was a punishment over and above that decreed in 3:17. . . it is simply the threat of another flood that is lifted."[89]

Wenham, however, does not seem to take into account that the flood is never referred to as a curse. What other curse could the author be referring to in 8:21 if not to the curse that has been wending its way through the last five chapters? Scharbert asks

> But what is the meaning of *leqallēl* in Gen. 8:21, since there is no mention of any actual curse in the whole deluge narrative? Here too we can probably follow the early versions (*katarásasthai, maledicere*) in translating the verse: 'I will never again curse the earth.'[90]

Scharbert argues that even with no other mention of a curse in the deluge narrative, it is appropriate to understand the mention of *qālal* as referring to the stronger notion of curse already familiar to the reader.

While I agree with Scharbert that no curse is mentioned in the deluge narrative itself, there is the mention of *'ārar* in 5:29 in reference to Noah, before the formal beginning of the deluge narrative in 6:9. The play of words on Noah's name, the relief of the sacrifice, combined with the emphasis on the ground and the curse seems a significant enough link to hold the two passages together. The promise of God is fulfilled as the lifting of the curse: it is the looked-for rest from the *'iṣṣābôn*, the toil and pain, resulting from the curse on the ground. The relief is made tangible, when, after the flood Noah plants a vineyard that is so abundantly fruitful that he becomes magnificently drunk.[91]

Why does the author not use *'ārar* in 8:21? Perhaps it is because *qālal* has already appeared twice in the 8th chapter, referring to the abating of the water, and the author wishes to include a pun about the abating sea and the end of the curse. In the end, it is not certain why the author moves over to this other word. Still, it is significant that the word *'ārar* occurs four times in quick succession in these chapters all in close proximity to the word *'ădāmâ* and then the two never occur together again in the remaining 59 occurrences of the word *'ārar* in the Hebrew Bible. It seems strongly to suggest that the curse on the *'ădāmâ* is no longer in effect in the mind of the authors of the Hebrew Bible.

Conclusion to Genesis 1–9

There is good reason to see the curse laid on the ground in 3:17 as having been lifted in the new order of creation after the flood. Norman Habel concludes

> The removal of the curse means that nature is fully alive once again, fully green and vibrant. Now there is no fallen creation, no dark side to nature because of human sin. Nature is free of the curse, liberated to become lush, green and plentiful.[92]

Drawing out the lexical connections between 3:17, 5:29, and 8:21, I have drawn the line of a simple narrative thread: curse, prophecy of the relief of the curse, and then the lifting of the curse. The difficulties in this story, particularly the use of *qālal* rather than *'ārar* in 8:29, do not pose insurmountable objections to this interpretation. Rather, the ending of the curse lends coherence to the story: chaos has receded, the curse is lifted, and a new covenant is made with all living creatures as the creation gets off to a fresh start. Where, in the cursed earth, thistles and thorns were brought forth to man, now they have resumed their proper order, only to be renewed in disorder if people actively disobey the law, as the Israelites are warned in Deuteronomy 27 and 28. The particular type of toil referred to as a result of the curse, the *'iṣṣābôn*, is never again brought up in the Hebrew Bible.

Similar to the example of childbirth pain earlier, there is a tradition of reading into the curse narrative cosmic effects that are not evident from the text. Weeds and thistles were not necessarily *introduced* to the world because of the curse, only given a new relationship to humanity through humanity's misdeeds.[93] Predation and natural disasters, traditionally also assigned to the cosmic effect of the human fall, are not even mentioned. Instead, the ground is cursed in relation to humanity in Genesis 3, and the curse is lifted in Genesis 8. The cosmic fall as a result of the human fall, which is also the traditional narrative explaining the existence of natural evil, simply does not exist in the opening chapters of Genesis. One cannot look here for an explanation of the abundant suffering of the non-human world.

Romans 8

In addition to the text of Genesis, there is often an appeal to Paul's writing in Romans 8:18–23 as the reason a Christian worldview must hold an anthropogenic cosmic fall.[94] The passage in question reads:

> I consider that the sufferings of this present time are not worth comparing with the glory about to be revealed to us. For the creation waits with eager longing for the revealing of the children of God; for the creation was subjected to futility, not of its own will but by the will of the one who subjected it, in hope that the creation itself will be set free from its bondage to decay and will obtain the freedom of the glory of the children of God. We know that the whole creation has been groaning in labor pains until now; and not only the creation, but we ourselves, who have the first fruits of the Spirit, groan inwardly while we wait for adoption, the redemption of our bodies.[95]

Most interpreters hear in Paul's veiled references to "the subjection of nature to futility" and its "bondage to decay" an allusion to the Adamic narrative of sin in Genesis 3 and the subsequent curse on the ground.[96] The difficulty of the passage is contained, according to James Dunn, in the fact that, "Paul was attempting to convey too briefly a quite complicated point: that God subjected all things to Adam, and that included subjecting creation to fallen Adam, to share in his fallenness."[97] If these commentators are right and Paul is alluding to the curse narrative in Genesis, then (apart from the type of exegesis shown earlier in this chapter) those who wish to take the Bible seriously would be hard-pressed to deny the human fall causing a cosmic fall – or at least that Paul thought it was so.[98]

However, there is another perspective on this passage that avoids this problem. Laurie Braaten suggests instead, and Richard Bauckham agrees, that Paul is alluding to the Hebrew Bible's motif of the earth going into mourning found in the prophets, rather than to Genesis 3.[99] Hosea 2:3–14; 4:3; Jeremiah 4:23–28; 12:1–11; 23:9–12; and Amos 1:2 all use the motif of the mourning earth to describe the dysfunction of the earth as a direct result of human sinfulness and often of subsequent divine punishment. Their argument begins by dividing up the terms συστενάζει καὶ συνωδίνει in verse 22 and refusing to see the phrase as a hendiadys (meaning "groaning in labour") but rather as two separate terms "groaning" and "travailing." Separated in this way, the terms do not seem to point together to a one-time event in the past, such as the Genesis 3 curse, but rather point to two different spheres of meaning. The groaning refers to – based on Paul's use in 2 Corinthians 5:2 and the regular use in the LXX[100] – mourning and lament.[101] The travailing is associated with Hebrew Bible images of divine judgement.[102] There are nine passages in the Hebrew prophets where the earth is said to mourn in response to human sin or divine judgement on sin.[103] In Hosea 4:1–3, for example, the earth languishes because of the sin of the people:

> Hear the word of the Lord, O people of Israel;
> for the Lord has an indictment against the inhabitants of the land.
> There is no faithfulness or loyalty,
> and no knowledge of God in the land.
> Swearing, lying, and murder,
> and stealing and adultery break out;
> bloodshed follows bloodshed.
> Therefore the land mourns,
> and all who live in it languish;
> together with the wild animals
> and the birds of the air,
> even the fish of the sea are perishing.[104]

In Jeremiah the suffering caused by the demise of the earth stands as one of the outcomes of divine judgement:

> I looked on the earth, and lo, it was waste and void;
> and to the heavens, and they had no light.
> I looked on the mountains, and lo, they were quaking,
> and all the hills moved to and fro.
> I looked, and lo, there was no one at all,
> and all the birds of the air had fled.
> I looked, and lo, the fruitful land was a desert,
> and all its cities were laid in ruins
> before the Lord, before his fierce anger.[105]

In other prophetic passages the absence of fruit on the vines (Isaiah 24:7) or the departure of birds (Jeremiah 4:25) are the outcomes of human abuse *and* the sentence of punishment. In each of these instances the earth mourns and, Bauckham argues,

> what the Earth mourns is the withering and destruction of inhabitants, flora and fauna, and so Paul's phrase 'bondage to decay' or 'bondage to a process of destruction' (v 21) is an appropriate description of the state to which God has assigned creation because of human sin.[106]

Yet, these are localised responses to localised human sins, not a cosmic fall scenario where all of nature is inherently bound to decay because of a one-time curse. Instead, because the whole earth is filled with people, and "all have sinned" (Romans 3:23), so too Paul can say the "whole creation" is subject to the effects of sin.

Perhaps the link between Romans 8 and the Hebrew Bible prophets is most clearly seen in Isaiah 24–27. Although this passage is primarily one of lament and judgement, it contains prophecies of hope for the deliverance of both humanity and the wider creation. There are numerous lexical links that might suggest this passage was foremost in Paul's mind. In Isaiah 24:1, in response to sin, the earth will be "utterly laid waste and utterly despoiled,"[107] or more literally, "destroyed with decay (φθαρήσεται φθορᾷ) – the same term used by Paul in Rom 8:21 to characterize the decay to which creation has been subjected."[108] Note that the term φθορᾷ, or decay, is absent from the LXX of Genesis 3, yet in Isaiah it is used of the future judgement that will occur in response to sin. The decay is associated with a curse on the earth (Isaiah 24:6 "Therefore a curse devours the earth, and its inhabitants suffer for their guilt"), but it is distinct from the curse pronounced in Genesis 3 since it has just come into effect. So too, waiting in hope is not mentioned in Genesis 3, but waiting on the future deliverance of the LORD is made explicit in Isaiah 25:9:

> It will be said on that day,
> Lo, this is our God; we have waited for him, so that he might save us.
> This is the Lord for whom we have waited;
> let us be glad and rejoice in his salvation.[109]

Other thematic and lexical links draw the two passages together. Jonathan Moo in particular has found strong parallels between Isaiah 24–27 and Romans 8.[110] He notices that the common themes include:

> the suffering of the earth due to the Lord's punishment of human sin, the personification of creation's response to judgment, the promise that God's glory will be revealed, the present waiting of the righteous in expectant hope, the use of birth-pang imagery, the defeat of death, and the possibility of life beyond death.[111]

However Moo, unlike Braaten and Bauckham, does not deny that Paul was referencing Genesis 3. In fact, he considers it "nearly certain" that Paul has been influenced by the Genesis narrative, but finds that though Paul indeed links the subjection of creation back to Adam, he interprets this narrative in such a way that the effects of the subjection of creation continue to be worked out in the context of a dynamic and ongoing relationship between God, Adamic humanity, and the rest of creation.[112]

I agree that the Adam event is central to Paul's thought in Romans as a whole, and it is probable that some echo of it is in view here. Yet, the uniqueness of the language of the groaning creation and travail (Paul does not use this language in the rest of Romans) may indicate that he is not drawing from Genesis, but from the prophetic literature.[113] Moo's final conclusion, is:

> if Rom 8.19–22 is to be read in light of Paul's possible use of Isaiah 24–27, the *effects* of creation's subjection may not have entailed for Paul a once-for-all ontological change in the created order, or a 'fall of nature' in the traditional sense.[114]

There is also an often overlooked and very positive outcome if Paul is drawing from the prophets: the prophets focus on salvation for those who mourn and the eventual release for the mourning earth. The mourning of the land in Isaiah 33:7–9 and the mourning women in Isaiah 32:11–13 are promised the peaceful reign of God in Isaiah 32:15–20, including the animals who live in peaceable relationship with humans:

> Until a spirit from on high is poured out on us,
> and the wilderness becomes a fruitful field,
> and the fruitful field is deemed a forest.
> Then justice will dwell in the wilderness,
> and righteousness abide in the fruitful field.
> The effect of righteousness will be peace,
> and the result of righteousness, quietness and trust forever.
> My people will abide in a peaceful habitation,
> in secure dwellings, and in quiet resting places.
> The forest will disappear completely,
> and the city will be utterly laid low.
> Happy will you be who sow beside every stream,
> who let the ox and the donkey range freely.[115]

The devastated and withering fields will be fruitful, the ox and donkey will range freely.[116] Similarly in Joel, the destruction of the earth sends the land and animals into mourning:

> The fields are devastated,
> the ground mourns;
> for the grain is destroyed,
> the wine dries up,
> the oil fails.[117]

How the animals groan!
The herds of cattle wander about
because there is no pasture for them;
even the flocks of sheep are dazed. . .
Even the wild animals cry to you
because the watercourses are dried up,
and fire has devoured
the pastures of the wilderness.[118]

Yet, as the inhabitants join in the mourning and repent (1:11–15), fruitfulness is restored to the people, to the land and to the animals:

In response to his people the Lord said:
I am sending you
grain, wine, and oil,
and you will be satisfied;
and I will no more make you
a mockery among the nations.
Do not fear, O soil;
be glad and rejoice,
for the Lord has done great things!
Do not fear, you animals of the field,
for the pastures of the wilderness are green;
the tree bears its fruit,
the fig tree and vine give their full yield.[119]

The curses brought upon the earth by human sin are not irreversible or immutable, but subject to repentance and restoration: hints of the restoration that Paul refers to as the creation being made subject "in hope."[120]

There is a correlation between the redemption of humanity and the release of creation from sin's damaging effects. Until that day of full redemption, the creation is made subject (by God) to *mataiotēs*, to a frustrated state, where the world displays the "ineffectiveness of that which fails to attain its goal."[121] The frustration of the created order echoes the book of Ecclesiastes, with its continual refrain that all is *hebel*, subject to frustration and fleeting good.[122] C.E.B. Cranfield likens this frustration to the members of a concerto group being frustrated by the soloist failing to play his or her part.[123] It is an analogy that may be worth some further exploration.

If the whole creation can be likened to a symphony of praise, the meaning of creation's ματαιότης – its futility and frustration – the sense of Paul's intentions, can be parsed in a new way. Imagine a symphony orchestra arranged to play one of Mozart's concertos. The horns and woodwinds and large stringed instruments all begin in unison and in harmony, and the sound builds into a beautiful melodic theme. But, suddenly, the violins – brashly ignoring the conductor and the music – interrupt on untuned instruments with whatever strikes their fancy. One starts with a loud rendition of "Happy Birthday," another with "God save the Queen," and a third simply emits a series of cacophonous squeaks. The performance is utterly ruined because a key set of players have refused their part and gone their own way.

If we were to imagine the same scene with the theology of the traditional cosmic fall, the violins' rebellion would cause all the other instruments to immediately go out of tune, so that they could no longer play in harmony with each other, or produce in-tune music themselves. In my suggested alternative scenario, the rest of the instruments all continue to follow the music, and through gritted teeth continue the performance until its conclusion. In this case, all the instruments apart from the violins have performed their duties and have fulfilled what they could fulfil of their potential: their music was well-played and their ability to emit good sound to the audience was not compromised. However, the performance was still ruined by the errant violin section, and the gathered purpose of the orchestra (to perform Mozart's concerto) is brought to meaningless futility by the interruption. The purpose of each individual player is therefore two-fold: to perform their own part well, and for their own efforts to be gathered with all the others into a pleasing performance for the audience. If either one of these objectives is lost, the other is lost as well. A good personal effort is made almost meaningless if the overall performance of others is poor. Equally, if the personal performance is poor (as in the case of the violins), it will result in the overall performance being ruined. Simply by being part of one orchestra, the fates of the two outcomes are tied together.

In a similar way, the individual purpose of each non-human animal to glorify God in its participation in life is not necessarily compromised by human sin because of some ontological shift in the nature of its being. That is, non-human animals have not "gone out of tune" due to a cosmic fall. However, the effects of sin are still such that the corporate purpose of the non-human creation is frustrated, both through the languishing of the creation due to the direct action of humans, but also through the playing out of divine judgement, as seen in the prophetic material.

Paul's statement in Romans 8, then, does not necessarily require that the exegete adhere to a cosmic fall scenario. Once again, this has implications for those theologians who want to hold the ontological corruption of creation by human sin. If creation's work is futile, it is not necessarily so because of an immutable condition tied to the initial sin of Adam, but it may be because of the continual sin of humanity that causes discord and dissonance in the work of creation.

Conclusion

In this chapter, I set out to show that there is not sufficient biblical merit for the familiar notions of the cosmically fallen or corrupted creation. I started by looking at the initial state of creation in Genesis 1. Was the earth, as Oord's proposal suggests, created out of a chaos that resisted divine shaping? Oord did not sufficiently acknowledge the sovereignty and power of God displayed in that chapter: God is portrayed as thoroughly in control of the limits and boundaries of the chaos, and is satisfied with the "very good" finished work. Second, I investigated the proposal that some malicious force may have intentionally ruined the creation, as argued by Boyd, Griffiths, Lewis, Pannenberg, and Lloyd. Once again the proposal was lacking in Scriptural support. The creation is ubiquitously attributed to God's work; God claims even the violent and dangerous elements as divine masterpieces. Third, I investigated Webb's proposal that the firmament was a dome to protect Eden from the effects of a satanically corrupted cosmic fall. However, I rejected this due to its adherence to the questionable Gap Theory of Genesis 1:1–2 and the dubitable exegesis surrounding the firmament.

Approaches which claim that a primordial cosmic fall occurred, whether by satanic origin or mysteriously, all have to meet the challenge that the world is pronounced "very good" and that even a violent creation is continually attributed to God's work.

The second half looked at the language of the curse in Genesis 3–8 to see if the curse in the garden narrative could account for the presence of disvalues. However, I argued that the lexical similarities and narrative structure of Genesis 1–8 pointed toward the curse being lifted after the flood. The world was given a new beginning. The new start meant that although future human sin could still damage the creation, as portrayed in the prophetic books, the non-human world was not bogged down by an ontological shift due to a curse from the entrance of human sin in Genesis 3. Finally, I looked at Romans 8 and the groaning of creation. I argued, in line with Braaten, Bauckham, and Moo, that this enigmatic passage could be understood as drawing primarily from the prophetic literature where the earth is seen to mourn in response to localised human sin. This interpretation removes the necessity of accepting a cosmic fall scenario, either due to the human fall or some primordial fall.

Neil Messer has written:

> the biblical witness, in short, requires us to say of the world we inhabit both that it is created and that it is fallen; both that it is the work of God, pronounced 'very good,' and that it is badly astray from what God means it to be.[124]

While this might be true of humanity, there is no necessary reason why a person who desires to take the biblical witness seriously has to hold to a version of the cosmic fall for the non-human creation, or think that evolution as God's method of creation is in any way corrupted by opposing spiritual powers.

This chapter has opened the way Scripturally to explore the option of leaving a cosmic fall behind. The next chapter will move from the Biblical texts into the realm of philosophy and theology. The scope will widen from simply the question of a fallen creation to include many of the ways scholars have tried to account for the violence of the created world.

Notes

1 William Dembski is a notable exception, who argues that the effects of the human fall were applied retroactively to the creation. William Dembski, *The End of Christianity: Finding a Good God in an Evil World* (Nashville, TN: B&H, 2009). I exclude outright those young earth creationists who do not accept that evolution happened.

2 C. S. Lewis, *The Problem of Pain* (San Francisco: HarperCollins, 1940, 1996), 138; Wolfhart Pannenberg, *Systematic Theology*, vol. 2, trans. Geoffrey W. Bromily (Göttingen: Vanderhoeck & Ruprecht, 1991), 274; Michael Lloyd, "Are Animals Fallen?" in *Animals on the Agenda*, eds. Andrew Linzey and Dorothy Yamamoto (London: SCM Press, 1998), 147–160; Paul J. Griffiths, "Impossible Pluralism," *First Things* (June/July 2013): 44–48; Nicola Hoggard Creegan, *Animal Suffering & the Problem of Evil* (Oxford: Oxford University Press, 2013), 10; Gregory Boyd, "Evolution as Cosmic Warfare: A Biblical Perspective on Satan and 'Natural Evil'," in *Creation Made Free*, ed. Thomas Oord (Eugene, OR: Wipf & Stock, 2009), 125–145; Gregory Boyd, *Satan and the Problem of Evil: Constructing a Trinitarian Warfare Theodicy* (Downers Grove, IL: IVP, 2001); Stephen H. Webb, *The Dome of Eden: An New Solution to the Problem of Creation and Evolution* (Eugene, OR: Cascade, 2010), 139–180.

3 See Chapter 3, 67–70.

4 The term "fall" here is still not the best, since it assumes an original "height" from which to fall, which inevitably pictures an Augustinian-type fall from moral perfection, rather than allowing for an Irenaean-type of "fall forward" from innocence.

5 Other primordial fall narratives include William Dembski's retroactive applications of the effects of the human fall, Origen's pre-material fall, Neil Messer's ambiguous creation with "nothingness," and Celia Deane-Drummond's shadow sophia. Dembski, *The End of Christianity*; Neil Messer, "Natural Evil after Darwin," in *Theology after Darwin*, eds. Michael S. Northcott and R. J. Berry (Milton Keynes: Paternoster, 2009), 149; Celia Deane-Drummond, "Shadow Sophia in Christological Perspective: The Evolution of Sin and the Redemption of Nature," *Theology and Science* 6:1 (2008): 13–32.

6 See, for example, John J. Bimson, "Reconsidering a 'Cosmic Fall'," *Science & Christian Belief* 18 (2006): 63–81.

7 The cosmic fall is never seen as caused by direct human action, as if humans could force lions to become carnivorous, but some of the satanic fall scenarios do imagine that kind of effect.

8 This is a view most famously enshrined in John Milton's Paradise Lost. The view that the fall of Satan had no effect on the goodness of the world was held by most Christian thinkers during the Patristic period. Bernard J. Bamberger, *Fallen Angels: Soldiers of Satan's Realm* (Philadelphia, PA: Jewish Publication Society, 1952), 82.

9 Or, at least, I accept the plausibility of a satanic fall.

10 Athanasius, *On the Incarnation of the Word* (Grand Rapids, MI: CCEL, 2005), 34–35.

11 Augustine, *The Literal Meaning of Genesis*, vol. 1., bk. 3, Chapter 18., trans. J. H. Taylor (Mahwah, NJ: Paulist Press, 1982), 93–94.

12 Augustine, *Literal Meaning of Genesis, I:3:16,* 92. Augustine goes on to argue "To wish that this were otherwise would not be reasonable. For all creatures, as long as they exist, have their own measure, number, and order. Rightly considered, they are all praiseworthy, and all the changes that occur in them, even when one passes into another, are governed by a hidden plan that rules the beauty of the world and regulates each according to its kind."

13 See N. P. Williams, *The Idea of the Fall and of Original Sin* (London: Longmans, Green and Co., 1927).

14 Thomas Oord, "An Open Theology Doctrine of Creation," in *Creation Made Free: Open Theism Engaging Science*, ed. Thomas Oord (Eugene, OR: Pickwick, 2009),

28–49; Boyd, "Evolution as Cosmic Warfare," 125–145; Webb, *The Dome of Eden*, 144–146, 165–166.

15 Genesis 1:2, NRSV.

16 Gordon J. Wenham, *Genesis 1–15*, Word Biblical Commentary 1 (Nashville, TN: Thomas Nelson, 1987), 16.

17 The only other place the exact same phrase is used is in Jeremiah 4:23 to describe a ruined land. The words tōhû and bōhû are also found together in Isa 34:11 where they describe the confusion and emptiness of a land under God's judgement. Examples of tōhû being used to describe a wilderness include Deuteronomy 32:10 and Psalm 107:40. An extensive etymology of both words, and their use in the Hebrew Bible, can be found in David Tsumura, *Creation and Destruction: A Reappraisal of the Chaoskampf Theory in the Old Testament* (Winona Lake, IN: Eisenbrauns, 2005), 10–35.

18 John H. Walton, *The Lost World of Genesis One: Ancient Cosmology and the Origins Debate* (Downer's Grove, IL: IVP, 2009), 47.

19 Norman Habel, *The Birth, the Curse and the Greening of the Earth: An Ecological Reading of Genesis 1–11* (Sheffield: Sheffield Phoenix, 2011), 29.

20 Oord, "An Open Theology Doctrine of Creation," 28–49.

21 Hermann Gunkel, *Genesis*, trans. Mark E. Biddle (Macon, GA: Mercer University, 1997), 126–132.

22 Gunkel, *Genesis*, 127. See also Wenham, *Genesis 1–15*, 16.

23 Jon D. Levenson, *Creation and the Persistence of Evil: The Jewish Drama of Omnipotence* (Princeton, NJ: Princeton University, 1994), 122.

24 Oord, "An Open Theology Doctrine of Creation," 40.

25 Levenson, *Creation and the Persistence of Evil*, 122. Oord, in his article, has a direct quotation from page 121.

26 Levenson, *Creation and the Persistence of Evil*, 123.

27 This claim about the divine ability is reinforced by the hope that God can and will entirely do away with dark and chaotic elements in the new creation. See Revelation 21:1–4.

28 Throughout the Hebrew Bible God regularly claims responsibility for these darker aspects of creation, as will be explored in the next section.

29 Lewis, *Problem of Pain*, 138.

30 Boyd, "Evolution as Cosmic Warfare," 127.

31 Paul J. Griffiths, "Impossible Pluralism," *First Things* (June/July 2013), 48. When I challenged him on the biblical difficulties of his view, he responded: "I do think that Scripture tells the story of an angelic fall. I recommend a close reading of books eleven and twelve of Augustine's City of God, together with the scriptural texts he engages. It's an invigorating exercise." "Good from Evils," *First Things* (October 2013): 13–14.

32 Genesis 1:31a, NRSV.

33 Psalm 24:1–2, NRSV.

34 Psalm 104:24, NRSV.

35 Psalm 95:5–6, NRSV.

36 Job 38–41.

37 Boyd, "Evolution as Cosmic Warfare," 134–135.

38 Gregory Boyd, *God at War: The Bible & Spiritual Conflict* (Downers Grove, IL: InterVarsity, 1997), 84–85.

39 Boyd, *God at War*, 86.

40 Boyd, *God at War*, 87.

41 That the Chaoskampf motif has more to do with the present appeal of Israelites to work in history than God's work in creation is argued by Dennis McCarthy and Andrew Angel over against John Day. Dennis McCarthy, "'Creation' Motifs in Ancient Hebrew Poetry," *Catholic Biblical Quarterly* 29 (1967): 393–406; Andrew R. Angel, *Chaos and he Son of Man: The Hebrew Chaoskampf Tradition in the Period 515 BCE to 200 CE* (London: T & T Clark, 2006), 9; John Day, *God's Conflict*

with the Dragon and the Sea: Echoes of a Canaanite Myth in the Old Testament
(Cambridge: Cambridge University Press, 1985), 3–4.

42 Boyd, *God at War*, 87. "This passage, which is possibly echoing another Canaanite
hymn, seems to identify yām with "the dragons of the sea," and the monster is clearly a
mocking enemy of Yahweh. . . . In short, even though God is in an ultimate sense sovereign, for the psalmist his battles with evil are not on this account in any sense a sham.
In contrast to Augustine, the psalmist sees that evil and thus warfare are absolutely real
for God just as they are for his creation."

43 See Psalm 74:4–7.

44 Rebecca S. Watson, *Chaos Uncreated: A Reassessment of the Themes of "Chaos" in
the Hebrew Bible* (New York, NY: Walter de Gruyter, 2005), 376.

45 Boyd, *God at War*, 89.

46 E.g. Job 41:25; Genesis 1:21; Psalm 104:26, 146:6.

47 There is only one passage, Isaiah 27:1, that could contradict the idea that the monsters
of creation were utterly defeated: "On that day the Lord with his cruel and great and
strong sword will punish Leviathan the fleeing serpent, Leviathan the twisting serpent,
and he will kill the dragon that is in the sea." Here alone in the Hebrew Bible is there
a sense that a brooding chaos monster might have been allowed a continued existence,
and one that merits "punishment." The passage, however, forms part of the "Isaiah
Apocalypse," is highly figurative, and describes the eschatological event of Leviathan's defeat alongside the prediction that "Jacob shall take root, Israel shall blossom
and put forth shoots, and fill the whole world with fruit" (Isa 27:6). As an idealised
future order, it pictures redemption in a similar way to how Revelation 21:1 pictures
the new heaven and the new earth without a sea. The author of Revelation does not
picture no sea because it was against the ability of God to subdue or eliminate the sea,
but because the time for the disorder caused by the sea is finished and a new order is to
take place. Indeed, strong thematic links between Isaiah 24–27 and the book of Revelation have been pointed out. See Day, *God's Conflict with the Dragon and the Sea*,
143–144.

48 The one exception to the absence of Satan in these narratives might be Genesis 3 and
the snake in the garden. However, identification of the snake in Genesis 3 with Satan
has long been rejected by biblical scholars. Von Rad writes: "The serpent which now
enters the narrative is marked as one of God's created animals (Chapter 2.19). In the
narrator's mind, therefore, it is not the symbol of a 'demonic' power and certainly not
of Satan." Gerhard von Rad, *Genesis: A Commentary* (London: SCM Press, 1961), 87.

49 Boyd, "Evolution as Cosmic Warfare," 141. Reflecting on the history of interpretation,
Rebecca Watson concludes "The term 'chaos' is unclear, inconsistently applied – and
from the first, it was contested whether it accurately described the situation in Genesis
1" *Chaos Uncreated*, 18.

50 Tsumura, *Creation and Destruction*.

51 See von Rad, *Genesis*, 49; Day, *God's Conflict with the Dragon and the Sea*, 4; Susan
Niditch, *Chaos to Cosmos: Studies in Biblical Patterns of Creation* (Chico, CA: Scholars Press, 1985), 18.

52 Habel, *The Birth, the Curse and the Greening of the Earth*, 29. Ellen van Wolde, "Facing the Earth: Primaeval History in a New Perspective," in *The World of Genesis: Persons, Places, Perspectives*, ed. Philip R. Davies (Sheffield: Sheffield Academic, 1998),
25. Van Wolde writes "This is the primaeval situation: no 'nothing,' nor a chaos that
needs sorting out, but a situation of 'before' or 'not-yet' in view of what is coming."

53 Tsumura, *Creation and Destruction*, 56–57. The refusal to see chaos in the creation
narratives is not simply a recent phenomenon though: it was characteristic of the Patris-
tics (Clement and Hippolytus), and many post-enlightenment writers as well (Herder).
See Watson, *Chaos Uncreated*, 14–15. Watson also adds that "the association of the
supposed 'Chaoskampf' theme with creation seems not to be original or central in the
Hebrew Bible" *Chaos Uncreated*, 379.

54   William P. Brown, *The Seven Pillars of Creation: The Bible, Science, and the Ecology of Wonder* (Oxford: Oxford University Press, 2010), 36. Watson's voice can also be helpfully added: "The notion of combat with or the suppression of the sea is nowhere clearly expressed in the Old Testament and indeed there could be no place for such a notion within the monotheistic framework of which is it ultimately an expression" *Chaos Uncreated*, 398.

55   Brown, *Seven Pillars of Creation*, 31–32, 36.

56   In place of the chaos myth, Habel suggests a birth metaphor: the earth is surrounded by waters just as an infant in the womb is surrounded by fluid. Habel defends that primal birth images also emerge elsewhere in Scripture: the earth as mother is found in Psalm 139:13–15 and Job 1:21, and the birth of the sea is pictured in Job 38:8, and of the mountains in Psalm 90:2. Habel, *The Birth, the Curse and the Greening of the Earth*, 31. I do not agree that this is primarily what is going on (one would expect birth-type language to appear in Genesis 1, with words such as yālad, if that were the case), but it is a helpful way to re-imagine this text without the chaos motifs.

57   Psalm 29:10, NRSV.

58   Webb, *Dome of Eden*, 143–145.

59   Webb, *Dome of Eden*, 143.

60   Boyd, as we saw above, admits that no divine battle motifs are found in Genesis 1.

61   Michael Lloyd, "The Cosmic Fall and the Free Will Defence," (PhD Dissertation, Worcester College, University of Oxford, 1996), Chapter 5.

62   Webb, *Dome of Eden*, 166–167.

63   Wenham, *Genesis 1–15*, 20. Actually, where Webb does mention ancient depictions of the world, it is to say that the depiction of the earth as flat with a hard dome above it is "widespread in the ancient world." Webb, *Dome of Eden*, 214.

64   For more on the firmament and ancient cosmology, see Denis O. Lamoureux, *Evolutionary Creation: A Christian Approach to Evolution* (Eugene, OR: Wipf & Stock, 2008), 120–131.

65   Webb, *Dome of Eden*, 225. At one point, Webb seems to imply that the dome is still in existence around the whole earth: "Scientists have long puzzled about the increasing rate of the universe's outward expansion, and physicists have posited a dark energy to account for it. The latest thinking, however, is that the earth might be located in a kind of space-time bubble that is particularly void of matter. This domically shaped bubble would explain why things look further away than they actually are, because light is distorted in a void. The bubble of low density matter surrounding the Earth would thus make speculations about dark matter unnecessary" Webb, *Dome of Eden*, 215. If the dome were still in existence around the world, one would expect the Edenic conditions underneath it that Webb attributes to its presence in Genesis.

66   Indeed, when highly destructive events happen in the Hebrew Bible, whether whirlwinds, earthquakes, fire, or lightning storms, they are usually associated directly with God's presence: Exodus 19:18; Psalm 77:18; Isaiah 29:6; Habakkuk 3.

67   Hoggard Creegan, *Animal Suffering*, 77–78.

68   Deane-Drummond, "Shadow Sophia in Christological Perspective," 13–32.

69   Messer, "Natural Evil after Darwin," 139–154.

70   Genesis 3:14–19, NRSV.

71   I am grateful to Iain Provan for first pointing out the linguistic discrepancies that led to this work. His work can be found in "Pain in Childbirth? Further Thoughts on 'An Attractive Fragment' (1 Chronicles 4:9–10)," in *Let Us Go Up to Zion: Essays in Honour of H.G.M. Williamson on the Occasion of his Sixty-Fifth Birthday*, Supplements to *Vetus Testamentum* 153, eds. Iain Provan and Mark Boda (Leiden: Brill, 2012), 285–296.

72   This is maintained even in contemporary commentaries: Habel, *The Birth, the Curse and the Greening of the Earth*, 61, 131.

73　Wenham, *Genesis 1–15*, 81.

74　Such as דְּלִי הַשֵׁק‎, or לוּחַ‎.

75　The one possible exception is in 1 Chronicles 4:9 where the mother of Jabez names him "sorrow" because she bore him "with sorrow" (KJV) or "in pain" (NRSV): בְּעֹצֶב‎. However, considering this to be specifically his birth pains is problematic, since in the next verse Jabez prays to be delivered from evil so that he would be "kept from hurt and harm" using the same root word for pain: יַבְעֵץ יִתְלְבֵל‎. It would be a strange man indeed who was motivated to pray for deliverance from birth pains! Even in this passage, the implication is toward a generalised circumstance of pain into which the woman gave birth.

76　C. Meyers, "asab," in *Theological Dictionary of the Old Testament* (*TDOT*), Vol. 11, eds. G. Johannes Botterweck, Helmer Ringgren, and Heinz-Josef Fabry (Grand Rapids, MI: Eerdmans, 2001), 279.

77　Meyers, "asab," 280.

78　Alternatively, and more darkly, it may mean that more conceptions will be needed because of increased child mortality rates.

79　There are, of course, other aetiological claims made by the Hebrew author that would conflict with science, such as the monogenesis of humanity and the lack of evolutionary development of life forms.

80　Helpfully, for my case, the link between the marriage covenant between Israel and Yahweh and the covenant between Yahweh and Noah is made evident by the following lines in 54:9 "This is like the days of Noah to me: Just as I swore that the waters of Noah would never again go over the earth, so I have sworn that I will not be angry with you and will not rebuke you."

81　On occasion, though, it is ambiguous which root is meant. Wellhausen, in Psalm 16:4 argues that ʿaṣṣābôṯ should be connected with ʿōṣeb instead of with ʿaṣṣebeṯ. A. Graupner, "āṣāb," *TDOT*, Vol. 11, 281.

82　Wenham, *Genesis 1–15*, 189.

83　Ellen van Wolde, *Stories of the Beginning: Genesis 1–11 and Other Creation Stories*, trans. John Bowden (London: SCM Press, 1996), 127.

84　Habel, *The Birth, the Curse and the Greening of the Earth*, 105.

85　Genesis 4:11 and 9:25.

86　Genesis 4:11, NRSV.

87　The closest to the ground being cursed after this is in Deuteronomy 28:16–18 when the people are assured that if they fail to keep the law they will be cursed in the field, and the fruit of the ground.

88　Wenham, *Genesis 1–15*, 190. David Clines also thinks this is the case, but argues that it is because of the parallelism with God promising not to destroy all living things again. David J. A. Clines, *The Theme of the Pentateuch*, 2nd ed. (Sheffield: Sheffield Academic, 1997), 77.

89　Wenham, *Genesis 1–15*, 190.

90　J. Scharbert, "qll," *TDOT*, Vol. 13, 40.

91　W. M. Clark also links this fruitfulness to the lifting of the curse. "The Flood and the Structure of the Pre-Patriarchal History," *Zeitschrift für die alttestamentliche Wissenschaft* 83:2 (1971): 208.

92　Habel, *The Birth, the Curse and the Greening of the Earth*, 111.

93　See Augustine's point earlier.

94　E.g. Boyd, "Evolution as Cosmic Warfare," 139.

95　Romans 8:18–23, NRSV.

96　This is the usual interpretation in the standard commentaries: Ernst Käsemann, *Commentary on Romans*, trans. Geoffrey W. Bromiley (Grand Rapids, MI: Eerdmans, 1980), 234–235; C. E. B. Cranfield, *The Epistle to the Romans*, Vol. 1, *International Critical Commentary* (Edinburgh: T & T Clark, 1975), 413; James D. G. Dunn,

Romans 1–8, Word Biblical Commentary 38a (Dallas, TX: Word Books, 1988), 469–471; Joseph A. Fitzmyer, *Romans*, Anchor Bible Series 33 (New York, NY: Doubleday, 1993), 505–507; Thomas R. Schreiner, *Romans, Baker Exegetical Commentary on the New Testament* (Grand Rapids, MI: Baker Academic, 1998), 436; Douglas J. Moo, *Epistle to the Romans* (Grand Rapids, MI: Eerdmans, 1996), 515; Brendan Byrne, "An Ecological Reading of Rom. 8.19–22: Possibilities and Hesitations," in *Ecological Hermeneutics: Biblical, Historical and Theological Perspectives*, eds. David G. Horrell, Cherryl Hunt, Christopher Southgate, and Francesca Stavrakopoulou (London: T & T Clark, 2010), 83–93, 90–91; Cherryl Hunt, David G. Horrell, and Christopher Southgate, "An Environmental Mantra? Ecological Interest in Romans 8:19–23 and a Modest Proposal for its Narrative Interpretation," *Journal of Theological Studies* 59:2 (October 2008): 569. Hunt et al. do emphasise that a broader background than just Genesis 3 is likely in view; Ben Witherington III, *Paul's Letter to the Romans: A Socio-Rhetorical Commentary* (Grand Rapids, MI: Eerdmans, 2004), 223. Andrew Linzey, "Good News for the World?" *Third Way* 26:6 (2000): 24; Harry A. Hahne, "The Birth Pangs of Creation, the Eschatological Transformation of the Natural World in Romans 8:19–22," Paper presented at the annual meeting of the Evangelical Theological Society, November 1999. Accessed 18 September 2013. Online: www.balboa-software.com/hahne/BirthPangs.pdf; Harry A. Hahne, *The Corruption and Redemption of Creation: Nature in Romans 8:19–22 and Jewish Apocalyptic Literature* (London: T & T Clark, 2006), 1, 187–188. For a history of interpretation, see David G. Horrell, Cherryl Hunt, and Christopher Southgate, *Greening Paul: Rereading the Apostle in a Time of Ecological Crisis* (Waco, TX: Baylor University, 2010), 65–70.

97 Dunn, *Romans 1–8*, 471. Hahne shares this view: not that creation fell because of rebellion, but "Creation is not in the state in which it was originally created. Yet it is not correct to speak of a fallen creation, as if the subhuman creation disobeyed God. . . . Rather, nature is a victim to human sin" *The Corruption and Redemption of Creation*, 192.

98 Some scholars are willing to say both that Paul thought the cosmic fall was incited by a historical Adam, and that Paul was mistaken in this respect. Lamoureux, *Evolutionary Creation*, 324.

99 Laurie J. Braaten, "All Creation Groans: Romans 8:22 in Light of the Biblical Sources," *Horizons in Biblical Theology* 28 (2006): 131–159; Richard Bauckham, *Bible and Ecology: Rediscovering the Community of Creation* (London: Dartman, Longman & Todd, 2010), 92–101.

100 See Braaten, "All Creation Groans," 138–141.

101 Braaten, "All Creation Groans," 152–154.

102 Jeremiah 4:31, Isaiah 21:2–3. See also Conrad Gempf, "The Imagery of Birth Pangs in the New Testament," *Tyndale Bulletin* 45:1 (1994): 122–125.

103 Amos 1:2; Hosea 4:1–3; Jeremiah 4:23–28, 12:1–4, 12:7–13, 23:9–12; Isaiah 24:1–20, 33:7–9; Joel 1:5–20. See Katherine M. Hayes, *"The Earth Mourns": Prophetic Metaphor and Oral Aesthetic*, Academia Biblica 8 (Leidin: Koninklijke Brill, 2002).

104 Hosea 4:1–3, NRSV.

105 Jeremiah 4:23–26, NRSV.

106 Bauckham, *Bible and Ecology*, 97.

107 Isaiah 24:3, NRSV.

108 Braaten, "All Creation Groans," 145. Note that φθορᾷ in this context does not mean the instantiation of all decay that has ever happened, as might be imagined in a cosmic fall scenario. It means undue decay, or lack of fruitfulness from expected sources, such as the languishing vine (v.7) causing a lack of wine (v. 7 & 9), or the earth ending up "polluted under its inhabitants" (v.5).

109 Isaiah 25:9, NRSV. Waiting on the LORD's deliverance is also mentioned in Isaiah 26:8.

110 Jonathan Moo, "Romans 8:19–22 and Isaiah's Cosmic Covenant," *New Testament Studies* 54:1 (2008): 74–89.

111 Moo, "Romans 8:19–22," 84.

112 Moo, "Romans 8:19–22," 84.

113 Elsewhere, Paul uses the word for "travail," ὠδίνω, only in Galatians 4:19 and 4:27. The second of these is a quotation from Isaiah 54:1, reinforcing the link with prophetic material in his use of this verb. The Greek verb for "groaning," συστενάζω, is derived from the root verb στενάζω which is used elsewhere by Paul only in 2 Corinthians 5:2&4, where the context is the believer's groaning in longing for the redemption of the body "so that what is mortal may be swallowed up by life." Nowhere else is the creation described as mourning or in travail in the Pauline material.

114 Moo, "Romans 8:19–22," 89. Italics original. Emil Brunner is more emphatic: "The Bible knows nothing of a 'fallen world'. . . . We have no right to turn the divine promise that things will one day be different from what they are now, in to the conclusion that 'once they were not.'" *The Christian Doctrine of Creation and Redemption, Dogmatics*, Vol. 2, trans. Olive Wyon (London: Lutterworth, 1952), 128.

115 Isaiah 32:15–20, NRSV.

116 Verse 19's description of the forest disappearing, or being laid low by hail, has been problematic for interpreters. Kaiser suggests the verse "consists entirely of allusions" and "that the forest destroyed by the hail is in fact the enemy army, which has overwhelmed the city of God (cf. 10.33f., 18: 30.30)" Otto Kaiser, *Isaiah 13–39: A Commentary*, trans. R. A. Wilson (Philadelphia, PA: Westminster, 1974), 335–336.

117 Joel 1:10, NRSV.

118 Joel 1:18, 20.

119 Joel 1:19, 21–22, NRSV.

120 For further work on the theme of Paul's hope, see Horrell et al., *Greening Paul*, 175–176.

121 C. E. B. Cranfield, "Some Observations on Romans 8:19–21," in *Reconciliation and Hope: New Testament Essays on Atonement and Eschatology Presented to L. L. Morris on His 60th Birthday*, ed. Robert Banks (Exeter: Paternoster, 1974), 227.

122 Chris Wright, "Theology and Ethics in the Old Testament," *Transformation* 16:3 (1999): 82; Cranfield, *The Epistle to the Romans*, 413. Hahne, *The Corruption and Redemption of Creation*, 190.

123 Cranfield, "Some Observations on Romans 8:19–21," 227.

124 Messer, "Natural Evil after Darwin," 149.

3   Joining the conversation

When I talk to scientists about my work, I am often asked, "What is it you actually *do?*" Research without experiments is confusing. My usual reply is that my task is to join a conversation that is happening with any new insights I can muster from interdisciplinary knowledge. This chapter is intended to outline the conversation that has come before so that what I say in Chapters 4–6 is placed in its relevant context.

There are vast oceans of literature concerning theodicy,[1] and many who have addressed the question of non-human animal suffering. This chapter will be limited in two ways. First, I will focus almost exclusively on the literature that covers non-human suffering, as opposed to theodicy inclusive of human concerns. Second, I will largely confine myself to the contemporary discussion, rather than explore all possible historical debates. With very few exceptions, my sources are from the last 30 years – publications that are largely motivated by the growing ecological crisis that has brought the question of non-human suffering ever more to the forefront of theological consideration.[2] All four extant book-length treatments of evolutionary theodicy are recent, with Christopher Southgate and Michael Murray both publishing in 2008, Nicola Hoggard Creegan adding her contribution in 2013, and Trent Dougherty his in 2014. Most of the relevant articles have all been published within the last decade. The long tradition of Christian theodicy is less relevant to this question of evolutionary suffering because it either advances arguments that are not applicable to non-humans (such as the moral freewill defence) or because the particular sharpening of the question through evolutionary sciences (that the disvalues are necessary to the values) was simply not available. There was a sophisticated argument about animal suffering in the late Victorian period (post 1859)[3] that would make an interesting study. However, the scientific data and theories today have changed so much since Darwin's day that it would take a rather substantial piece of work to translate the concepts they were working with into the present debate. That research is simply beyond the scope of this work.

This chapter is structured to journey from the clearer and simpler philosophical positions that hold few presuppositions through to the increasingly difficult and complex theological positions. This path of exploration is intended to allow the reader to build layer upon layer of complexity as the arguments become increasingly multi-faceted.

Chapter overview

The philosophical section begins by exploring and rejecting the positions that simply evade the problem of reconciling a good God with the existence of evolutionary evil, such as the inscrutability response advanced by Michael Bergmann, William Alston, and Daniel Howard-Snyder.[4] The rest of the philosophical positions, most notably those advanced by Michael Murray, but also including Peter van Inwagen, Richard Swinburne, Trent Dougherty, and Robin Attfield,[5] are explored through the grid of Christopher Southgate and Andrew Robinson's "Good-harm Analyses."[6] Southgate and Robinson's identification of defences as either property-consequence, developmental, or constitutive helps to reduce these complex arguments into their component parts for analysis and evaluation. At the end of the philosophical section, there is a bridging section exploring the limits of philosophy, followed by a contrast of philosophical with theological approaches.[7] I argue that along with different resources and limitations, the theological project is written for a different audience than most philosophical theodicies.

In the second half of the chapter I explore the theological positions in evolutionary theodicy. As with the philosophical section, the theological section begins by exploring some positions that evade the problem – this time through radical redefinitions of God that eliminate the divine qualities of goodness or omnipotence that are central to the question.[8] Next, I go on to investigate the theological positions that posit a fall scenario. While my own rejection of the fallenness of the natural world was made clear in the first two chapters, here I investigate in greater depth the theological and philosophical reasons for rejecting a fallen world. Finally, I will investigate more moderate redefinitions of God or God's action in the world as they relate to the natural world.

This chapter is like a map room. The purpose of looking at a map before a journey is to have some idea of the landscape that will be traversed. There is no rush in the map room, and the traveller is prepared for the challenges of the landscape to come. The reader will find, then, that many of the concepts, themes, and arguments found here will be revisited in later chapters. This chapter will also outline the types of debate I will not pursue, and knowledge of the strategies and approaches I will not use may prove valuable to the reader as well.

Philosophical positions

No problem of evil or impossible problem

The first two philosophical approaches to the problem of evil are the neo-Cartesian approach and the inscrutability response. Both end almost before they begin. The first approach, called by Michael Murray "neo-Cartesianism" due to its initial attribution to Descartes, simply states that there is no problem of animal suffering because non-human animals do not have the higher-order capacities necessary to suffer.[9] Non-human animals, in this view, only appear to suffer.[10] Pain-related behaviours are carried out without any conscious awareness of pain or particularly of suffering. This view has some experimental verification, where pain-avoidance behaviour and even simple learning tasks were exhibited in the bodies of rats whose spinal cords had been disconnected from their brains.[11] However, there is plenty of strong and convincing opposing evidence that shows the symptoms of psychological distress that we associate with suffering are regularly present in non-human animals.[12] Michael Murray explores this topic at length[13] and concludes: "few will find the neo-Cartesian position to be compelling or even believable."[14] The common-sense argument against neo-Cartesianism is simply too strong, and ultimately, since the position cannot be conclusively proved or disproved, most people prefer to err on the side of greater compassion, giving the benefit of the doubt to the non-human animals. At the very least, it is argued, non-human animal pain responses are similar enough to human pain responses that it would damage one's humanity to simply ignore them.[15] Were that not enough, shadows of seventeenth-century vivisectionists laughing about the pained cries of dogs as "mere creaking of the animal 'clockwork'" are revolting enough to keep most people away from contemplating such a position.[16] The evidence of non-human animals being "subjects-of-a-life"[17] continue to increase and distance people yet further from any contemplation of the neo-Cartesian perspective.

The strongest contemporary critique of the neo-Cartesian position comes from Trent Dougherty.[18] He thoroughly examines the arguments against non-human animal pain, including the purported inability to hold higher-order conscious thought (the ability to reflect on oneself being in pain) and the lack of a sufficiently complex neo-cortex (the large frontal lobe in humans that is the seat of higher-order thought). Dougherty undermines the position by drawing on contemporary pain theorists who identify pain as an "emotion like" state rather than a cognitive judgement.

> This evaluative account requires less cognitively than any other. Because the seeings as good and bad here are emotive, they are pure aversion or attraction, not the kind of considered judgments dependent upon the neocortex and not requiring higher-order thought that [non-human] animals plausibly don't have.[19]

These emotion-like responses rely on deeper, more common parts of the brain that are shared by humans with the rest of vertebrates. Many non-human animals share the same parts of the brain that process pain, and respond behaviourally in ways that are consistent with experiencing pain. This is not only a common-sense observation, but is also the scientific consensus as outlined in a 2009 report by the US National Research Council Committee on Recognition and Alleviation of Pain in Laboratory Animals.[20] I will, therefore, set aside the neo-Cartesian approach.[21]

The second approach, known as the inscrutability response, states that the reasons for the existence of suffering simply cannot be known; human capacity to understand the complexities of the world is too small. In order to evaluate the extent of evil, or prove that one good outweighs another evil, one would have to be able to describe all the necessary conditions for both, as well as describe every single outcome emerging from their initial occurrences. There are simply too many variables for a person to make a plausible judgement, even in a relatively simple situation. Humans are, therefore, not well positioned to make arguments about whether or not evils can or cannot outweigh respective goods at a cosmic scale. Defenders of this position include Michael Bergmann, Daniel Howard-Snyder, and William Alston.[22] Shrouded in mystery, the problem of non-human animal suffering remains intractable, and attempts to solve it only result in wasted philosophical and theological speculations. They distract from the more important work of discerning and responding to evil here and now.

The inscrutability response may seem attractive since it begins where all theodicy ultimately ends: in mystery. However, the advocates of this position miss many important discussions that emerge from thinking about suffering. Theodicy is not only attempting to find an answer to suffering, it also includes reflection on the nature of God and on the nature of the world. To attempt to reflect on the divine nature or the constitution of reality without including suffering would be obviously impossible, and so wrestling with theodicy must continue, even if only for the light it throws on other questions. So while a final comprehensive answer to suffering may never be found, I do not take the inscrutabilist's choice of refusing to engage the question. Let us turn instead to three sets of philosophical approaches that take the plunge in acknowledging and giving response to evil.

Analytical philosophical defences

Most philosophical defences attempt to show through analytical thinking that God has not built avoidable evil into the natural process of the world, thereby rescuing God from culpability for the extent and severity of animal suffering.[23] It is, as I argued in the first chapter, a proceeding of the courtroom. These defences[24] are built of several different types of strategies, helpfully distinguished by Christopher Southgate and Andrew Robinson[25] who outline three different categories of good-harm analyses (GHA), in each of which the good is supposed to outweigh the harm. The three categories are defined as:

> Property-consequence GHAs: a consequence of the existence of a good, as a property of a particular being or system, is the possibility that possession of this good leads to it causing harms.
> Developmental GHAs: the good is a goal which can only develop through a process which includes the possibility (or necessity) of harm. [These can be further divided into instrumental or by-product varieties of developmental GHAs].
> Constitutive GHAs: The existence of a good is inherently, constitutively, inseparable from the experience of harm or suffering.[26]

Southgate and Robinson further divide these categories by three different references: human, anthropocentric, and biotic. As only the anthropocentric and biotic references include consideration of the non-human animal world, they will be the only two explored here.

Property-consequence GHAs

Nomic regularity is a good example of a property-consequence GHA. The concept of nomic regularity states that the processes of change can be described in law-like forms with few or no exceptions.[27] If I drop a large rock, its fall will always adhere to certain law-like descriptions, as will the impact it would have on a body below. Great harms develop out of the fact that the world has extremely regular patterns of change and interaction. Fires do not stop burning when fawns are caught in them, nor does water cease carrying its properties because it is built into a tsunami. The world's physical properties continue to stay stable regardless of the suffering they inflict on living beings. Because these law-like forms cause so much suffering, Michael Murray argues that "theists must accept the claim that nomic regularity is either something that God values highly in creation or it is an inevitable by-product of something else valued highly."[28] What could constitute this highly valued something else?

Two varieties of possible goods are derived from nomic regularity: first, the anthropocentric perspective, which states that the entire universe is subject to law-like forms for specifically human goods, and second, the biotic perspective, which argues that nomic regularity is good for non-human animals themselves.

For Murray, the possibility of a moral universe is one of the outcomes of nomic regularity that could form part of an anthropocentric GHA.[29] It is only in a universe where actions have predictable effects that a person can have a chance to make real and effective moral choices. Without knowledge of what might occur if, say, one were to throw a hard object at another person, free and effective – and crucially, moral – choice becomes meaningless.[30] In this case, the suffering of non-human animals (who do not have moral capacities[31]) due to nomic regularities are simply a tragic by-product of the necessity for moral human freedom. Thus, non-human animal suffering serves human ends.[32] A second example of an anthropocentric approach is to argue that nomic regularity serves humans by providing intellectual satisfaction through scientific investigations. The nineteenth-century geologist George Frederick Wright, for example, wrote happily that in comparison to a trilobite's whole pleasure in its own life:

> a far higher purpose is served in the adaptation of his complicated organism and of the position of his tomb in a sedimentary deposit to arrest the attention and direct the reasoning of a scientific observer. The pleasure of one lofty thought is worth more, and so more fitted to be with the Creator an object of design, than a whole herd of sensational pleasures. A page of Darwin has to a single reader more 'value in use' than all the elements had to the whole race of Trilobites in Silurian seas.[33]

The first argument, that nomic regularity is necessary for moral choice, and that it necessarily causes non-human animal suffering as a by-product, would hold great merit if it could be shown that moral choice could not exist some other way that did not involve non-human animal suffering, or if non-human animals themselves benefited from moral choice. However, in the form that van Inwagen articulates the argument (which denies non-human animals any possibility of moral choice), it is hard to accept that billions of organisms' suffering and death is outweighed by the possibility of human moral choice alone. Any valid solution must attribute value to the lives of the non-human animals themselves.

The second argument, Wright's approach of the intellectual satisfaction of the palaeontologist, is even more outrageous to suggest, since all the satisfaction of the pursuit of physics and mathematics and present-day biology would have been available to investigate without the suffering and death of past non-human animals. Palaeontology would certainly have suffered, but not the scientific endeavour as a whole. Furthermore, the great majority of non-human animals have left no trace able to be investigated by science, and so we cannot use this argument to explain their travail. It is morally vacuous to attribute so much suffering to no greater good than a particular branch of intellectual satisfaction, unknown to the vast majority of humans.

A slightly stronger point to be made here is that without nomic regularity no science would be possible, since science depends on the repeatable law-like functioning of the natural world. Robin Attfield points out that without natural regularities:

> There would be no science and no scope for rationality, there would be no creatures of the kinds that have evolved by natural selection within the framework of the laws of nature to which we are accustomed, and if there were any life at all, it would be unrecognizably different, with no recognizable goods or ills remaining. For conscious life, indeed, some system of nature not too different from that of the actual world seems essential.[34]

Two objections arise in response to Attfield's statement. First, the applicability of rationality is almost entirely a human value, and does not ascribe worth to the non-human animals themselves. Second, an "unrecognizably different" life would not necessarily be better or worse than the current state of affairs, so pointing out that it would simply be different does not constitute an argument. In a hypothetical "other order" without non-human animal suffering, there could still remain goods and ills of a different order, and so the question would have to land on whether or not those goods and ills outweigh the goods and ills currently in operation. Unfortunately, with no concrete knowledge of another world (it will always be hypothetical) and with only a very limited knowledge of this world, the question remains unanswerable. It is better to argue, as I will later, that nomic regularity gives non-human animals the chance to develop skills and abilities, to "selve" and form themselves in ways that would be unavailable to them without nomic regularity, even if the present order does cause suffering.[35]

A different sort of anthropocentric argument comes from Peter van Inwagen, who asserts that the co-creator destiny of humanity requires a world with the properties of nomic regularity, because one could not have dominion over a world of massive irregularity.[36] A world constantly interfered with by direct divine intervention could not be handed over to human rule in the eschaton because they would not be able to intervene in the same ubiquitous and supernatural way. Although God might be able to constantly intervene to prevent harm, for example by transforming a falling tree limb into water so as not to hurt the creature below, humans would not be able to do this. The world system, built upon such interventions, would collapse into chaos upon being handed over to humans. This is not a developmental argument because van Inwagen does not imply that the regularities are necessary for humans to learn their roles as governors of creation, but only that their task would be impossible to perform without said regularities. Once again, there is little in this argument that can justify the long past of non-human animal suffering, particularly when the eschaton is usually envisioned to work under different "rules of being" anyways.[37] In the end, anthropocentric property-consequence GHAs are unsatisfactory, and therefore have little to contribute to the contemporary debate.

Property-consequence arguments with a biotic reference can also focus on nomic regularity. Murray points out "embodied creatures cannot successfully reproduce, acquire adequate nutrition, constitute a suitably interdependent ecosphere, and so on, unless the physical world in which they are embodied is appropriately nomically regular."[38] Here, at least, the goods of nomic regularity benefit the individual non-human animals themselves. They are enabled to have autonomous and effective lives because the reliability of the world opens up the possibility of developmental values such as learning, adapting, and responding to the environment. Nomic regularity insofar as it is part of a creature's ability to selve, and thus exists with a biotic reference, forms part of a successful defence.

Apart from nomic regularity, a more generalised property-consequence argument with biotic reference looks to the consequences of some natural processes, such as plate tectonics. The anguished death of many non-human animals swept out to sea by a tsunami – caused by plate movement – is measured against the innumerable and necessary goods that plate tectonic movement provides. An earth with moving plates will harm creatures through earthquakes, volcanoes, and tsunamis. Yet, without the goods that plate tectonics bring, there would be no possibility of life on earth.[39] Property-consequence arguments, particularly with a biotic reference, are helpful starting points but they do not address the imbalance of harms: why one individual suffers more than another. To answer that, one needs to draw on wider theological and philosophical resources.

Developmental GHAs

Developmental GHAs argue that certain processes include the possibility (or necessity) of harm for certain goods to develop. Anthropocentric arguments in this category abound. The moral choice argument explored earlier can easily, and is often, argued from this perspective. That is, human moral choice can only be developed through involvement in a world like ours that involves suffering and pain. Michael Corey concludes his book *Evolution and the Problem of Natural Evil* with this point:

> Now we are in a position to understand why an omnipotent Deity would have opted to create the universe in a gradual, evolutionary manner, instead of instantaneously by divine fiat. He presumably did so in order to facilitate the human growth process as much as possible; but in order to do this He seems to have been compelled to implement the same evolutionary processes in the natural world that appear to be an essential part of the Human Definition.[40]

If the scope of value is widened beyond humans to sentient beings, the GHA can take on a biotic reference. Murray, in his Chaos-to-Order argument, argues that the present state of synchronic order – that is, order that is displayed at a given instant by an array of different organisms,[41] including creatures like human beings – could only have emerged from the early chaotic state of the universe through a process "which tends to allow for an overall increase in organismic complexity over time."[42] Murray explores the possibility that the evolution of complex beings necessitates the long chain of creatures beforehand. The suffering of creatures finds meaning in the values of progress, narrative structure, and the necessity of divine hiddenness. He concludes that none of these instrumental goods adequately stands as a defence, but goes on to say that chaos-to-order can be viewed as an intrinsic good, and thus succeed as a defence. The intrinsic good of chaos-to-order is found in analogy to the idea that a man who can make a watch-making machine is more worthy of praise than a man who can simply make a watch. In a similar way, God making the world with the ability to carry on creative processes of its own – to be seeded with developmental possibilities of aesthetic, moral, and religious value that emerge over time – "is of greater value than creation of the finished project by divine fiat."[43] Murray argues that this is not an ad hoc argument in light of evolution because it was attested to by Christian thinkers long before Darwin, such as Gregory of Nyssa and Augustine.[44] As such, Murray considers this the most compelling defence in light of non-human animal suffering. This developmental GHA is only very subtly different from the biotic property-consequence GHA. The difference lies mainly in a longer timeframe: the developmental GHA argues that a creature has the opportunity to change over its lifetime due to nomic regularity, while the property-consequence GHA argues that the creature can make a meaningful decision here and now, without the thought of how that decision might shape its future self. However, the two arguments are very close, and naturally overlap with each other.

A philosophical route more focussed on the individual creature itself is the developmental instrumental GHA. This defence argues that many good goals are only developed by use of the harms in question. Pain is the classic example – a defensive mechanism that the body uses to protect itself. People who do not feel pain, or who do not associate pain with suffering, end up seriously damaging their bodies because they do not avoid destructive situations. Paul Brand and Philip

Yancey explain pain's tremendous value in their book, *The Gift of Pain*.[45] Brand was a doctor in India working with patients with Hansen's disease (leprosy) and began to suspect that the damage patients suffered was from their lack of ability to feel pain rather than from any "flesh-eating" properties of the bacteria. Mysterious wounds were investigated, and invariably preventable causes were found. In one memorable case, rats were found eating flesh off patient's fingers while they slept. Without the warning signals of pain, patients simply slept through the attacks.[46] The inability to feel pain led the patients into countless situations where their bodies were irreparably damaged because they did not learn to avoid harm.

From this perspective, every creature that feels pain, and can therefore respond to harmful stimuli in its environment, gains far more from the harm of pain than from its lack. "That capacity to suffer" writes Attfield, "drives the capacity for focussed consciousness; thought cannot happen in plants, and emerges in the course of evolutionary history partly so as to secure wellbeing while at the same time averting pain."[47] The benefit of pain is attributable directly to the creature who experiences it, so it is considered an instrumental harm. Indeed, the very *hurtfulness* of pain is what makes it so valuable: everything else is put aside until the damage is responded to in some way.[48] The benefits that pain brings cannot be separated from its harm. If pain did not hurt, it would lose its protective function. Pain is part of a biological "package deal." Developmental instrumental GHAs, insofar as the harms benefit the individual themselves, are very strong arguments. New challenges arise regarding the goodness of God when the instrumental argument begins to extend beyond the individual. For example, those who argue that "the pain of the one causes the harmony of the whole," raise questions about why God should use tactics that are so brutal to the allegedly loved individual.[49]

One of the ways the suffering of individuals is accounted for in the larger evolutionary scheme is through a developmental GHA known as the "Only Way" argument.[50] The basic argument is that an evolutionary process, with all the harms it possesses, is the only way to create life without constant intervention.[51] The "only way" argument is advanced by both philosophers and theologians, and I will review both here since the essential point is scientific and philosophical. Arthur Peacocke sums up this type of argument when he writes:

> There are inherent constraints on how even an omnipotent Creator could bring about the existence of a law-like creation that is to be a cosmos not a chaos, and thus an arena for the free action of self-conscious, reproducing complex entities and the coming to be of the fecund variety of living organisms whose existence the Creator delights in.[52]

A process like evolution may be one of those "inherent constraints" – there are only so many ways to grow a creature. Attfield shows convincingly how biological values – such as organisms with quick neural capacities and fleet-footedness – could only have developed independently in predator-prey relationships.[53] Attfield admits that in a totally different created order these skills might have been implanted directly by divine action, thus diminishing the need for violence, yet he asserts that no other non-interventionist system would provide the skills and attributes we value.[54] Attfield writes, "Though evolution by natural selection is not logically necessary, it is probably the only kind of non-interventionist world-system which could give us those capacities found in nature that we value."[55] Christopher Southgate agrees that this argument is unprovable, but still maintains that it is "common sense to a scientist."[56] If there was another way to begin with a Genesis-like *de novo* creation where animals appeared fully developed with their various skills, competition for food and resources would soon come to govern ongoing evolution in any case, unless animal interactions were constantly prevented by divine intervention. Interestingly, the atheist Richard Dawkins joins theists in this assertion that God had no other choice. Dawkins insists that only natural selection could account for the adaptive complexity we see in nature.[57]

The "only way" argument does not only apply to the evolutionary development of life, but can equally apply to the physical constants of the entire universe. Robert Russell surveyed the research assessing the possibilities in determining the cosmological constants for the universe to be fine-tuned for life, and concluded: "God had little choice."[58] John Barrow has also outlined Gerald Whitrow's investigation of the possibility of life in the universe with different time and space dimensions, and concluded that the universe had to be exactly as it is to sustain complex life. Barrow writes,

> the alternatives are too simple, too unstable, or too unpredictable for complex observers to evolve and persist within them. As a result we should not be surprised to find ourselves living in three spacious dimensions subject to the ravages of a single time. There is no alternative.[59]

If there was no alternative for physical, complex beings to flourish in than a world where physical constants ensured that values would be mixed with disvalues, and the possibility of life is mixed with the possibility of suffering, then God cannot be at fault for creating the world with the physical constants and properties that it requires. Even creation *ex nihilo* is subject to logical constraints. Robert Russell, Nancey Murphy, Denis Alexander, and John Polkinghorne, have advanced similar "only way" arguments.[60] Theologians as well as philosophers argue that it is reasonable to assume that although every possibility of creation was available to God's divine power – with regard to dimensions, universal constants, attributes of matter, etc. – God still had to create the universe within relatively constrained limits (including the possibility of suffering) if God desired physical life, and in particular, sentient life. Similarly, if creatures are to have some autonomy in their process of selving – if they are to be creatures who make themselves – then natural selection is inevitable. The "Only Way" argument is a developmental by-product approach, where the focus of the good achieved reaches beyond the individual who actually suffers and the harms do not affect every creature equally.[61] The suffering is a by-product of the development, rather than instrumental to the development as in the case of pain.

Another common example of the developmental type, and an example now immortalised in the literature by Jay McDaniel, is the example of the second white pelican chick.[62] White pelicans regularly lay two eggs, with the strategy of raising only one chick. After birth, the second (and usually smaller) sibling is pushed from the nest by the older sibling and ignored by its parents until it dies of exposure or is eaten by a passing predator. However, the advantage of this evolved behaviour is that in a small percentage of cases, the first chick dies, and the parents raise the second chick instead, thus insuring that each reproductive cycle is fruitful. To find value in the death of an insurance pelican chick for the ongoing survival of white pelicans is a developmental by-product approach. The same is true of Holmes Rolston's observation that "adversities make life go and grow. The pressure, before extremity, for doing better is steadily a blessing in disguise. The cougar's fang has carved the limbs of the fleet-footed deer, and vice versa."[63] The suffering of millions of deer as they are painfully brought down by cougars is an unfortunate by-product of a process that is strengthening and stretching deer into beautiful forms as a species, developing specialised skills and senses. Without the bite of the cougar, these rich aspects of the deer's being would soon be lost, just as fish living in dark caves eventually lose their eyes from lack of selective pressure.

Darwin's theory of natural selection rests heavily upon a developmental argument, whether instrumental or by-product. Famously he wrote: "Thus, from the war of nature, from famine and death, the most exalted object which we are capable of conceiving, namely, the production of the higher animals, directly follows."[64] Ruthless competition refines life into "endless forms, most beautiful and most wonderful" yet, Darwin assures us,

> when we reflect on this struggle, we may console ourselves with the full belief, that the war of nature is not incessant, that no fear is felt, that death is generally prompt, and that the vigorous, the healthy, and the happy survive and multiply.[65]

According to Darwin, the goods emerge out of the harms, and heavily outweigh them.

However, the value of Darwinian mechanics is critiqued by those who assert that there are other possibilities available: other paths that would have led to the same goods without the bloodshed and suffering. Martin Nowak presents this sort of riposte by showing how altruistic and cooperative strategies of survival are beneficial to reproductive success.[66] Lynn Margulis goes even farther to argue that complex life, as seen in the origin of eukaryotic cells and many speciation events, could not have developed by random mutation and natural selection alone, but had to have been developed by symbiotic relationships.[67] Indeed, Margulis states, "symbiogenesis, while it can clearly lead to new species, also set up the conditions for speciation itself."[68] If it can be shown that the same or similar goods, such as physical skills and consciousness, could have evolved without the harms of predation, then the case for the developmental by-product GHA's is considerably weakened. At the same time, it is difficult to know how this could be shown conclusively. The problem with these cooperative approaches is that they ignore the eventual necessity of competition: even though a new symbiotic relationship may promote peace between two organisms, the two now work as a new unit within natural selection against other beings. Although two organisms might perhaps even merge to create a new species, that new species must now compete for resources and reproduction rights. Darwin himself, when confronted with the self-sacrificial nature of individual bees and ants, simply assumed that the hive or the nest must now be considered the "unit" of selection, as one hive competes against another.[69] So the essential problem of suffering is not eliminated by symbiotic relationships, only pushed back a step.

Developmental GHA's can begin to address the imbalance of suffering, but only when they are used in light of the suffering individual. Often, developmental arguments get swept up into addressing the grand processes of evolution. They are effective, but are in danger of overlooking the central question of the individual suffering of creatures. Both property-consequence and developmental GHA's are necessary for a theodicy, but they are not in themselves sufficient to convince of the goodness of God or the universality of God's benevolence since there are always so many remaining instances of severe suffering which are not adequately addressed by these approaches.

Constitutive GHA's

Constitutive GHA's find that the goods and harms are linked, not causally as in the two previous types of analyses, but constitutively. This type of defence is used often when ecosystem dynamics are taken into account, exemplified by Holmes Rolston and Loren Wilkinson.[70] Energy transfer up and down trophic levels through predation and decay emerges into the richness and orderliness of the natural world. The circles of life and death encompass the suffering individual, drawing the narrative of their life into a systemic whole that Holmes Rolston describes as "a passion play."[71] Wilkinson outlines the Christology in Revelation of the Lamb who was slain and writes "worthy are all lambs, all victims of the world's carniveroisty [*sic*], for out of their death comes life."[72]

In such considerations, the good is less mechanical and more aesthetic. When the outweighing goods proposed are the existence of beauty or harmony, one enters into the realm of constitutive arguments. Murray argues, for example, that, "there is something grand, beautiful, and artful about a universe which contains within it everything that is necessary in order for it to yield the results God intends for it."[73] In many cases, as with Murray here, the constitutive arguments quickly break down into what are actually developmental instrumental arguments: the harm is good for developing such-and-such an end. Most true constitutive positions become almost entirely theological in nature because theological positions do not need to set the weigh scales mechanically. Theology can affirm the mysterious and paradox-laden non-reductive truths that are found in constitutive arguments. Philosophical thought tends to baulk at what cannot be broken down into its component reasons and analysed, and so there are not any really good examples of a true philosophical constitutive position. In a later section of this chapter I will unpack the extant theological positions.

Compound defences

Most defences do not rest on a single premise, nor on one type of philosophical strategy alone. Philosophers mix together the different approaches to try and build a stronger compound case. Consider Peter van Inwagen's compound approach.[74]

He begins with the statement that nomic regularity is intrinsically good. Or, at least, he says that a world of incongruity or massive irregularity would be extremely bad – worse than a world with suffering. He bases this thesis around three main arguments of intrinsic disutility and one of extrinsic disutility. The three intrinsic arguments are as follows: first, he attempts to show that every world would (for all we know) have to contain either suffering or massive irregularities (a property-consequence GHA). Second, some good comes from the existence of higher-level sentient creatures, and these creatures could only have developed through a process that involves suffering (a developmental instrumental GHA).[75] Therefore, the whole ladder of intermediate forms is a necessary good to the full expression of God's creativity (a constitutive or developmental by-product GHA, depending on how it is elaborated).[76] Third, massive irregularity would be a defect in the world equally morally problematic to the suffering of animals (another property-consequence GHA). Therefore, between the choice of suffering beasts or massive irregularity, the option of suffering is *possibly* the greater good. Extrinsically, as I mentioned earlier, van Inwagen argues that the world is meant to be handed over to human rule in the eschaton and that it would be hard to see how a world of massive irregularity could be handed over if it continually depended on direct divine intervention.[77] Thus, a world of nomic regularity is good for the sake of the humans who will one day rule it (an anthropocentric property-consequence argument). Argument builds upon argument into a whole that is vastly stronger than any one argument alone.

It is now becoming commonplace to suggest that combined or compound defences are the only admissible way to deal with both the complexity of the world and the varieties of natural evil which occur.[78] Both Michael Murray and Christopher Southgate advocate compound theodicies. Murray writes:

> Indeed, it seems quite implausible to think that an evil as widespread as the evil in question here, animal pain and suffering, could or would be explained only by appeal to one narrow range of goods. It seems far more likely that there would be a whole host of goods that God aims to bring about through creation, and that certain types of permitted evil are aimed at securing more than one of these goods.[79]

A compound explanation makes a stronger case, and allows for greater strength against arguments that falsify one or two of the cases made. More than this, a compound defence allows one to bring a variety of goods into focus, not all of them immediately obvious. The promise of eschatological renewal, for example, stands as a great good that can complement many of the other positions, but would be hard to defend if it was the only good. Furthermore, there are a variety of harms to address: the harms caused by a tsunami are different than the harms caused by a predator. It is only natural to assume that different types of defence might apply to each. A compound theodicy or defence allows for the flexibility of addressing these various harms.[80]

All the GHA approaches hinge on one critical point: that it is possible for humans to effectively judge measures of good and evil, or to make compelling arguments about what an outweighing good or evil would look like.[81] In the next section, I will outline how these philosophical approaches contrast with the theological approaches, and how this central assumption has been called into question.

Philosophical and theological approaches compared and contrasted

There are many differences between the philosophical and theological approaches to theodicy. Perhaps the prime difference is one of setting and audience. The philosopher sets him or herself in the courtroom, defending God against the accusations of God's non-existence in light of evil.[82] The audience is sceptical and the purpose is essentially negative: to dismantle arguments brought against God. Peter van Inwagen set up his Gifford Lectures defence to try and convince a "neutral agnostic" that the theistic argument is more compelling than the atheistic argument that God cannot and does not exist.[83] In a similar way, Michael Murray states that his aim is simply to engage the critics of theism on the difficult problem of animal suffering.[84] A theological approach may seek to address critiques from outside a circle of faith or to destabilise atheistic doubts, but its purpose is essentially more constructive than that – to engage in an enquiry about the nature of the God-world relationship and one's own being in that world.[85] By and large, theology assumes God's existence and seeks to encourage, instruct, or aid the believer who is troubled by the suffering they see but who already has a commitment to faith. Theological theodicy seeks to build or reinforce a theological foundation upon which faith can build. In Anselm's famous line, it is "faith seeking understanding."

Methodologically, philosophers seek to approach the question of theodicy with as few theological presuppositions as possible.[86] They often begin with whether the existence of God is plausible at all. Because of the focus on logic and lack of initial assumptions, a philosophical approach often becomes what Thomas Tracy calls a "thin defense," something that deals only with the logical incompatibility of evil with the existence of a god.[87] By contrast, a Christian theological approach starts explicitly with foundational assumptions and with stated sources of authority, such as the Bible and tradition. Holding to these initial beliefs and commitments allows for what Tracy calls a "thick defense." A thick defence attempts to weave a narrative that explains how suffering is consistent with beliefs held about God.[88] While a thick defence offers a theodicy limited by certain conceptual constraints (i.e. it cannot explore any possibility, since some are ruled out by prior belief), it allows for a more in-depth engagement with evidential and existential arguments about evil.

Finally, theology and philosophy are separated by different limits and responsibilities. The philosopher is bound primarily by the constraints of logic and is responsible only for following the argument to its conclusion. The theologian is boundaried by the teachings of Scripture, and is responsible for being faithful to the tradition and the needs of the Church, as well as staying inside the boundaries of orthodox belief.[89]

Theologians should also be more sensitive to the affective and pastoral nature of their endeavour, while philosophers are primarily concerned about whether or not the problem of evil has been "formally satisfied." Such an approach can lead to startlingly problematic claims. Take, for example, philosopher Richard Swinburne who claims that his book formally satisfies the need for showing that God does everything possible to bring about an overall good state of affairs in the evil of the world.[90] He goes on to illustrate his point by listing the overall goods coming from the eighteenth-century African slave trade:

> But God allowing this to occur made possible innumerable opportunities for very large numbers of people to contribute or not to contribute to the development of this [slave] culture; for slavers to choose to enslave or not; for plantation-owners to choose to buy slaves or not and to treat them well or ill; for ordinary white people and politicians to campaign for its abolition or not to bother, and to campaign for the compensation for the victims or not to bother; and so on. There is also the great good for those who themselves suffered as slaves that their lives were not useless, their vulnerability to suffering made possible many free choices, and thereby so many steps towards the formation of good or bad character.[91]

Swinburne may "formally satisfy" the strictly logical needs of a defence through such argumentation, but he does nothing to satisfy the sense of outrage one feels in contemplating human slavery, then and now. If anything, Swinburne's confident description increases the sense of protest and outrage one feels – that the suffering, persecution, and enslavement of millions of people should be considered a great good because it allows rich, free, white people the decision to *perhaps* campaign for the slaves' freedom – it is not convincing as an outweighing good, whatever logical terms it might satisfy.

Compare Swinburne's approach to Christopher Southgate's summary of a theological approach:

> All theodicies that engage with real situations rather than philosophical abstractions, and endeavour to give an account of the God of the Christian Scriptures, arise out of protest and end in mystery. Theodicies never 'work,' in the sense of solving the problem of suffering in the world.[92]

A theodicy arising out of protest and ending in mystery allows the whole person, mind and heart, to engage with the problem, though theological approaches do not often produce the tight, neat packages one finds in analytical philosophy.

My approach in this work is theological. I do not set out to create a watertight case for the plausibility of God, but rather from a wide range of sources I seek a rich description of the God-world relationship in a way that recognises the goodness of God and yet can sustain the burden of suffering.

There are other thinkers who also find the analytical philosophical approach unsatisfactory. The next section will explore three critical responses to "thin defence" philosophical theodicy: rejection of theodicy, "thick defence" philosophy that addresses and engages with the existential issues raised by suffering, and theological approaches. These critiques give further rationale for not pursuing this question from a strictly philosophical angle.

Rejection of theodicy

One of the strongest critiques of the analytical philosophy of theodicy is found in Kenneth Surin's *Theology and the Problem of Evil*.[93] In the introduction he shows how the ahistorical approach of post-Leibniz theodicies badly misrepresents the theological endeavours of figures such as Augustine and Irenaeus. Augustine, he argues, was concerned with the problem of evil in the human heart, and the solution was not to be found in philosophical reasoning but in conversion.[94] For Augustine, "the goal of the true *Christian* philosophy, is the attainment of blessedness, and there is no way to blessedness except that which God has revealed in Jesus Christ."[95] In a similar way, Irenaeus's real goal in historical context was to combat gnosticism and the perversion of the human heart, not to solve an abstract philosophical question. Here it is useful to quote Surin at length:

> There is a 'problem of evil' for Irenaeus, but it has absolutely nothing to do with this kind of 'soul-making' or with anything resembling a theodicy. For as Irenaeus sees it the real problem concerning evil arises in quite another area of theological territory, one occupied by beings who,
>
>> puffed up by the pretence of knowledge, fall away from the love of God, and imagine that they themselves are perfect, for this reason . . . they set forth an imperfect Creator . . . it is therefore better . . . that one should have no knowledge whatever of any reason why a single thing in creation has been made, but should believe in God, and continue in His love, than that, puffed up through knowledge of this kind, he should fall away from that love which is the life of man; and that he should search after no other knowledge except [the knowledge of] Jesus Christ the Son of God, who was crucified for us, than that by subtle questions and hair-splitting expressions he should fall into impiety.
>>
>> (*Against Heresies*, II, 26, 1)[96]

The individualistic and rationalistic activity that philosophers such as Swinburne, Hick, and Plantinga are involved in has nothing to do with the holiness-persuasion writings that formed the tradition of the church. Furthermore, Surin argues, the spiritual formation that consists of the practical defeat and overcoming of evil – which was the goal of the Patristic writings – is, in essence, a trans-individualist task. Holiness is a communal quest, and a theodicy with the goal of holiness cannot survive within the narrow confines of a solitary rationalistic thinker.[97] Surin even goes so far as to say that the state of philosophical theodicy post-Leibniz "must be reckoned to constitute a grave and even insurmountable obstacle" to a theodicy of conversion and holiness.[98]

Surin's approach can be used not only to critique the ahistorical elements of philosophical thought, but also philosophy's tendency to reduce the complexities of the world into thought experiments that are vastly improbable.[99] Once reduced, philosophers set out criteria to be met that have nothing whatsoever to do with either the real world or even theological abstraction, and result in grave troubles of severe anthropocentrism, a myopic view of earth history, and an entrenched utilitarian approach to creation that has no relation to the God of love.

Take the article "Open Theism: does God risk or hope?" by James Rissler as a case study.[100] It is a fairly standard discussion of the questions of providence, evil, and free will explored in relation to an open theist theology. Rissler rightly begins by pointing out that the essential logic of open theism is based on love; that freedom in the world is not an end in itself but a means and necessary grounding point for love. So far so good. Then he writes:

> Let us make the simplifying assumptions that God's sole purpose in creating was that we would freely enter into loving relationships with Him, and that the proportion of free creatures who enter into loving relationships with their Creator relative to those who do not is an appropriate measure of the degree to which God's purpose is achieved. I will call this the proportionality measure. Let us also arbitrarily assume that God's purpose for creation will be achieved if a simple majority of persons freely choose to love Him.[101]

And with that shift, with these self-admittedly arbitrary assumptions, the reader is transported to a world quite alien to the God of the Scriptures, or at least, of Jesus of Nazareth. Jesus spoke of God being like the shepherd who leaves the 99 sheep behind to chase after the lost one, or of discipleship being like the treasure-hunter who joyfully sells all he possesses for the pearl of great price; of abandoned and scandalous risk-taking. One cannot imagine the father of the prodigal son considering his purposes in fatherhood fulfilled if a simple majority of his sons chose to love him. What of the divine care for the two sparrows, sold for a penny? Or the lilies of the field that God attires more splendidly than the great kings of old? Even if Rissler chose the number 99% instead of 50%, it still pictures God in entirely the wrong frame: as a calculating God trying to figure out if the bet of creation is worthwhile. Rissler's appraisal is not faithful to the open theist conception of God that stresses the limitlessness of God's love.[102] Where love is concerned, there can be no fulfilment by a simple majority.

Keep listening to Rissler, and one hears further snippets of the conversation:

> Even if the long-term probability of any particular action having an overall beneficial or deleterious effect on His goal is very close to 0.5, the probability of particular actions having a positive impact in the short term might well be significantly higher.[103]

Or, "Eventually, as the end of time approaches, God will be able to increase the odds of the final proportionality measure being favourable."[104] The reader is left wondering what this discussion could possibly have to do with the God of the Bible who constantly argued, bargained with, begged, rebuked, raged at, forgave, and redeemed people. The colour and dimensions – the very life – of the rich God-world relationship are stripped away by the confines of the philosophical laboratory. The laboratory becomes a mortuary. The irony becomes even more acute when (as with Rissler) the dissections and calculations are intended to show the reasonableness of the scandal of a God who undertakes the always-precarious project of love! This sort of philosophical work draws one ever farther away from the theological project of theodicy.

'Wandering in Darkness'

There are, however, philosophers who do enter the mysteries, who are at home amongst the paradoxes of the complexity of life, and who do not try to fit suffering into small logical boxes. One of these is Eleonore Stump, whose magisterial work *Wandering in Darkness* explores a Thomist theodicy through the frame of four biblical narratives.[105] Although her work only refers to normally functioning human adults, she establishes several important perspectives that help bridge the usual gap between philosophical and theological approaches.

She insists on using narratives as the basis for her philosophical reasoning for two reasons. First, narratives include uncomfortable complexities and nuances that force the philosopher to engage with the three-dimensional full-colour complexities of the world. There are no "suppose a trolley cart full of people is headed for a defective bridge" scenarios. The few created narratives in her work are fastidiously quotidian and probable. Second, the narratives include knowledge and situations that cannot be reduced to the sorts of simple propositions or just-so stories that analytical philosophers tend to prefer. Stump distinguishes between the irreducible narrative-type knowledge, which she calls "Franciscan knowledge," and propositional knowledge, which is dubbed "Dominican knowledge." Analytical philosophy usually proceeds by Dominican knowledge, but Stump performs her work through Franciscan knowledge.

A second merit of Stump's work is that it is wholehearted. If a proposition is soundly logical, meeting all the formal requirements of philosophy, but has the added effect of making the common person cringe at the cold ruthlessness of it, she rejects it. Use of the Holocaust is a good example. Where many will bandy about arguments with reference to the Holocaust, Stump writes:

> Although it is vitally important for us to remember the Holocaust and to reflect deeply on it, taking it simply as one more example or counterexample in academic disputation on the problem of evil strikes me as unspeakably awful. It is enough for me that I am a member of the species that propagated this evil. Stricken awe in the face of it seems to me to be the only response bearable.[106]

The refusal to treat human suffering as simply an interesting datum set for philosophical argument is one of the valuable aspects of Stump's work, and draws her work closer to the pastoral and practical concerns of theology.

There are two aspects of Stump's work that will be important for the argument I will later develop. The first is her exploration of Aquinas's definition of love.[107] The second is Stump's view of the world's experiences adding up to make fractal patterns of nested narratives, in such a way that each individual is the centre of their own story, but is also a contributor to the stories around them.[108] Both of these will help me formulate a view of God's work of redemption, based on love and focussed on the individual, but allowing for a broader range of trans-individual goods as well.

The limitations of Stump's work for my project are clearly stated in her work: it is "limited to the suffering of unwilling, innocent, mentally fully functional adult human beings."[109] There is no case made for non-human animals, and the major centre of her argument – that suffering opens unique possibilities for a person to achieve his or her highest purpose of union with God – is not directly translatable to the wider natural world. Still, her work provides valuable foundational contributions that can be extended to the natural world, as I will explore in Chapters 4 and 6.[110] While Stump's philosophical approach is a great deal closer to the type of project I am working on than the earlier analytical philosophers, it is still entirely philosophical. My project will include philosophy, but will also draw from biblical studies and systematic theology. However, her wholehearted and narratival approaches have shaped my work when I draw on philosophical resources.

In summary, philosophical approaches have both strengths and limitations when considered in light of a theological approach to theodicy. Particular strengths include how the property-consequence and developmental GHAs help support the "only way" argument. The world needs various types of regularities for free creaturely interaction, for the development of skills, and for the possibility of creaturely selving. An evolutionary process may be the only sort of process that brings about complex life while maintaining the value of creaturely freedom.[111] Another advantage of some philosophical approaches – van Inwagen, for example – is that they demonstrate how different types of arguments can be combined into compound arguments that are stronger than their individual components. My goal, however, is to explore contested territory and map out a thick defence – a narrative that holds God and suffering together. Now we turn to explore the available theological approaches to see what resources they offer.

Theological positions

There are various theological positions that seek to account for evolutionary suffering. Some of them would fit well in the organisational grid of good-harm analyses used for the preceding philosophical viewpoints, but several of them cannot be easily reduced to those categories of balancing goods and harms. I will proceed, therefore, with a different organisational approach. I will first explore the strategies that seek to dismiss the problem as either non-existent or intractable. Then I will explore the theodicies that seek to redefine God in such a way that the problem no longer exists. Third, I will outline the strategies that seek to get God "off the hook" by denying in one fashion or another that the world really is God's creation. Finally, I will look at the remaining theodicies that argue for various values and constitutive elements arising from evolutionary harms and explore them through a grid of different creational standpoints.[112]

It should be remembered as I proceed that the process of defining these arguments requires an element of reduction. Many of the arguments here are parts of larger compound arguments and they are not usually proposed alone, as if one argument should be expected to hold the full weight of explanation for natural evil.

Dismissal of the problem

There are some thinkers who, when confronted with the horrors of nature, simply shrug their shoulders, and fail to see the problem. Kenneth Miller, for example, raises the question of natural evil only to conclude, "the brutality of life is in the eye of the beholder."[113] There is no ontological problem to be solved, only a perspective to be changed. Viewed from the right perspective nature's most horrific inhabitants – from cordyceps and Ichneumonidae to necrotizing bacteria – are all beautiful creatures, splendid in adaptation and complex in developmental strategies. The wilful destruction of one creature by another is simply the way the world works. Nor are non-human animals culpable for their actions. As amoral agents, to ascribe evil to their actions is, as Holmes Rolston points out, a "category mistake."[114] Therefore, there is no real problem of natural evil to be solved; only a certain distaste to be overcome.

I agree that non-human creatures are either amoral or pre-moral, and that natural processes do not reflect rational moral choice, and therefore are not "evil" in the same sense as a murder or a war would be.[115] Still, this does not in itself excuse the question of why a good and all-loving God would create a world in which harms occur, nor why a God would allow suffering and death to be intrinsic to the process of development. Even if creatures are amoral, God should still be expected to act in moral ways in respect of them. The vast disjunction between the Gospel message that the "meek shall inherit the earth" and the wild's "law of club and fang"[116] raises many theological questions which cannot be answered by a simple redefinition of evil.[117] Ted Peters and Martinez Hewlett write,

> the tendency among theistic evolutionists to collapse the theodicy problem into natural process – to see violence, suffering, and death as merely natural and hence value-neutral – represents a failure of theological nerve. It is a sellout to naturalism and a loss to theism.[118]

Mystery response

Celia Deane-Drummond views the world as penetrated by a mysterious evil, and dismisses the problem of evil by naming natural disvalue as creation's "shadow sophia" and placing the debate in the dark realms of mystery. Drawing from Bulgakov's Orthodox tradition, the notion of sophia (wisdom) and shadow sophia (anti-wisdom) stand as the cosmic goods and evils. Deane-Drummond follows an Augustinian definition of evil as *privatio boni*, the deprivation of good. Therefore, shadow sophia is present as a possibility simply because true sophia exists in a world where it can be lost or resisted.[119] The shadow sophia is the chaos and non-being of creation, the source of death and opposition to God. Deane-Drummond writes that one of the advantages of the shadow sophia position is that: "it resists too ready an explanation as to why [shadow sophia] exists." [120] In other words, we are not told why it is "inevitable that shadow sophia surfaces in creation in the way that is envisaged, [where] human wisdom is confronted by its own limitations."[121] Deane-Drummond denies that this is "an easy escape into the idea of evil as mystery" and insists that "the depth of evil and suffering in the world are ultimately beyond human understanding."[122] If one accepts her caveat that it is not an "easy escape" into the concept of mystery, her conclusion still lands the theologian in a place where no more can be said because reasoning has reached its limits. To some extent this is a necessary admission,[123] but one cannot move to her conclusion of shadow sophia too quickly because it lacks important nuance. When it comes to some of the developmental arguments, to draw a conclusion of mystery too quickly ends up overlooking very simple and persuasive arguments to the contrary. The necessity of pain for a flourishing life outlined earlier by Paul Brand and Philip Yancey is a good example. They show that pain is a protective element that keeps creatures from harm. If, instead, one concluded with Deane-Drummond that suffering caused by pain is the absence of a good, or that it is simply beyond human wisdom, we would miss the constructive elements of pain. In the end, evolutionary disvalues as shadow sophia may be the last step a theologian must take, but there are many paths to explore before one gets there. Jumping to the end immediately sets the problem too quickly into the realm of intractable mystery, and misses accounting for the complex goods emerging out of complex harms.

Radically redefining God

The second set of theological strategies seek to radically redefine God in such a way that the problem of disvalues disappears. I call these "radical" redefinitions of God because, unlike later strategies we will see, these approaches have no issue with entirely divesting God of attributes that have long been considered central to the divine character and make no effort to retain the values that were held by those attributes. The three strategies are to divest God of love, of power, and of activity.

The first strategy is to totally divest God of love. Wesley J. Wildman forcefully advances this thesis as the logical outcome of observation of the natural world and the exhaustion of other theological or philosophical options. For Wildman, a loving God who created a world with as much suffering as we now see, and who has not yet relieved it, would be guilty of gross neglect or incompetence. Instead of levelling such an accusation Wildman would rather describe God as the source of all being – the ground of all existence – but not as particularly concerned about what form that existence takes. When Dawkins describes the universe as a place of blind, pitiless indifference, Wildman agrees and simply states: "God is not in the caring business."[124] Disvalues do not pose a difficulty for God's existence from a ground-of-being theistic perspective, but they do pose a challenge for God's alignment with any particular moral path. Wildman's view of God as uncaring does not descend into utter nihilism because he also thinks that goodness and purpose can be found if humans look for it. "The divine particularity" he writes, "is expressed in the structured possibilities and interconnections of worldly existence; wanting and choosing is the human role."[125] God meets the righteous in hope and the unrighteous in purposelessness and despair.

As interesting as ground-of-being theism is, it cannot be a help to people who wish to maintain anything of the character or nature of traditional Christian theism. Wildman's challenge of divine neglect is an important one, but his solution is inadmissible to those who wish to hold any form of Christian faith, because God's love for creatures is intrinsic to that faith (see for example Psalm 100:5, 119:64, 136:1–26, 145:8; Isaiah 54:10; John 3:16; Romans 5:8, 8:35–39; Ephesians 2:4–5, 1 John 4:7–8, etc.).

The second option for radical divine redefinition is process theism, which divests God of power. In process thought, God cannot direct any events, nor can God unilaterally alter the world or its inhabitants in any way. The only activity available to God is to lure the agents of events by divine love into a preferred pathway. In addition, God is understood as evolving with the world, growing in understanding of the world as well as self-understanding throughout the ages. God does not – and could not – have foreknowledge of any kind,[126] but simply observes the world and has perfect knowledge of things present and all things past.

In one sense, process theism offers an elegant solution to the problem of disvalues. God, having given creation freedom to be,[127] is powerless to take it along any other track than that which it chooses. God suffers with the suffering creation, and so takes on the cost of a suffering world. Process theists such as David Griffin will extend the freedom of created things not only to living creatures, but also to the simplest elements of matter such as quarks and electrons.[128] Creation is free to explore various possibilities of being, including many that are against the divine will and end in harm, and God is powerless to stop those harms from occurring. Griffin states frankly, "My solution dissolves the problem of evil by denying the doctrine of omnipotence fundamental to it."[129] Kenneth Surin challenges Griffin's solution by pointing out that if we take the process description of God seriously it fails to actually provide a theodicy at all, since it "cannot legitimately claim to have reconciled the proposition 'There is a God who is *omnipotent*, omniscient and benevolent' with the proposition 'Evil exists'."[130] Process theism "solves" the problem by redefining God in such a way that the problem does not arise in the first place.

A further problem is that a God who is essentially unable to bring about events or direct history in any effective way will not be able to bring about the eschatological recreation of the world either. There is no guarantee left that good will triumph over evil, for the divine lure towards the good has (evidently) already failed many times. Process thinkers are often, troublingly, willing to concede this. But sacrificing the substance of hope for redemption ends up with a greater problem of evil and suffering, not a lesser one, since there is no clear end to evil. Evil simply exists, parasitic upon the good around it, threatening like a black hole to wipe out purpose and meaning, and even God is powerless before it.

Furthermore, as Surin notes, the process approach does little to give comfort or courage to those who suffer. I advance the notion that God co-suffers with each creature, but if co-suffering is advanced on its own, it gives little hope even to those creatures who can understand what comfort divine co-suffering might offer.[131] "To the person in urgent need of succour, it would conceivably be just as efficacious to look to unicorns and centaurs for salvation."[132] Instead, the Christian theodicist looks to the cross, to the defeat of evil, and the in-breaking Kingdom. "What the process theist lacks" writes Surin, "is an eschatology, a resurrection-perspective, in which the almighty God on the cross of the powerless Nazarene is affirmed in faith to have inaugurated a radically new world by this very deed on the cross."[133] Without an eschatology of hope no valid theodicy can exist.

The third strategy is to divest God of activity. If God is all-powerful and all-loving, but cannot use that power in the world in any way, God ends up with tied hands when it comes to rescuing creatures from harm. Philip Clayton and Steven Knapp claim that if God were to rescue a suffering subject from unnecessary harm even once, then God would be morally obliged to do so every time. For God to submit to that moral requirement and rescue creatures every time they were in peril of suffering would undermine the nomic regularity (in Murray's phrase) that is so important to the development of life. If God turned tsunamis into cool mist when they threatened living animals, or if God transformed rocks into feather duvets when creatures stumbled, the world would soon turn into a place where no real learning could take place, and thus rational and autonomous beings could not develop.[134] Clayton and Knapp articulate the "Not-even-once" principle: that even one physical intervention would undermine either God's morality or the world's physical regularity. Clayton and Knapp allow for God influencing thoughts, even on a subconscious level (and thus, presumably, with non-human animals as well), as long as the creature is not compelled to take action in response.[135] While Clayton and Knapp hold that God might possess the traditional attribute of omnipotence, hope for the future is sacrificed since the recreation of the world would certainly require more than simply mental enticement. Also, their approach raises the question whether the Incarnation would count as a violation of the "not-even-once" principle, and what implications that might have if it is. A longer discussion of divine action and the "not-even-once" principle will take place in Chapter 5.[136]

In the end none of the radical redefinitions of God satisfy. Either they do not even remotely resemble the Christ-like God portrayed in the Bible, or they so deeply undermine the basic attributes of God that they sacrifice the future hope of redemption as well. God, in these definitions, may be able to evade accusation of the problem of evolutionary disvalues and even of evil, but the emaciated God left over is not the kind of God who can be trusted to "make all things well." What other theological maps are around?

Fall scenarios, satanic and otherwise

A surprisingly popular contemporary option for those who wish to account for nature's brutality comes from the long theological tradition of the fall. There are two basic categories: event-based fall theories, which blame natural evil on sinful action, satanic or human, and mysterious fallenness theories, where the origin and even the content of evil is unknown or shrouded in mystery.

Of event-based fall theories, the most important is that which roots the origin of natural evil in the angelic fall and the consequent corruption of the world. Augustine most notably developed the idea within the Christian tradition that the fall of Satan and the angels was responsible for the human fall, and that there was evil present in God's good creation before a human fall.[137] Since Darwin, several thinkers have picked it up as a possible solution to pre-human disvalues, including C. S. Lewis, Wolfhart Pannenberg, Michael Lloyd, Stephen Webb, and Gregory Boyd.[138]

The problems are manifold. First, there is no biblical evidence for a satanic fall corrupting the world. Modern biblical scholars would strongly challenge Augustine's notion that a fall, particularly a satanic fall, is present in the Genesis narrative. Second, despite its presence in the tradition, the ancient thinkers who developed this position did not know that it is the very presence of the disvalues that give rise to so much of nature's value. Would we then be forced to honour the fallen angels for the fleet-footedness of the deer or the coordination and strength of the orca? Satan would end up being the (possibly unintentional) originator of the diversity generated by cellular mutation and all the speciation events arising from predation or natural disasters.[139] Finally, this position contradicts the continual biblical refrain that God created the world good. The goodness of creation is constantly affirmed, including at the end of the first account of creation when all the creatures, even the great leviathan and the beasts of the field, are present.[140] In the Hebrew Scriptures, the complexity of the natural world in its totality – even in its more troublesome elements – brings honour and glory to God.[141]

Another related event-based strategy is that of blaming disvalues in the non-human world on the effects of human sin. Very few thinkers still adopt this move, given the chronological difficulties posed by proposing that human sin could affect processes in place millions of years before human existence. But a version of this argument is still advanced by William Dembski.[142] Instead of pointing to Satan for the corruption of the evolutionary world to solve the timeline problem, he wraps the responsibility back around on human sin by arguing that the effects of the fall were retroactively applied at the beginning of time on the created world. Just as – it is sometimes said – the saints before Jesus's time were saved through Jesus's saving work on the cross in light of God's foreknowledge of that saving work, so too the effects of sin were applied to the world in God's foreknowledge of mankind's fall.

Not only is Dembski's theory biblically inadmissible – as was argued in Chapter 2 – but his approach also fails to convince that God is in fact good. A God who would inflict untold suffering on uncounted numbers of non-human animals over hundreds of millions of years without any good emerging out of it for the creatures themselves (and only a very indirect benefit for humans[143]) is morally repulsive. The same is true of Dembski's thoroughgoing anthropocentric focus. Southgate points out "Dembski's theodicy is marked by an anthropocentrism that is breathtaking to anyone who has followed contemporary debates in ecotheology. His only concern is with humans and human sin."[144] God allows the pointless suffering of billions of individuals just to make a point. It does not constitute an adequate theodicy.

David Clough takes a different tack and makes a unique contribution to event-based fall theories by arguing that some particular disvalues, such as predator/prey relationships, are actually forms of sinful rebellion amongst non-human animals.[145] Clough amasses evidence from the Hebrew Bible and from law courts almost up to the present day, and shows that non-human animals were regularly treated as ethically responsible and therefore subject to the same consequences humans would receive for sinful actions: stoning for violence toward, or sexual relations with, people (Lev 15–16), not fasting during times of repentance (Jonah 3), death for touching Mt. Sinai during a theophany (Exodus 19).[146] Interestingly, Clough does not assume that an understanding of God's moral requirement is necessary for sin.[147] His primary scientific case study concerns a family of cannibalistic chimpanzees. Are their actions right or wrong, sinful or morally neutral, when they slaughter and eat each other's young? Clough argues convincingly that:

> We might judge the ability of chimpanzees to make considered choices about their actions to be closer to a human child than to a human adult, but we do not believe that children go from automata to responsible subjects at a particular age and so this judgment of degree is not a reason for considering chimpanzees outside the boundary of sinful action.[148]

However, it is slightly misleading to present a case study using the most mature members of the most intelligent non-human animal to argue that sin might manifest itself as violence beyond the boundaries of humanity. Clough's main argument is that the existence of violence in general is a result of non-human action against the will of God. While there may indeed be proto-moral violence amongst the highest of sentient non-human animals, it would be impossible to attribute any sort of moral rebellion amongst the creatures extant when predation first occurred, estimated to be in the early Cambrian period.[149] And while Clough references the biblical tradition of punishing non-human animals for their actions, such as stoning an ox for goring a human, this applies only to the most intelligent orders of life. There is no such provision in the law codes for locusts, for example. Nor does Clough engage with the places where God seems only too happy to provide a violent creation with the sustenance it needs (Psalm 104:21–27; Job 39:30). Finally, Clough draws primarily from sources (such as the biblical narrative of the Garden and mediaeval law cases) that had no understanding of evolution. Clough does not wrestle with the paradox that the values are often directly attributable to the disvalues. So while Clough writes of the biblical text that:

> the most obvious reading of these texts concerning the [*sic*] God's will for peace and harmony between creatures is that relationships of predation where the life of one creature is sustained only at the expense of the lives of others are not original or final indications of God's creative and redemptive will,[150]

Clough cannot reconcile with evolution. It is a point he himself acknowledges.[151]

Clough eventually argues that the clearest evidence that creatures have turned from God and are mired in sin is that according to Colossians 1:20 Jesus came to reconcile "all things."[152] Since "all things" includes non-human animals, then they must stand in need of reconciliation. In Chapter 6, I will make an attempt to build a picture of non-human creaturely reconciliation that does not involve sin. For now, let it suffice to say that in Colossians 1:20 the "all things" referred to is defined as all things "whether on earth or in heaven." The line of Clough's logic is that because all things on earth need to be reconciled to God, all things on earth are mired in sin. Would he say the same about all heavenly things? Is there sin in heaven? If not, then I argue that there is some way to be reconciled to God through Christ that does not involve sin.[153]

The second category of fallenness is mysterious fallenness. These theories do not clearly state either the origin or effect of evil in the world. Nicola Hoggard Creegan, for example, does not identify natural evil with biological selfishness,[154] but thinks it might have something to do with the second law of thermodynamics,[155] and perhaps with predation.[156] Elsewhere, in complete contradiction, she says that evil is not necessarily to be identified with "the earthquake and the tsunami and the eating of one animal by the other and natural disasters."[157] There is no clear way to distinguish good from evil in her work, nothing she can point to (apart from moral evil) and say "this is evil." Instead, Hoggard Creegan's work is punctuated with statements such as: "I believe there is something opposed to God"[158] or "I am convinced of the reality of this [evil] something and its subtle interplay with life at all levels,"[159] though not being able to point to any concrete evidence, while also freely mixing natural and moral categories of evil.[160] The result is a theological muddle in which anything aesthetically unappealing becomes "evil" and where the very basis of her argument – that draws on the parable of the wheat and tares – is actually overlooked.[161] In her argument, the parable of the wheat and tares (Matthew 13) is comparable to the way that good and evil are mixed in the natural world. However, in the parable, it is not the *identification* of tares that is the problem (the wheat having already borne grain), but the impossibility of uprooting one without the other as the result of their intertwining roots.[162] In contrast, Hoggard Creegan's arguments do not allow for a helpful identification of good and evil. Furthermore, the origin of the tares is clearly stated as "an enemy" in the parable, a concept that Hoggard Creegan sometimes accepts and sometimes challenges.[163] Also, as I explored in Chapter 2, there is little scriptural support for the idea that nature has been corrupted by a satanic force, or that the earth ever was or is corrupted by evil independently of direct human action.

Where Hoggard Creegan views evil as having real ontological substance, Deane-Drummond and Neil Messer argue that the world is pervaded by a mysterious evil which is anti-being. Deane-Drummond, as recounted earlier, argues that evil is the shadow of creation, the necessary counterpart to light. Neil Messer argues that the created world is constantly in conflict with "nothingness" – a concept borrowed from Barth. The nothingness (*das Nichtige*) "is what God rejected, and *did not will*, in creating everything that exists."[164] Messer draws from Barth's view that the world was fallen before the beginning of history, and therefore places the "golden age" of goodness beyond any history we can investigate. Critiques of Messer, raised by Southgate, include whether he really is as faithful to Barth's ideas as he claims, and whether or not God can really be the sovereign Creator if God was unable to expunge this nothingness that is contrary to God's will.[165] I am inclined to agree with Southgate's critiques, but would also point out the difficulty of advocating that the world which God claims is "very good" in Genesis 1:31, was in fact deeply corrupted before the process of development ever began.

There are plenty of other strategies that do not rely on either a radical redefinition of God's activity or essence and that do not invoke a fall scenario either. What are these remaining paths?

Redefining God's attributes and actions

Rather than completely redefining God in the radical ways described previously, there are attempts to redefine divine attributes, or limit God's actions, in more moderate and subtle ways. These strategies do not deny God's omnipotence, omni-benevolence, or omniscience, but they do redefine these traits in ways that are more amenable to the problem of suffering and natural disvalue. A primary example of this sort of approach is exemplified by kenotic theology.

Kenotic approaches generally do not deny God's power, knowledge, or ability to act in the world. Rather, they argue that, by merit of God's love or God's interest in creaturely freedom, God voluntarily self-limits the expression of these attributes.

The idea of kenosis is drawn from the first part of the great Christ hymn in Philippians 2:5–7:

> Let the same mind be in you that was in Christ Jesus,
> who, though he was in the form of God,
> did not regard equality with God
> as something to be exploited,

but emptied himself [ἐκένωσεν],
taking the form of a slave,
being born in human likeness.[166]

The Christ who emptied himself in the Incarnation stands as the central revelation of divine being. If Christ emptied himself, then self-emptying must be a part of God's nature, and as such would characterise God's actions in spheres other than the Incarnation. In his contribution to *The Work of Love: Creation as Kenosis*, John Polkinghorne sets out four different kenotic types: of omnipotence, of simple eternity, of omniscience, and of causal status.[167]

By the kenosis of omnipotence, God allows creation to be something truly other than God. Creation is free to be itself, and to have independence from divine determination. Therefore, states of affairs may arise in the world which are not according to the divine will, leading to the emergence of various types of disvalue. God is totally free and powerful in that God has no external impositions that limit the expression of power (unlike process theology), but God can and does self-limit the active expression of power in order to not overwhelm or coerce the creaturely other, and to allow it space to be itself.[168]

Kenosis of simple eternity is God's giving up of simple existence outside of time. Polkinghorne points out that "since Augustine, theologians have understood the created nature of time, so that the universe came in to being *cum tempore*, not *in tempore*."[169] God chooses to know the world in the temporal terms to which it is limited: the successive slip of moments from future through present to past. Kenosis of simple eternity allows God to learn from and respond to the world since God is thought to experience time in similar successive ways to what we do.

If God has given up knowledge of the simple future, the definition of what is included in God's omniscience changes. Instead of having all knowledge, held from one eternal vantage point, the future is not something that is it is logically possible to know. If omniscience is defined as knowing everything that can logically be known, the future is not included. In kenotic thought, God has full knowledge of the past and present, and so has the best possible vantage point for knowing what is likely to happen in the future, without knowing exact details of what will unfold.

Finally, Polkinghorne suggests the kenosis of causal status, which he defines as the belief that "*the Creator's kenotic love includes allowing divine special providence to act as a cause among causes.*"[170] As a cause amongst causes, God is not the ground of all causes, but humbly shares power with creation and even enters into the creation as an agent, most notably in the Incarnation.[171] Polkinghorne suggests that God may act alongside other causes by inputting energy or information, but does not expand further on the discussion.[172]

Kenotic theology offers a promising family of solutions to the problem of evolutionary suffering: God could not create others in free relationship without their having independence.[173] Once the decision to make a free creation was chosen, the possibility of those creatures acting apart from divine purposes was also created (this, therefore, is a property-consequence GHA). The world displays harms that are not in themselves according to divine purpose, but which are the inescapable result of a world of free beings. Yet, unlike process theism or Clayton and Knapp's approach, kenotic theology does not say that God's power and expression are limited in identical ways, in all circumstances, or at all times. When the purposes for which they are now limited are fulfilled, the expression of God's power can and will be displayed differently. John Polkinghorne calls this the denial of the kenosis of novelty.[174] Therefore, future hope for eschatological renewal and salvation are not ultimately at risk in the way they are with the radical redefinitions of God's being explored earlier.

Still, for all its strengths, kenosis does not explain why God does not intervene in cases of extreme suffering. Voluntary self-limitation could conceivably be voluntarily self-renounced for extreme situations. Thomas Oord is particularly emphatic on this point, arguing:

> A God who voluntarily chooses to refrain from controlling others remains culpable for failing to prevent genuine evils. A voluntarily self-limited God should at least occasionally become un-self-limited, in the name of love, to prevent the suffering and pain that victims of genuine evil experience.[175]

Oord's solution is to propose "essential kenosis," which proposes that God's kenosis is so complete that God could not intervene to prevent suffering.[176] He writes, "Because of God's immutable nature of self-giving, others-empowering love, God cannot prevent genuine evil."[177] In this aspect, Oord's theology is very close, if not identical, to process theism's claim that God is powerless to prevent evil and subject to all the same critiques about eschatological hope.

Equally, kenotic theology has come under critique for misrepresenting the nature of divine relationship to the world. Ted Peters and Martinez Hewlett have, in particular, levelled the critique that a kenotic argument "presupposes a conflict between divine power and creature power; whereas the classic Christian view, we contend, emphasizes that God's power empowers and thereby liberates God's creatures."[178] Instead of divine power limiting or diminishing creaturely power as if everyone were fighting over a limited supply of power, God's power actually creates the freedom to make creaturely power possible.[179] If a kenotic approach gives a loose rein to natural selection (which, in turn, privileges the ruthless and strong), Peters and Hewlett ask, "What could a doctrine of the self-limitation of God in favor of natural selection mean other than to give theological blessing to the strong to dominate, if not destroy, the weak?"[180]

Finally, while kenosis may explain the origin of suffering, it does not – by itself – offer hope to individuals who suffer. There is no redemption or recapitulation in kenotic theology itself.[181] While kenotic theology will form an important part of my approach to theodicy, it does not stand alone, as I will develop a strong theology of redemption.

So while kenosis offers several of the advantages that the radical redefinitions offer while maintaining a more traditional view of God and eschatological hope, it is sometimes challenged by being overstated into essentially process theism.

It seems to imply a divine condoning of evolution's valuation of the fit and it lacks an inherent eschatology, especially for the suffering individual.

The value of suffering: biocentric approaches

If individual creatures are to suffer because of evolution, what goods do they gain themselves through the harms of evolutionary development? In one sense, each new creature born benefits from the long line of those who suffered before them. Rolston's classic phrase rings true: "the cougar's fang has carved the limbs of the fleet-footed deer."[182] The pains of the evolutionary process produce glorious beauty, skill, and power on the part of both the cougar and the deer. These goods are experienced by many of the creatures in their process of selving.

Yet, something more than mere development is present in the evolutionary process: freedom.[183] If creatures are to be free, then the biological paths toward some of the desired values will be limited. The limited possibilities available to a God who wants to make creation truly free invokes all the "only way" arguments outlined previously about the scientific constraints of such an endeavour. Southgate also outlines a theological line of "only way" reasoning: if there was a better way for God to create, that would have entailed less suffering, one could expect that a good and loving God would have used it.[184]

If God has indeed created a world that creates itself through evolution, then creatures really do have some autonomy in choosing their own methods of survival. This is not to say that the choices are necessarily rational, but the choices made are innovative, or self-generated.[185] The outworking of processes brings forth varied and novel survival strategies, and God has given them the freedom to do so. John Polkinghorne has called this the "free process defence." He explains:

> In his great act of creation I believe that God allows the physical world to be itself, not in Manichaean opposition to him, but in that independence which is Love's gift of freedom to the one beloved. That world is endowed in its fundamental constitution with an anthropic potentiality which makes it capable of fruitful evolution. The exploration and realization of that potentiality is achieved by the universe through the continual interplay of chance and necessity within its unfolding process.[186]

"Love's gift of freedom" is given to the world with a potentiality for fruitfulness that the creation explores in an ongoing way. The gift of freedom is kenotic insofar as God surrenders the ability to determine the outcome of all things. Free process is not a freedom that denies God's essential ability to act, as Oord or the process theists argue earlier, but a "letting-be" that is essential to the nature of love. Peters and Hewlett define the freedom of continuing creation as "the abiding divine activity of continuing to provide the world with an open future."[187] Ruth Page borrows the term *Gelassenheit* (an active "Letting-be") from Heidegger to make the same point: *Gelassenheit* is a valuable way to understand God in creation, for it is more creative and supportive than mere permission, but not determining in the way that causation is normally understood. It therefore expresses freedom without loss of power on the part of the one releasing, and a consequent freedom to experiment and explore for those let be.[188]

To let creatures explore their own potentiality of being is not weakness, or neglect, but the necessary starting point for the expression of divine love.[189] Equally, creatures could not be given true freedom to develop valuable attributes without also being given the freedom to develop harmful attributes.

Yet, there is a strong objection: does God's letting be in instances of horrific evil not undermine all the good of God's *Gelassenheit*? When freedom turns to violence, and self-expression victimises the innocent, is not a loving God allowing the whole show to go too far? Many, including William Rowe, Richard Dawkins, and Wesley Wildman, have argued that this is the case.[190] But Page and others have responded that the letting-be of creation must also be paired closely with God's being-with creation. *Mitsein* is another Heideggerian term that Page adopts to express this "pansyntheism."[191] God not only lets creation be, but is also intimately present with creation in its brokenness, its suffering, and also in its healing. There is no "cost" of evolutionary development that God does not also "pay," and no creature is left to suffer alone. Whether or not this is of comfort to the non-human animals themselves is debatable,[192] but it does imply that God has taken full responsibility for the sufferings which God has also allowed. It keeps us from imagining God as one who sacrifices others without regard for the benefit of God's own plans and purposes. Niels Gregersen and Christopher Southgate in particular go on to stress that it is in the cross of Christ that God most clearly takes the responsibility of evolutionary suffering.[193] Arthur Peacocke also tentatively suggests that God's co-suffering with creatures may – in itself – have creative potential:

> God, we find ourselves having to conjecture, 'suffers' the natural evils of the world along with ourselves because – we can but tentatively suggest at this stage – God purposes *inter alia* to bring about a greater good thereby, namely, the kingdom of living organic creatures, delighting their Creator, and even free-willing, loving persons who have the possibility of communion with God and with each other. Indeed, the creation may in one sense be said to exist *through* suffering: for suffering is recognized to have creative power when imbued with love.[194]

Just as childbirth is suffering with creative purpose, the co-suffering of God may, Peacocke suggests, have some creative affect beyond the comfort of co-presence. How this might be the case, however, is not spelled out.

The free process defence and the co-suffering arguments are powerful together, but they leave out one important aspect: what is the final fate of animals that die?

Redemption approaches[195]

Many of the solutions explored so far have focussed on the beginning: how God had to set up the universe in such a way that suffering would ensue in order to bring the glories of the present. There is another realm of theological approach that begins instead with the future, with the hope that present sufferings will bring about, or be solved by, future harmonies.

Some redemption approaches are this-worldly, that is, they look to how the suffering individual finds redemption either in the midst of its own suffering, or in how its suffering will contribute to lives beyond its own, in ecological or historical senses. Ruth Page and Holmes Rolston defend these positions, which will be explored in much greater detail in Chapter 6.[196] Other theologians look beyond the grave to find redemption for the suffering creation. To these I now turn.

The question of whether or not non-human animals have an existence beyond death is one that has long been speculated on by theologians. Most of the early theologians, wedded as they were to certain neo-Platonic views of the world, did not think non-human animals had the capacity to endure beyond death, usually citing the lack of a rational soul in non-human beings.[197] As the rational soul was the part of humanity that had an ability to endure beyond death, non-human animals simply passed away without remainder. Others, however, were not so sure. John Wesley preached his suggestion that in the resurrection:

> The whole brute creation will then, undoubtedly, be restored, not only to the vigour, strength, and swiftness which they had at their creation, but to a far higher degree of each than they ever enjoyed . . . as a recompense for what they once suffered, while under the 'bondage of corruption,' when God has 'renewed the face of the earth,' and their corruptible body has put on incorruption, they shall enjoy happiness suited to their state, without alloy, without interruption, and without end.[198]

In Wesley's mind, God's redemption would be extended to all life, which would all also be perfected. It is interesting to note that Wesley does not think that animals will be restored to what he thought was their pre-fallen state, but that their eschatological being would be "to a far higher degree" than any earthly reality. He even suggests at one point that their intelligence would increase to the present human level, just as human intelligence would reach that of the angels.

Contemporary theologians also often defend the resurrection of non-human animals.[199] Some do so anthropocentrically, such as Paul Griffiths, who thinks that non-human animals will only be included in the resurrection because they are necessary for human delight to be made complete.[200] John Polkinghorne argues that only tokens of the different types of species are needed to complete heaven, but not every living creature. Where John Wesley argued that the individuals would be raised in recompense for their suffering, Polkinghorne is only concerned with a representation of species, either for human or divine benefit, but the actual case of the individual creatures who suffered is ignored. Polkinghorne does make an exception for animals that have had particular significance to humans, such as pets. Polkinghorne speculates that they "could be thought to have acquired enhanced individual states through their interactions with humans"[201] and thus could be included in the resurrection in more numbers than needed for mere representation. In short, there will be many dogs, and few dinosaurs.

Other contemporary theologians are more concerned about the fate of individual non-human animals themselves, regardless of their interaction with human beings. Jay McDaniel and Christopher Southgate in particular are convinced of the resurrection of members of the non-human creation. McDaniel delineates four different types of redemption, only two of which concern us here: redemption as the contribution to a life beyond one's own, and redemption as a transformation of being.[202] The first type of redemption sees individuals as contributing to the life and experience of God, and thus their lives are redeemed in meaning, though with little advantage to the creature itself. The second redemption sees the creature – in McDaniel's example, a pelican chick – transformed into a higher state of affairs. The chick would find itself in "pelican heaven;" a place of ultimate satisfaction of its needs and desires. Yet, McDaniel does not envision this resurrection to be eternal. "The hope is not necessarily that all living beings live forever as subjects in their own right; rather, it is that they live until they enjoy a fulfillment of their needs as creatures."[203] Once the individual has found fulfilment and recompense for its suffering, it can pass out of existence without a problem. Compensation for the lack of earthly fulfilment is the central tenet of McDaniel's redemption.

Southgate advocates redemption in several more ways.[204] While he does hold that resurrection for the suffering individual who has not experienced flourishing is important as compensation, he also grounds non-human redemption as part of the full work of Christ. Not only do biblical passages such as Isaiah 11 and Romans 8 hint at the whole creation being present in the new life, but humans themselves are always understood in their relationship to creation. Full redemption would require the fulfilment of all those relationships. Also, he argues that it would be curious if a Cosmic Christ only actually redeemed a very small part of the cosmos. Finally, Southgate argues that for a theodicy to be complete, the importance of non-human resurrection must be included to maintain the goodness of God.

Yet, despite his focus on the individual and insistence on divine care for each creature, Southgate also admits that redemption for "simple organisms" who "possess little distinctive experience or agency . . . may be represented in the eschaton as types rather than as individuals."[205] Creatures without sentience, in his view, do not suffer, and so do not need individual compensation for suffering, though they may still be represented in the final new creation. Still, he advises that theologians ought not to be frugal in their speculations on the inhabitants of the new creation. Southgate writes that, along with the elimination of the second law of thermodynamics in the new creation, "must surely go the implication that there is no competition for resources, no shortage of space in heaven. We should therefore be bold in our trust of the redemptive grace of God that will populate it."[206] Later in this work, I will argue that the nature of divine love will necessitate the resurrection of every creature, even those who have little personal agency, or do not seem to vary much one from another.[207] Particularity is essential to love, and perhaps not even bacteria can be substituted one for another by the God who loves them.

Trent Dougherty takes up a view that is closest to John Wesley's suggestion. He not only suggests the subjective physical redemption of non-human creatures, but he also suggests that for their earthly suffering to be outweighed, their capacity to know and experience God's love must be expanded enough to allow each creature to individually understand and affirm their place in the narrative of God's creation and be drawn into eternal communion with God. *"If God exists and animals suffer,"* he writes, *"then animals are resurrected and deified."*[208]

We have thus explored several different possibilities for the resurrection of individual non-human animals. What about wider-scope schemes? What other forms are there for redemption?

Southgate argues that whilst creatures will be resurrected on their own merit, redemption for them can also come through the work of humans. As humanity takes up its priestly role, it will offer up creation's praise to God and use human ingenuity to act as partners with God in bringing the creation into fulfilment.[209] Humanity as priests and created co-creators act in the now-present eschatological age to bring relief to creation's groaning and liberate it from its bondage to decay.[210] This particular approach of Southgate's is interesting because it is anthropocentric, but unlike most anthropocentric schemes that are concerned only with the cost and benefit to humans and the place of humans as agents in eschatological fulfilment, Southgate is anthropocentric for the sake of wider life.[211] Southgate assumes the place of humanity is central, but that humans are to live out this central role in a Christ-shaped way, as servants who give themselves up for the good of the wider creation. If Southgate is anthropocentric, he is at least redeemingly so.

Approaches to redemption focussed on divine action come from thinkers such as Jürgen Moltmann, Karl Rahner, and Denis Edwards. For them, God will tie up all of cosmic history through the work of Christ. Humans will be part of that redemption, but will not be key to it. In Rahner's thought, redemption is tied to God's self-bestowal to the world. As God gives Godself to the world, the world then finds in itself – through the indwelling presence of God – the capability for self-transcendence.[212] Thus, God's work in the world in self-giving will be consummated in the self-transcendence of world history.[213] Edwards, drawing conclusions from Rahner's theology, argues for the companionship and co-suffering of God in creation, and "sees the resurrection as a promise that creaturely suffering and death will be redeemed and healed as each creature finds its meaning and fulfillment in God's self-bestowing love."[214] Moltmann, by contrast, does not see history as moving forward into the eschatological period, but rather sees the eschaton as breaking back into the present. The culmination of creation is coming – the *adventus* – not as something that will proceed out of the past and present, but as something which exists already and will meet the present.[215] Heaven is not simply a future reality, but "the beginning of heavenly bliss is already present – and is also already experienced – in the grace of Christ and in the church of Christ; and this means that heaven has already been thrown open here."[216] The outpost of heaven created here in the church is the promise to the wider cosmos of the redemption that will come.

Peters and Hewlett do not hold to the in-breaking eschatology of Moltmann. By contrast, they assert that the future coming into being will change the meaning of the now. "It is the divine act of redemption that determines what creation will have meant, and this can be determined only eschatologically."[217] God's redemption actually creates the meaning of what is past, and the whole of creation cannot be understood before that moment, for its meaning is not yet determined.[218] Theodicy for individuals, then, is an issue only resolved in the eschatological age, as the meaning of suffering is forged in light of the whole work of God. Robert Russell claims with Peters and Hewlett that: "It is only when the new creation is the starting point for reflecting on evil that we can hope to give a response to its origin and meaning in this present, broken world."[219]

Each of these teleological schemes does find a solution for the individual creature that suffers. Whether resurrection is seen as recompense or as fulfilment, the creature finds that all things have been made well. Yet, this places an enormous weight of meaning on the creature's being that does not directly relate to its life on earth. Celia Deane-Drummond rightly asks whether or not teleological explanations are used too quickly "to escape the conundrum of suffering and evil?"[220] If we are too quick to point to the eschaton as the residing place of all value and meaning, it makes the lives lived here vapid and hollow.

Ruth Page objects strenuously to future-oriented redemption models, arguing that they prioritise a distant God and a lack of concern for present suffering or present creaturely value. Her particular objection is to those who consider non-human lives as unimportant stepping-stones to the development of humans as the teleology of creation. Her pattern of thought, however, would equally object to those who place the true value of a creature in its "completion" in a final state of redemption.[221] Page writes, "A distant teleology goes with belief in a distant God who will sort everything out at the end. But when God is believed to be present, then every moment becomes eschatological, an end in itself, so to speak."[222] Instead of a distant teleology, Page advances an argument of "Teleology Now!," where the value of creatures is found as they live and participate in relationship to God and in relationship to the world around them. As opposed to David Ray Griffin who asks, "why a God whose power is essentially unlimited would use such a long, pain-filled method, with all its *blind-alleys*, to create a world,"[223] for Page there are no blind-alleys. There are simply creatures who did not pass on their DNA to successive generations, but who were nonetheless delighted in by God and who participated in relationships around them in meaningful ways.[224] Relationships are the primary purpose of creation for Page, and nothing separates a creature from its primary relationship with God. Thus, disvalues do not and cannot speak against the love of God because even the worst disaster cannot separate a creature from having participated in relationships.[225]

Theocentric approaches to suffering

There are also a few additional perspectives that are essentially theocentric rather than biocentric in their treatment of evil and suffering. Two examples here will suffice. The first sees the cross as the central moment where God takes responsibility for the suffering of the world, the second places the meaning of creaturely lives (and indeed of all creation) in God and not in creation.

The cross of Christ is perhaps the most difficult and paradoxical concept in Christianity. This, perhaps, also makes it one of the most powerful. At the cross, extremes meet together. The God of life dies. Perfect innocence carries sin. Good triumphs over evil by submitting to death. Love is found in the domain of hate. The greatest expression of God's power comes through the experience of entire weakness. Although precisely what happened at the cross is widely debated, Southgate and Gregersen argue that at the cross God took responsibility for all the evil and disvalue in creation.[226] Gregersen in particular remarks how Jesus, who died without descendants, identifies with the losers of the evolutionary race, and thus *"co-carries the costs of creation."*[227] Certainly, the concept that God meets the creation in the cross, and fully experiences its worst aspects helps justify God in allowing evil, since there is no suffering God does not also experience. At the same time, the mysteries of the cross will never be fully pierced by theological enquiry, though we will return to it throughout this study. Instead of a focus on the suffering of the individual, the focus here is on the God willing to suffer for creation.

Moltmann's theocentric approach is quite different. Moltmann places all the value of creation in its meaning, and finds that meaning in God. He writes:

> Theologically speaking, the meaning and purpose of human beings is to be found in God himself, like the meaning and purpose of all things. In this sense, every single person, and indeed every single living thing in nature, has a meaning, whether they are of utility for evolution or not. The meaning of the individual is not to be found in the collective of the species, and the meaning of the species is not to be found in the existence of the individual. The meaning of both is to be found in God. . . . We have to overcome the old anthropocentric world picture by a new theocentric interpretation of the world of nature and human beings.[228]

If the meaning of a creature is not found in itself – neither in its evolutionary contribution nor its own fulfilment – but in God, then every life has meaning and value regardless of its circumstances or suffering. Utility, on any conceived level, is no longer a measure for worth.

Compound approaches

Just as Murray was the main advocate for articulating a compound defence in the philosophical realm, so Southgate is the clearest expositor of the need for compound approaches to theodicy in the theological realm.[229] While he recognises the power and necessity of each argument, he attests that no one position alone is sufficient. Rather, various positions must be drawn together in order to address the problem of natural evil. For Southgate, (1) God must be seen as originally creating a good world: a good world with constraints that provide values that can come about in no other way (the "only way" argument). (2) God must also be seen as responding to, companioning, and suffering with each creature, taking the responsibility for suffering most especially at the cross. (3) God works redemption in, and for, and through creatures – providing for them either fullness of life here, or in a life to come. (4) Finally, humanity has a particular role in redemption as co-redeemers of the world, and so suffering cannot be divided from the work of humans.[230] Together, Southgate argues, these lines of argument help us account for non-human animal suffering.

I follow Southgate and Murray in thinking that for a theodicy to be robust and satisfying it has to be a compound of various different lines of approach. An adequate understanding of creation needs to be complex and multi-faceted if we are to nuance the various natural disvalues we encounter. An entire population wiped out by a volcano requires a different sort of approach than a baby seal skinned alive by an orca. Holding various strands of argument together allows the flexibility to account for different values and disvalues, without simply painting all disvalues with one brush or looking for only one source of disvalue.

Conclusion

We have now explored the various resources available to the study of non-human animal theodicy. The maps of major territories lie before us. First explored was the territory of analytical philosophy. I began with rejecting the neo-Cartesian and inscrutability arguments because they do not engage the question of evil, but only evade it. Property-consequence GHAs (such as the necessity of nomic regularity) with anthropocentric references were rejected as inadequate, while those property-consequence GHAs with biotic reference I accepted as necessary, but not sufficient on their own. Developmental defences also were shown to be strong arguments, but not strong enough to stand in isolation. A compound defence, allowing for varieties of goods and harms, was deemed the strongest approach.

Then, the analytical philosophical positions were compared and contrasted with theological positions, and three critiques were explored. Some simply refuse to engage in theodicy. Some philosophical approaches did not retreat behind unfeeling logic, but chose to engage the affective realm and are comfortable with mystery and theological concerns. Surin's refusal of traditional philosophical theodicy in favour of practical theodicies and Stump's example of sensitive philosophical engagement with theodicy will both stand as examples of how analytical philosophy will be drawn upon in this work.

The exploration of theological approaches began with attempts to radically redefine God in order to dissolve the theodicy problem. I rejected these largely for their lack of hope. A god divested of goodness, power, or activity could not satisfy a Christian theodicy. Theodicies centred on the fall, by contrast, I critiqued as denying the central insight of Darwin, ignoring that much good and value emerges out of the harms that those theodicies condemn as the result of sin. Finally, I explored the various theodicies stemming from theological considerations, whether theocentric or biocentric. The usefulness of kenotic and relational theologies was noted.

The maps are behind us. It is time to set forth. The rest of the project will concentrate on just one small piece of this vast landscape: the attempt to develop a compound theological approach that does not radically redefine God or incorporate a theology of the fall, but which will draw on the resources of relational and redemptive theologies.

Notes

1 An entire book cannot even contain a completely comprehensive bibliography. See Barry L. Whitney, *Theodicy: An Annotated Bibliography on the Problem of Evil 1960–1991* (Bowling Green, OH: Bowling Green State University Philosophy, 1998).

2 One earlier exception is the pioneering work of Loren Wilkinson, who wrote in 1976 on ecology and the theological implications of death. Loren Wilkinson, "A Christian Ecology of Death," *Christian Scholar's Review* 5:4 (1976): 319–338.

3 Particularly of interest to this topic are the writings of Asa Gray, the Harvard botanist who championed Darwinism in the United States. Gray and Darwin corresponded several times – puzzling together over the question of natural evil – and the themes of design and suffering entered regularly into Gray's writings about evolution. See Bethany Sollereder, "The Darwin-Gray Exchange," *Theology and Science* 8:4 (2010): 417–432; John Hedley Brooke, "Darwin, Design, and the Unification of Nature," in *Science, Religion and the Human Experience*, ed. James D. Proctor (Oxford: Oxford University Press, 2005), 165–184; Sara Joan Miles, "Charles Darwin and Asa Gray Discuss Teleology and Design," *Perspectives on Science and Christian Faith* 53:3 (2001): 196–201. Other thinkers also realised how problematic non-human animal suffering was as evidenced in Lux Mundi and Clement C. J. Webb's comment that "the problem of suffering of the lower animals is the most difficult part of the problem of pain." Clement C. J. Webb, *Problems in the Relations of God and Man* (London: James Nisbet & Co, 1911), 268. Webb is referenced by Christopher Southgate, *The Groaning of Creation: God, Evolution, and the Problem of Evil* (Louisville: Westminster John Knox, 2008), 11.

4 Martin Bergmann, "Skeptical Theism and Rowe's New Evidential Argument from Evil," *Noûs* 35:2 (2001): 278–296; William Alston, "Some (Temporarily) Final Thoughts on Evidential Arguments from Evil," in *The Evidential Argument from Evil*, ed. Daniel Howard-Snyder (Bloomington, IN: Indiana University Press, 1996), 320–321; Daniel Howard-Snyder, "The Argument from Inscrutable Evil," in *The Evidential Argument from Evil*, ed. Daniel Howard-Snyder (Bloomington, IN: Indiana University Press, 1996), 286–310.

5 Michael J. Murray, *Nature Red in Tooth and Claw: Theism and the Problem of Animal Suffering* (Oxford: Oxford University Press, 2008); Peter van Inwagen, *The Problem of Evil: The Gifford Lectures Delivered in the University of St. Andrews in 2003* (Oxford: Clarendon Press, 2006); Richard Swinburne, *Providence and the Problem of Evil* (Oxford: Clarendon Press, 1996); Trent Dougherty, *The Problem of Animal Pain: A Theodicy for All Creatures Great and Small* (New York, NY: Palgrave Macmillan, 2014); Robin Attfield, *Creation, Evolution and Meaning* (Aldershot: Ashgate, 2006).

6 Christopher Southgate and Andrew Robinson, "Varieties of Theodicy: An Exploration of Responses to the Problem of Evil Based on a Typology of Good-Harm Analyses," in *Physics and Cosmology: Scientific Perspectives on the Problem of Natural Evil*, eds. Nancey Murphy, Robert J. Russell, William R. Stoeger, S. J. (Vatican City and Berkeley, CA: Vatican Observatory, CTNS, 2007), 67–90.

7 Kenneth Surin, *Theology and the Problem of Evil* (Oxford: Basil Blackwell, 1986); Eleonore Stump's, *Wandering in Darkness: Narrative and the Problem of Suffering* (Oxford: Clarendon Press, 2010).

8 Championed by Wildman and Griffin. Wesley J. Wildman, "Incongruous Goodness, Perilous Beauty, Disconcerting Truth: Ultimate Reality and Suffering in Nature," in *Physics and Cosmology: Scientific Perspectives on the Problem of Natural Evil*, eds. Nancey Murphy, Robert Russell, and William R. Stoeger, S. J. (Vatican City: Vatican Observatory Foundation, 2007), 267–294; David R. Griffin, "Creation Out of Chaos and the Problem of Evil," in *Encountering Evil: Live Options in Theodicy*, ed. Stephen T. Davis (Edinburgh: T & T Clark, 1981), 101–136.

9 Murray, *Nature Red in Tooth and Claw*, 42. "Descartes and the Cartesians are reputed to have been seen torturing animals and marveling how well their behaviour mimicked the behaviour of organisms, like ourselves, who *really do* experience pain and suffering." Italics original.

10 This view has been advanced by C. S. Lewis, *The Problem of Pain* (New York, NY: HarperCollins, 1940, 1996), 135–136.

11 Michael Domjan and James W. Grau, *The Principles of Learning and Behaviour* (Belmont, CA: Cengage Learning, 2006), 179–180.

12 Evidence extends from very short term-effects of trauma, such as being hunted, to long-term effects similar to post-traumatic stress disorder. See Patrick Bateson and Elizabeth L. Bradshaw, "Physiological Effects of Hunting Red Deer," *Proceedings of the Royal Society London B* 264 (1997): 1707–1714; K. S. Gobush, B. M. Mutayoba, and S. K. Wasser, "Long-Term Impacts of Poaching on Relatedness, Stress Physiology, and Reproductive Output of Adult Female African Elephants," *Conservation Biology* 22:6 (2008): 1590–1599. For more general discussions of animal distress see David DeGrazia and Andrew Rowan, "Pain, Suffering, and Anxiety in Animals and Humans," *Theoretical Medicine* 12:3 (September 1991): 193–211. Evidence suggests not only that animals experience deep distress in circumstances such as being hunted, but also that psychological and physiological impacts can continue for more than a decade after a traumatic event. One innovative clinic for the orphans of poached African elephants has found success by treating the young elephants as having post-traumatic stress disorder. Charles Siebert, "Orphans No More," *National Geographic* (September 2011): 40–65. Accessed 1 January 2013. Online: http://ngm.nationalgeographic.com/2011/09/orphan-elephants/siebert-text.

13 Murray, *Nature Red in Tooth and Claw*, 41–72.

14 Murray, *Nature Red in Tooth and Claw*, 71. See also Bethany Sollereder, "When Humans Are Not Unique: Perspectives on Suffering and Redemption," *The Expository Times* 127:1 (2015): 17–22.

15 Thomas Aquinas, *Summa Contra Gentiles*, trans. Vernon J. Bourke (Notre Dame, IN: University of Notre Dame Press, 1975), III. 112–113.

16 Nicolaas A. Rupke, *Vivisection in Historical Perspective* (London: Francis & Taylor, 1987), 27.

17 Tom Regan, *The Case for Animal Rights* (Berkeley, CA: University of California Press, 2004), 243–248; Holmes Rolston III, *A New Environmental Ethics: The Next Millennium for Life on Earth* (New York, NY: Routledge, 2012), 64–66. For Regan, a "subject-of-a-life" is any organism capable of felt experience, which is mostly mammals. For Rolston, it also includes organisms like octopi, which have sentient experience but which may be very different from our own.

18 Dougherty, *The Problem of Animal Pain*, 56–95.

19 Dougherty, *The Problem of Animal Pain*, 81.

20 National Research Council Committee on Recognition and Alleviation of Pain in Laboratory Animals, *Recognition and Alleviation of Pain in Laboratory Animals* (Washington, DC: National Academies Press, 2009). Accessed 26 March 2016. Online: www.ncbi.nlm.nih.gov/books/NBK32655/.

21 My own longer critique of the neo-Cartesian position, particularly critiquing the neocortex argument, is found in Bethany Sollereder, "When Humans Are Not Unique: Perspectives on Suffering and Redemption," *The Expository Times* 127:1 (October 2015): 17–22.

22 Murray, *Nature Red in Tooth and Claw*, 26; Nicola Hoggard Creegan, *Animal Suffering and the Problem of Evil* (Oxford: Oxford University Press, 2013), 65; Bergmann, "Skeptical Theism and Rowe's New Evidential Argument from Evil," 278–296; Howard-Snyder, "The Argument from Inscrutable Evil," 286–310; William Alston, "Some (Temporarily) Final Thoughts on Evidential Arguments from Evil," in *The Evidential Argument from Evil*, ed. Daniel Howard-Snyder (Bloomington, IN: Indiana University Press, 1996), 320–321.

23 Neil Messer, "Natural Evil after Darwin," *Theology after Darwin*, eds. Michael S. Northcott and R. J. Berry (Milton Keynes: Paternoster, 2009), 143.

24 I will use the language of defence in this context because most of the philosophical approaches are not attempting to build a theological framework to explain God, and so the language of theodicy is inappropriate. Alternative language, such as Michael Murray's Causa Dei, is acknowledged but seems an unnecessary proliferation of terms. See Chapter 1, 3–5.

25 Southgate and Robinson, "Varieties of Theodicy," 67–90.

26 Southgate and Robinson, "Varieties of Theodicy," 70.

27 Murray, whose definition I use here, is careful to say that the law-like forms can include "chance" as it exists in the quantum world, "as long as the probabilities were well-behaved" *Nature Red in Tooth and Claw*, 135.

28 Murray, *Nature Red in Tooth and Claw*, 135.

29 Murray, *Nature Red in Tooth and Claw*, 136.

30 For a theological development of the same point, see the arguments of Clayton and Knapp later, 103.

31 "Since non-human animals presumably do not have free will, and since some (most, in fact) of the sufferings of non-human animals occurred before there were human beings, no extension or elaboration of the free-will defense can account for all animal suffering" van Inwagen, *The Problem of Evil*, 113.

32 "All past and present human and animal natural evils of which we know thus contribute to the widening of human choice when we learn about them" Swinburne, *Providence*, 192.

33 George Frederick Wright, *Studies in Science and Religion* (Andover: Warren F. Draper, 1882), 204–205. This quotation is used by Murray, *Nature Red in Tooth and Claw*, 142.

34 Attfield, *Creation, Evolution and Meaning*, 124.

35 See the section on selving in Chapter 1, 6–8.

36 van Inwagen, *The Problem of Evil*, 123.

37 See Chapter 6, 156–165, for various models of redemptive existence.

38 Murray, *Nature Red in Tooth and Claw*, 143.

39 See Peter Ward and Donald Brownlee, *Rare Earth: Why Complex Life Is Uncommon in the Universe* (New York, NY: Copernicus, 2004), 191–220.

40 Michael A. Corey, *Evolution and the Problem of Natural Evil* (Lanham, MD: University Press of America, 2000), 113.

41 Murray contrasts synchronic order with diachronic order. Diachronic order is the general orderliness of natural systems unfolding over time according to natural laws.

42 Murray, *Nature Red in Tooth and Claw*, 168.
43 Murray, *Nature Red in Tooth and Claw*, 184.
44 Murray, *Nature Red in Tooth and Claw*, 184–185. I find Murray's use of Gregory of Nyssa and Augustine very problematic. These church fathers were not arguing for a chaos-to-order universe as a good in its own right, as Murray is trying to do. Instead, they were attempting to harmonise the day-by-day account of creation in Genesis 1 with the (to them) self-evident truth that the only way an eternal God could interact with a world of time is instantaneously. The chaos-to-order element of their argument is simply a spandrel, an unintentional by-product of their discussion on time. To argue that Augustine thought a world of unfolding development was inherently better than a world made by divine fiat is a misrepresentation of Augustine's view since he argued for a creation by divine fiat of the seeds of possibility.
45 Philip Yancey and Paul Brand, *The Gift of Pain* (Grand Rapids, MI: Zondervan, 1997).
46 Yancey and Brand, *The Gift of Pain*, 127.
47 Attfield, *Creation, Evolution and Meaning*, 142.
48 Murray, *Nature Red in Tooth and Claw*, 117–118.
49 Ruth Page utterly rejects instrumentalist GHAs that reach beyond the individual, but she writes from a theological perspective, and we will return to her work later.
50 This argument is held in various forms by Alexander, Attfield, Murphy, Russell, and Southgate.
51 Attfield, *Creation, Evolution and Meaning*, 128–131, 139–141, 145–146. For more on this topic, see Denis Alexander, *Creation or Evolution: Do We Have to Choose?* (Oxford: Monarch, 2008), 279–281; Niels H. Gregersen, "The Cross of Christ in an Evolutionary World," *dialog* 40:3 (Fall 2001): 192–207, 197–199; Attfield, *Creation, Evolution and Meaning*, 121–131; Bethany Sollereder, "Evolutionary Theodicy: Towards an Evangelical Perspective," (MCS Thesis, Regent College, 2007), 19–39; See also Southgate's exposition of why the package deal is not enough to solve the problem in Southgate, *Groaning of Creation*, 12–13, 42–48.
52 Arthur Peacocke, "The Cost of a New Life," in *The Work of Love: Creation as Kenosis*, ed. John Polkinghorne (Grand Rapids, MI: Eerdmans, 2001), 37.
53 Attfield, *Creation, Evolution and Meaning*, 129.
54 Attfield, *Creation, Evolution and Meaning*, 129.
55 Attfield, *Creation, Evolution and Meaning*, 129.
56 Southgate, *Groaning of Creation*, "Cosmic Evolution and Evil," in *The Cambridge Companion to the Problem of Evil*, eds. Chad Meister and Paul K. Moser (Cambridge: Cambridge University Press, 2017), 147–164.
57 Dawkins's insistence on selection as the only way is pointed out by Michael Ruse and is cited by Robert Russell, "The Groaning of Creation: Does God Suffer with All Life?" in *The Evolution of Evil*, eds. Gaymon Bennett, Martinez J. Hewlett, Ted Peters, and Robert John Russell (Göttingen: Vandenhoeck & Ruprecht, 2008), 124. Dawkins as a supporter of the "only way" is also cited by Southgate, *Groaning of Creation*, 48.
58 Russell draws particularly on the work of John Leslie, *Universes* (New York, NY: Routledge, 1989) and Max Tegmark, "Is 'the theory of everything' merely the Ultimate Ensemble Theory?" *Annals of Physics* 270 (1998): 1–51. Robert Russell, "Physics, Cosmology, and the Challenges to Consequentialist Natural Theodicy," in *Physics and Cosmology: Scientific Perspectives on Natural Evil* (Vatican City and Berkeley, CA: Vatican Observatory, CTNS, 2007), 126–128. See also, Martin Rees, *Just Six Numbers: The Deep Forces That Shape the Universe* (London: Weidenfeld & Nicolson, 1999).
59 John D. Barrow, *The Constants of Nature: The Numbers that Encode the Deepest Secrets of the Universe* (London: Random House, 2002), 223–224.
60 Cf. Russell, "Physics, Cosmology, and the Challenges to Consequentialist Natural Theodicy," 123; Nancey Murphy, "Science and the Problem of Evil: Suffering as a By-Product of a Finely Turned Cosmos," in *Physics and Cosmology: Scientific Perspectives on the Problem of Natural Evil*, eds. Nancey Murphy, Robert J. Russell, and

William R. Stoeger, S. J. (Vatican City and Berkeley, CA: Vatican Observatory, CTNS, 2007), 135–136; Denis Alexander, *Evolution or Creation: Do We Have to Choose?* (Oxford: Monarch, 2008), 279–280; John Polkinghorne, *Science and Providence: God's Interaction with the World* (London: SPCK, 1989, 2005), 77.
61 Southgate and Robinson, "Varieties," 88.
62 This is an example used by Holmes Rolston, and later appropriated by others, most notably McDaniel and Southgate. Holmes Rolston III, *Science and Religion: A Critical Survey*, 2nd ed. (West Conschohocken, PA: Templeton Foundation Press, 2006), 137ff. The first edition was published in 1987.
63 Rolston, *Science and Religion*, 134.
64 Charles Darwin, *On the Origin of Species* (London: John Murray, 1859), 490.
65 Darwin, *On the Origin of Species*, 490, 79.
66 Martin A. Nowak, "Evolving Cooperation," *Journal of Theoretical Biology* 299 (2012): 1–8; Martin Nowak and Roger Highfield, *Supercooperators: Altruism, Evolution, and Why We Need Each Other to Succeed* (New York, NY: Free Press, 2011).
67 Lynn Sagan (Margulis), "On the Origin of Mitosing Cells," *Journal of Theoretical Biology* 14 (1967): 225–274; Lynn Margulis and Dorion Sagan, "The Role of Symbiogenesis in Evolution," in *Back to Darwin: A Richer Account of Evolution*, ed. John B. Cobb Jr. (Grand Rapids, MI: Eerdmans, 2008), 176–184.
68 Margulis and Sagan, "Role of Symbiogenesis," 182.
69 This is a point also made by Christopher Southgate in "Does God's Care Make Any Difference? Theological Reflection on the Suffering of God's Creatures," in *Christian Faith and the Earth: Current Paths and Emerging Horizons in Ecotheology*, eds. Ernst M. Conradie, Sigurd Bergmann, Celia Deane-Drummond, and Denis Edwards (London: T & T Clark, 2014), 107.
70 Rolston, *Science and Religion*, 134–137. Loren Wilkinson, "A Christian Ecology of Death," 319–338.
71 Rolston, *Science and Religion*, 144.
72 Wilkinson, "A Christian Ecology of Death," 331.
73 Murray, *Nature Red in Tooth and Claw*, 146.
74 van Inwagen, *The Problem of Evil*.
75 This is similar to Christopher Southgate's "only way argument" but Southgate argues that the good is not found solely in the existence of the creature themselves, but in their unique flourishing, or selving. Southgate, *Groaning of Creation*, 29, 63–64.
76 Here, van Inwagen echoes Aquinas's argument that the great diversity of creaturely forms is a great good in and of itself, as the creative mind of God can be best reflected in a diversity of forms. Thomas Aquinas, *Summa Theologica*, trans. Fathers of the English Dominican Province (New York: Bazinger Bros, 1947), I, 47, 2.
77 van Inwagen, *Problem of Evil*, 119–123.
78 See Murray, *Nature Red in Tooth and Claw*, 193–199; Southgate, *Groaning of Creation*, 15–16.
79 Murray, *Nature Red in Tooth and Claw*, 195.
80 The beginning of Chapter 4 will spend a little time on the tsunami-type harms, whereas most of my project deals with the predator-type harms.
81 Murray, *Nature Red in Tooth and Claw*, 186. van Inwagen, *Problem of Evil*, 120.
82 The courtroom setting is common to van Inwagen and Murray. Murray even uses the alternative term for theodicy of "de causa dei": a legal term for the case made by the defending lawyer for the innocence of the defendant. Murray, *Nature Red in Tooth and Claw*, 40. Van Inwagen, The *Problem of Evil*, 7.
83 Van Inwagen, *Problem of Evil*, 113. "In my view, the question we should attend to is not what I think of a defense or what you think of it, not what religious believers or committed atheists think of it, but what genuinely neutral agnostics think of it."
84 Murray, *Nature Red in Tooth and Claw*, 8, 36–37.
85 See Chapter 1 for the intended audience of this work.
86 Swinburne, *Providence*, 44.

87   Thomas F. Tracy, "The Lawfulness of Nature and the Problem of Evil," in *Physics and Cosmology: Scientific Perspectives on the Problem of Natural Evil*, eds. Nancey Murphy, Robert Russell, and William R. Stoeger, S. J. (Vatican City: Vatican Observatory Foundation, 2007), 152.
88   Tracy, "Lawfulness", 152.
89   Though a theologian may, of course, seek to argue that a particular position should be recognised as orthodox, if it is currently not recognised as such.
90   Swinburne, *Providence*, 238.
91   Swinburne, *Providence*, 245.
92   Southgate, *Groaning of Creation*, 132–133.
93   Kenneth Surin, *Theology and the Problem of Evil* (Oxford: Basil Blackwell, 1986).
94   Surin, *Theology and the Problem of Evil*, 10–11.
95   Surin, *Theology and the Problem of Evil*, 11.
96   Surin, *Theology and the Problem of Evil*, 18–19.
97   Surin, *Theology and the Problem of Evil*, 20–24.
98   Surin, *Theology and the Problem of Evil*, 23.
99   If a philosopher objects that the probability of a thought experiment is irrelevant because they are meant to reveal our attitudes, I would refer to the studies that show that vastly improbable thought experiments, such as the classic "Trolley Car" problem, actually do not provide us with valid results because they do not elicit the same psychological processes as real life moral events. They often evoke humour or a sense of the absurd, which changes the decision-making processes. Christopher W. Bauman, A. Peter McGraw, Daniel M. Bartels, and Caleb Warren, "Revisiting External Validity: Concerns about Trolley Problems and Other Sacrificial Dilemmas in Moral Psychology," *Social and Personality Psychology Compass* 8:9 (September 2014): 536–554.
100 James D. Rissler, "Open Theism: Does God Risk or Hope?" *Religious Studies* 42 (2006): 63–74.
101 Rissler, "Does God Risk or Hope?" 64.
102 See Vanstone's markers of love described in Chapter 4.
103 Rissler, "Does God Risk or Hope?" 66.
104 Rissler, "Does God Risk or Hope?" 66.
105 Eleonore Stump, *Wandering in Darkness: Narrative and the Problem of Suffering* (Oxford: Clarendon Press, 2010).
106 Stump, *Wandering in Darkness*, 16.
107 Stump, *Wandering in Darkness*, 85–107. See Chapter 4, 93–101.
108 Stump, *Wandering in Darkness*, 219–222. See Chapter 6, 165–171.
109 Stump, *Wandering in Darkness*, 378.
110 Faith Glavey Pawl at the University of Saint Louis is currently working on a dissertation focussed on extending Stump's work into the non-human animal realm, with a particular focus on baboons.
111 There is no way to prove this one way or the other.
112 For another survey of the theological positions, including many of those outlined below, see Southgate, *Groaning of Creation*, 3–39.
113 Kenneth Miller, *Finding Darwin's God: A Scientist's Search for Common Ground Between God and Evolution* (New York, NY: HarperCollins, 1999), 246.
114 Holmes Rolston III, "Naturalizing and Systematizing Evil," in *Is Nature Ever Evil? Religion, Science and Value*, ed. Willem B. Drees (London: Routledge, 2003), 67.
115 See my discussion of the difference between "natural evil" and "disvalue" in Chapter 1.
116 The "law of club and fang" comes from Jack London's Call of the Wild where the dog Buck learns that to survive in the north means to kill or be killed. Any show of weakness on the part of another was an opportunity to be taken advantage of for one's own

benefit. A human with a club was to be feared and respected; a human without one was to be mercilessly attacked. Jack London, *Call of the Wild* (London: Macmillan, 1903).

117 The term "natural evil" is sometimes discarded in favour of "harms" or "disvalues" because of its innate moral connotations.

118 Ted Peters and Martinez Hewlett, *Evolution from Creation to New Creation: Conflict, Conversation, and Convergence* (Nashville, TN: Abingdon, 2003), 158.

119 Celia Deane-Drummond, "Shadow Sophia in Christological Perspective: The Evolution of Sin and the Redemption of Nature," *Theology and Science* 6:1 (2008): 22.

120 Deane-Drummond, "Shadow Sophia," 23.

121 Deane-Drummond, "Shadow Sophia," 23.

122 Deane-Drummond, "Shadow Sophia," 23.

123 Remember Southgate's expression earlier that all theodicy "arises out of protest and ends in mystery."

124 Wesley J. Wildman, "Incongruous Goodness, Perilous Beauty, Disconcerting Truth: Ultimate Reality and Suffering in Nature," in *Physics and Cosmology: Scientific Perspectives on the Problem of Natural Evil*, eds. Nancey Murphy, Robert Russell, and William R. Stoeger, S. J. (Vatican City and Berkeley, CA: Vatican Observatory, CTNS, 2007), 282.

125 Wildman, "Incongruous Goodness," 282.

126 No foreknowledge, rather than foresight which God can possess. God can predict, but not foreknow with perfect certainty. This conclusion is held by both process theists and free will theists. See William Hasker, "An Adequate God," in *Searching for an Adequate God: A Dialogue between Process and Free Will Theists*, eds. John B. Cobb Jr. and Clark H. Pinnock (Grand Rapids, MI: Eerdmans, 2000), 218.

127 Although, it should be noted, in some process schemes, creation's freedom is eternally inherent, rather than something granted by God.

128 David R. Griffin, "Creation Out of Chaos and the Problem of Evil," in *Encountering Evil: Live Options in Theodicy*, ed. Stephen T. Davis (Edinburgh: T & T Clark, 1981), 105. All "actual entities" in process thought have some kind of experience and some kind of choice. Joseph Bracken, *Christianity and Process Thought: Spirituality for a Changing World* (Philadelphia and London: Templeton Foundation Press, 2006), 7.

129 Griffin, "Creation Out of Chaos," 105.

130 Surin, *Theology and the Problem of Evil*, 91.

131 Surin writes, "The merely suffering God might perhaps provide a half-consolation for the person who finds herself drinking the cup of suffering to its dregs, but this God is fundamentally unable to transform and to heal the world, or, to put it in more theological terms, to ensure that his Kingdom will become a reality" Surin, *Theology and the Problem of Evil*, 91.

132 Surin, *Theology and the Problem of Evil*, 91.

133 Surin, *Theology and the Problem of Evil*, 91–92.

134 Philip Clayton and Steven Knapp, *The Predicament of Belief: Science, Philosophy, Faith* (Oxford: Oxford University Press, 2011), 47–48. See also Philip Clayton and Steven Knapp, "Divine Action and the 'Argument from Neglect'," in *Physics and Cosmology: Scientific Perspectives on the Problem of Natural Evil*, eds. Nancey Murphy, Robert J. Russell, and William R. Stoeger, S. J. (Vatican City and Berkeley, CA: Vatican Observatory, CTNS, 2007), 179–194.

135 Clayton and Knapp, *Predicament of Belief*, 62.

136 See Chapter 5, 129.

137 For Augustine's account of fallen angels, see *The City of God*, books 10 and 11, and throughout The Literal Interpretation of Genesis.

138 C. S. Lewis, *The Problem of Pain* (New York, NY: HarperCollins, 1940, 1996), 138; Wolfhart Pannenberg, *Systematic Theology*, trans. Geoffrey W. Bromily (Göttingen:

Vanderhoeck & Ruprecht, 1991), 2:274; Michael Lloyd, "Are Animals Fallen?" in *Animals on the Agenda*, eds. Andrew Linzey and Dorothy Yamamoto (London: SCM Press, 1998), 147–160; Gregory A. Boyd, "Evolution as Cosmic Warfare: A Biblical Perspective on Satan and 'Natural Evil'," in *Creation Made Free: Open Theology Engaging Science*, ed. Thomas Oord (Eugene, OR: Wipf & Stock, 2009), 125–145; Stephen H. Webb, *The Dome of Eden: A New Solution to the Problem of Creation and Evolution* (Eugene, OR: Cascade, 2010), 139–152; Gregory A. Boyd, *Satan and the Problem of Evil: Constructing a Trinitarian Warfare Theodicy* (Downers Grove, IL: InterVarsity, 2001).

139 Cf. Southgate "Whatever processes science is able to understand as contributing to the evolution of complexity . . . must be presumed to be the gift of God in creation. . . . The tectonic movement that caused the Indian Ocean tsunami is an example of those processes that have made the Earth the lovely place that it is, and should not be regarded as in any way demonic" *Groaning of Creation*, 34.

140 Genesis 1:31.

141 See Psalm 104, Job 38–41 where God particularly points out the violent and uncontrollable parts of the natural world as special points of pride. See also the whole of Chapter 2.

142 William Dembski, *The End of Christianity: Finding a Good God in an Evil World* (Nashville, TN: B&H, 2009).

143 Dembski argues that the benefit granted to humans is that the corruption of the world teaches them of their own need for salvation.

144 Christopher Southgate, "Review of the End of Christianity by William A. Dembski," *Reviews in Science and Religion* 60 (November 2012): 43.

145 David Clough, *On Animals*, Vol. 1 of *Systematic Theology* (Edinburgh: T & T Clark, 2012), 119–127.

146 Clough, *On Animals*, 109–112.

147 Clough, *On Animals*, 116–117.

148 Clough, *On Animals*, 118.

149 Simon Conway Morris, *The Crucible of Creation: The Burgess Shale and the Rise of Animals* (Oxford: Oxford University Press, 1998), 160; Simon Conway Morris and Stefan Bengtson, "Cambrian Predators: Possible Evidence from Boreholes," *Journal of Paleontology* 68:1 (January 1994): 1–23; M. Y. Zhu, et al. "Direct Evidence for Predation on Trilobites in the Cambrian," *Proceedings of the Royal Society B* 271:5 (August 2004): S277–S289.

150 Clough, *On Animals*, 121.

151 Clough, *On Animals*, 122.

152 Clough, *On Animals*, 126.

153 See Chapter 6, "The Place of the Christ Event," 175–178.

154 Hoggard Creegan, *Animal Suffering*, 75.

155 Hoggard Creegan, *Animal Suffering*, 77.

156 Hoggard Creegan, *Animal Suffering*, 77.

157 Hoggard Creegan, *Animal Suffering*, 84.

158 Hoggard Creegan, *Animal Suffering*, 77.

159 Hoggard Creegan, *Animal Suffering*, 78.

160 She opposes Neil Messer's borrowed notion of "nothingness" accounting for the evil in the created world as not a sufficient explanation for the Holocaust or Jesus's temptation from demons, despite the fact that Messer uses these to explain natural evil, and not all moral evil. Hoggard Creegan, *Animal Suffering*, 76.

161 The muddle in Hoggard Creegan's categorisation is perhaps most clearly seen in her identification of the second law of thermodynamics as an element of evil. Without it, there would be no light dispersion, no heat dispersion . . . in short, there would be no chance for life and no history of creation at all.

162 See Matthew 13:24–30.

163 Hoggard Creegan, *Animal Suffering*, 77, 133, 148–149.

164 Messer, "Natural Evil after Darwin," 149.

165 Southgate, "Re-Reading Genesis, John, and Job," 379–382.

166 Philippians 2:5–7, NRSV.

167 John Polkinghorne, "Kenotic Creation and Divine Action," in *The Work of Love: Creation as Kenosis*, ed. John Polkinghorne (Grand Rapids, MI: Eerdmans, 2001), 102–105.

168 Polkinghorne, "Kenotic Creation and Divine Action," 95–96.

169 Polkinghorne, "Kenotic Creation and Divine Action," 102.

170 Polkinghorne, "Kenotic Creation and Divine Action," 104. Italics original.

171 See the discussion of God as a cause amongst causes in Chapter 5.

172 Polkinghorne, "Kenotic Creation and Divine Action," 105.

173 Kenotic theodicies have been offered, in various forms, by Jürgen Moltmann, Arthur Peacocke, John Polkinghorne, Denis Edwards, Paul Fiddes, and Keith Ward, amongst others. See essays in the volume edited by John Polkinghorne, *The Work of Love: Creation as Kenosis* (Grand Rapids, MI: Eerdmans, 2001).

174 Polkinghorne, "Kenotic Creation and Divine Action," 105.

175 Thomas J. Oord, "An Open Theology Doctrine of Creation and Solution to the Problem of Evil," in *Creation Made Free: Open Theology Engaging Science*, ed. Thomas J. Oord (Eugene, OR: Wipf & Stock, 2009), 49.

176 Essential kenosis is spelled out further in Thomas Oord, *The Uncontrolling Love of God: An Open and Relational Account of Providence* (Downer's Grove, IL: IVP Academic, 2015), 151–186.

177 Oord, *Uncontrolling Love of God*, 170.

178 Peters and Hewlett, *Evolution from Creation to New Creation*, 143.

179 Peters and Hewlett, *Evolution from Creation to New Creation*, 143.

180 Peters and Hewlett, *Evolution from Creation to New Creation*, 143.

181 Thus, Peters and Hewlett conclude "The doctrine of God's self-limitation on behalf of evolution would leave us with a Christian faith without hope." Peters and Hewlett, *Evolution from Creation to New Creation*, 143.

182 Rolston, *Science and Religion*, 134.

183 A great deal more on the nature of creaturely freedom is found in Chapter 4.

184 Southgate, *Groaning of Creation*, 48.

185 Celia Deane-Drummond might say that they reflect natural wisdom, rather than human wisdom. *Wonder and Wisdom: Conversations in Science, Spirituality and Theology* (London: Darton, Longman and Todd, 2006), 66–70. Equally, it is increasingly being shown that attributes and skills that have long been considered rational – and therefore uniquely human – such as educability, language, tool-use, number games, and self-consciousness, also exist to varying degrees in non-human animals. Clough, *On Animals*, 72–73. Cf. Mary Midgley, *Beast and Man* (New York, NY: Routledge, 1978), 265–272.

186 Polkinghorne, *Science and Providence*, 77.

187 Peters and Hewlett, *Evolution from Creation to New Creation*, 161.

188 Ruth Page, *God and the Web of Creation* (London: SCM Press, 1996), 7.

189 For John Haught, the "letting-be" of creation is linked with God's self-restraint or kenosis. Cf. John F. Haught, *God after Darwin: A Theology of Evolution* (Boulder, CO: Westview, 2000), 97.

190 William Rowe, "The Problem of Evil and Some Varieties of Atheism," *American Philosophical Quarterly* 16:4 (October 1979): 335–341; Richard Dawkins, *River Out of Eden: A Darwinian View of Life* (New York, NY: Basic Books, 1995), 154–155; Wesley J. Wildman, "Incongruous Goodness, Perilous Beauty," 277–278.

191 Page, *Web of Creation*, 40–43.

192 Southgate makes an "anthropomorphic guess" that God's co-suffering may "at some deep level take away the aloneness of the suffering creature's experience." See Southgate, *Groaning of Creation*, 54ff.
193 Southgate, *Groaning of Creation*, 76. Niels Henrik Gregersen, "The Cross of Christ in an Evolutionary World," *dialog* 40:3 (Fall 2001): 192–207. God's co-suffering in Christ is also emphasised by Arthur Peacocke, Ruth Page, Jürgen Moltmann, Robert Capon, W. H. Vanstone, John Polkinghorne, and others, though not all of them advance this thought with specific reference to the non-human creation. Cf. Arthur Peacocke, *Paths from Science Towards God* (Oxford: Oneworld: 2001), 85–88; Peacocke, "Cost of a New Life," 37–42.
194 Peacocke, "Cost of a New Life," 38. Italics original.
195 See also the further development of the theme of redemption in Chapter 6.
196 Page, *Web of Creation*, 63; Holmes Rolston III, "Does Nature Need to Be Redeemed?" *Zygon* 29:2 (June 1994): 205–229.
197 Paul J. Griffiths, "What Remains in the Resurrection? A (Broadly) Thomist Argument for the Presence of Nonrational Animals in Heaven," Paper presented at Blackfriars, Cambridge, 31 January 2013.
198 John Wesley, "The General Deliverance (Sermon 60)," The Wesley Center. Accessed 26 February 2013. Online: http://wesley.nnu.edu/john-wesley/the-sermons-of-john-wesley-1872-edition/sermon-60-the-general-deliverance/.
199 Including but not limited to the thinkers listed below as well as Keith Ward, Jürgen Moltmann, Ted Peters, Robert Russell, and Denis Edwards.
200 Griffiths, "What Remains?"
201 John Polkinghorne, *The God of Hope and the End of the World* (New Haven, CT: Yale University Press, 2002), 123.
202 Jay B. McDaniel, *Of God and Pelicans: A Theology of Reverence for Life* (Louisville, KY: Westminster John Knox, 1989), 42.
203 McDaniel, *God and Pelicans*, 45–46.
204 Southgate, *Groaning of Creation*, 82.
205 Southgate, *Groaning of Creation*, 84.
206 Southgate, *Groaning of Creation*, 85.
207 See Chapter 4 on the particularity and non-substitutability of love and Chapter 6 on the universality of resurrection.
208 Dougherty, *Problem of Animal Pain*, 136. Italics original.
209 Southgate, *Groaning of Creation*, 111–112.
210 Southgate, *Groaning of Creation*, 126.
211 Southgate makes a distinction drawn from Lukas Vischer between anthropocentrism and "anthropomonism." It is anthropomonism which sees humans as the only objects of concern in God's redemptive purposes, and every other creature as disposable or instrumental. However, Southgate and his co-authors "hold that a chastened and humble anthropocentrism, which strongly resists anthropomonism, can appropriately remain key to an ecological theology" David G. Horrell, Cheryl Hunt, and Christopher Southgate, *Greening Paul: Rereading the Apostle in a Time of Ecological Crisis* (Waco, TX: Baylor, 2010), 124.
212 See Denis Edwards, "Why Is God Doing This? Suffering, The Universe, and Christian Eschatology," in *Physics and Cosmology: Scientific Perspectives on the Problem of Natural Evil*, eds. Nancey Murphy, Robert J. Russell, and William R. Stoeger, S. J. (Vatican City and Berkeley, CA: Vatican Observatory, CTNS, 2007), 255–256.
213 Edwards, "Why Is God Doing This?" 262.
214 Edwards, "Why Is God Doing This?" 266.
215 Jürgen Moltmann, *God in Creation: A New Theology of Creation and the Spirit of God*, trans. Margaret Kohl (Minneapolis, MN: Fortress Press, 1993), 133–135.
216 Moltmann, *God in Creation*, 169.

217 Peters and Hewlett, *Evolution from Creation to New Creation*, 160.

218 I will explore this concept further in Chapter 5.

219 Russell, "Physics, Cosmology, and the Challenge to Consequentialist Natural Theodicy," 111.

220 Deane-Drummond, "Shadow Sophia," 24.

221 This objection would stem from her not thinking that creatures, as a whole, are either entirely saved or entirely lost, but rather that "only those parts of lives which please God, which bear the desired fruit from the seed of possibility, are saved." If a creature's life had no value in this world, it would be entirely lost. Page, *Web of Creation*, 170.

222 Page, *Web of Creation*, 63.

223 Griffin, "Creation Out of Chaos," 106. Italics mine.

224 The varieties and the shaping of meaning will be discussed later in Chapter 5, 144–146.

225 See also my discussion of extinction and teleology in Bethany Sollereder, "The Purpose of Dinosaurs," *The Christian Century* 130:20 (October 2013). Online: www. christiancentury.org/article/2013-09/purpose-dinosaurs.

226 Southgate, *Groaning of Creation*, 76; Gregersen, "Cross of Christ," 204.

227 Gregersen, "Cross of Christ," 203–204. Italics original. See also the discussion of biological telos in Chapter 5.

228 Moltmann, *God in Creation*, 197.

229 Southgate, *Groaning of Creation*, 15–17.

230 Southgate, *Groaning of Creation*, 16.

4 Creation, freedom, and love

Introduction

"How could a good and loving God create through an evolutionary process that involves so much suffering, death, extinction, and violence?" Implied in the question are assumptions about the attributes of God, particularly omnipotence and omni-benevolence. The unlimited power of God combined with the universal goodness of God seems deeply at odds with the disvalues in the natural world. Yet, the cosmos at large and the natural processes of evolution – I will now assume after the work of the last two chapters – are not fallen, corrupted, or cursed, but remain the "very good" creation of God. What do we make of a system where each flourishes at the expense of the other?

Along with Christopher Southgate and Michael Murray, I propose that only a compound theodicy that draws on several different approaches at once will be able to address non-human animal suffering.[1] The thick description of the God-world relationship will be spread over the next three chapters, but I will take a moment to sketch out the whole arc here.

I begin with the nature of love. I do not begin by focussing on a particular instance of animal suffering, like William Rowe's famous fawn in the fire, and then attempt to justify it by finding outweighing goods.[2] Instead, I start with the premise that God created the world in love, through love, and for love. Love involves vulnerability, precariousness, and an allowance of radical freedom of the other. The implication of this love is that God's action in the world involves various kenotic self-limitations that prevent a simple overpowering of the natural causes that lead to disvalues. I argue that God's love for non-human creatures requires granting them degrees of autonomy. Creatures can follow their desires into behaviours that do not always reflect God's loving character. Choices may involve strategies of survival that, as in the case of parasitism, capitalise on disvalues. I do not consider these free desires of creatures that lead to disvalues to be "fallen" because they are an integral part of one of God's aims: for creatures to develop the capacity to love. Love cannot be created *de novo* but must develop out of the "raw materials" of evolutionary desires.

The next chapter is devoted to the work of God in creation. The kenosis of God in creation does not imply the lack of God's creative action or presence. Instead,

God can be understood to be present in various complementary ways. I will explore in particular a four-fold combination of the fundamental gift of being, the work of co-suffering, the call of the divine lure, and participation through embodiment and the shaping of meaning.

The last chapter will explore the possibilities of redemption. Many creatures are denied the possibility of flourishing, so redemption for creatures is a key component of what makes the love of God comprehensible in light of suffering. I have three basic approaches. First, the nature of love requires that each creature is loved particularly, and therefore redemption must exist at the level of the individual creature that suffered. Second, the meaning, and therefore the value, of a life is only determined eschatologically. Therefore, God works to redeem meaning in every life in such a way that the creature who suffers experiences a new life that incorporates and glorifies previous suffering. Third, various extant models of redemption can be held together in the image of redemption as a fractal mosaic, composed of nested layers of redemptive meaning.

My compound approach to theodicy speaks more about the nature of God and God's love than it does about the traditional endeavour of theodicy. Theodicy is always (at least tacitly) a two-part process. It first asks, "How is God good or loving?" and then, second, applies that definition of God's goodness or love to the suffering world. The next three chapters are, in essence, an exploration of the nature of God. How does God love? How does God act? How does God redeem? In each of these, the suffering of creatures will appear, but the nature of God will be the primary focus.

While most of my work is concerned with how non-human creaturely suffering is addressed within its own frame of reference, I have to acknowledge that a theological account of evolution cannot leave out the place of humans entirely. In light of so many overwhelmingly anthropocentric approaches that have placed *all* the value of non-human suffering in human development, such as those of Dembski or Corey, this addition requires careful contextualisation so that the focus upon human development does not overwhelm every other good.[3]

Of divine love

The nature of love

Now we turn to the nature of love. "God is love," (1 John 4:8, 16) the Bible says. But what is meant by "love"? Love is a highly abused term in the English language. One can use "love" to express the highest, most difficult, and most noble realities of human life. Or one can "love" a hamburger. Despite thousands of years of songs, poems, books, and experiences of love, there is still little agreement as to what constitutes love's nature. Jules Toner remarks: "It is a strange and striking fact that even those who write best about love devote very little space to considering what love is."[4] It is worth taking some time to work out a definition.

I will follow a traditional definition, drawn from Thomas Aquinas and expanded upon by Eleonore Stump. Love is a compound desire made up of the desire for the good of the beloved and the desire for union with the beloved (appropriate to the type of relationship, or "office").[5] I add that love also includes an historical element – a faithfulness of particularity borne of shared history. The two desires of love, when they are truly desires of love and not some other desire disguised as love, will always converge. The desire for union with the beloved will always contribute to the good of the beloved, and the desire for the good of the beloved will always contribute (ultimately)[6] to union with the beloved.

Desire for the good of the beloved precludes controlling or manipulative behaviours. W. H. Vanstone has been an influential theological voice reflecting on the nature of love. His now-classic *Love's Endeavour, Love's Expense: The Response of Being to the Love of God* offers a highly regarded treatment of love's nature.[7] Vanstone writes, "When one who professes to love is wholly in control of the object of his love, then the falsity of love is exposed."[8] One cannot both love and control because love necessarily involves respect for the will and being of the other.[9] For God to control the creation entirely would be to determine and therefore destroy its capacity to selve insofar as it possesses that capacity. God's love means God will not control and thereby short circuit that process of development.

This does not mean that God has no control at all, that God cannot direct, encourage, persuade, or act. But it does mean that God cannot act in the overpowering ways that would be necessary to, for example, stop a starving animal from attacking another. Creatures find new food sources because they are hungry. Predation, parasitism, and other forms of creaturely violence have emerged out of deep-seated needs. If God were to prevent a creature (like the Pintail duck from the first chapter) from seeking a meal of meat in the face of starvation, God would be halting and overwhelming creaturely autonomy in ways that are irreconcilable to love. The horrors we see in evolutionary development are, in this sense, the expected outcome of God's love for creation.

Instead of preventing suffering, God engages with creatures, waits for them, works with them, and redeems them. God's nature of love, writes Australian theologian Denis Edwards, "is revealed in the Christ-event as radical self-giving love. This is a divine and transcendent love, a love that has an unimaginable capacity to respect the autonomy and independence of creatures, to work with them patiently, and to bring all things to their fulfilment."[10]

Desire for the good of the beloved can be a general, universal desire – one can desire the good of many. Nor is desiring the good of others a responsive love: it does not require any particular attribute or trait in the beloved. Desire for the good of the beloved would explain why love does not falter when encountered with change, and is faithful when others with similar or superior values emerge.[11] Love is inherently faithful, which has been a conundrum for some philosophers who situate love in the value of the beloved.

Niko Kolodny calls love conceived of as a response to certain characteristics in the beloved "the quality theory" of love.[12] As Gabriele Taylor writes: "if x loves y then he does so in virtue of certain determinate qualities which he believes y to have."[13] David Velleman nuances Kolodny by saying that it is not only the qualities themselves, but attention to the valuation of the qualities of the beloved that evokes love: "I am inclined to say that love is likewise the awareness of a value inhering in its object; and I am also inclined to describe love as an arresting awareness of that value."[14] For Velleman it is the rational nature of the beloved that is to be loved, not any particular qualities that the beloved's rational nature might bring forth. It is the choosing capacity itself that is to be loved, not the choices that are made. But what if that capacity is lost or does not exist? Intuition would advise that love which changes objects when a person of superior value walks by, or love which ceases to love the beloved after an accident or illness changes the valued characteristics, is not real love but somehow defective. By this definition of love alone, I would certainly not want to be the recipient of love.

God's love is faithful in at least two ways. First, it does not rest on the values or strengths of the beloved. Second, it is not limited. While a human might transfer their love to a new object after a loss of value occurs, God would not, for God already loves all other possible objects of love as well. God's love is not limited by capacity or attention – to love one is not to love another less. God's love never values one creature over another, rather, God's love is part of what gives value to creatures. The self-generated nature of God's love can be called the "volitional" aspect of love. Harry Frankfurt sees love as a choice that creates value, pointing out that his love for his children is precisely what causes them to have value, not vice versa.[15] In the classic work by Anders Nygren, *Agape and Eros*, Nygren identifies agape (the *Christian* love *par excellence* in his view) as this sort of value-creating, spontaneous love that arises entirely out of the character of the lover.[16] "We look in vain," he writes, "for an explanation of God's love in the character of the man who is the object of His love. God's love is 'groundless' . . . the only ground for it is in God Himself."[17]

While a volitional approach solves the problem of the beloved facing competition from someone with superior value and shows how love can be faithful when faced with changes, it has drawbacks too. Stump points out that if the beloved asks the reasonable question "why do you love me?" the volitional lover must answer "Oh, there is no reason, at least no reason having anything to do with *you*."[18] The love of volition can give no reason for its existence with respect to the beloved. In which case, any choice or particularity of love – say, to love one's husband more than a stranger on the street – is completely arbitrary.[19] Something more than volition is needed.

The second desire of love, the desire for union with the beloved, provides that something else. It introduces specificity and particularity to love that is responsive to the uniqueness of the beloved.[20] If I desire union with John or Valerie, they cannot be replaced by Peter or Karen, because I desire union with *this* person and not with another, based on their characteristics, a shared history, and the office of our relationship: it is a response to the beloved.

Since the desire for union must also converge with the good of the beloved, the union desired must be of an appropriate type.[21] For Stump, desire for union is closely tied to what she calls the "offices of love."[22] The office of love is, quite simply, the type of relationship one holds with another. That office might be mother, friend, lover, sibling, teacher, client, patient, or something else. It is important to note that offices are partly dependent on the characteristics of the beloved. Take, for example, an office like "mother" which seems general and universal enough. Yet, no one is only "mother." Everyone who is a mother is a "mother to so-and-so." The limits and boundaries of the office change depending on the identity of the beloved. A woman may be mother to both Julia and Steve, but if her relationships with both were identical in every way, something would be wrong. Circumstances, needs, and inherent abilities all shape how the love of the mother for the child will be expressed, and how far – as well as what type of – union will be achieved. Stump uses the example of a man who composes music trying to share his joy with a very beloved but tone-deaf sister. Her capacity to share in his music, and thus her ability to be united with him in that aspect of their love is dependent upon her innate qualities and abilities (or lack thereof).[23] Each relationship is unique, and each relationship must be weighted on all the considerations of office, inherent qualities of the lover and the beloved, and the circumstances in which love is to be expressed.

The specificity (or particularity) of love solves the problem that so antagonised Nygren: it seemed to him that to love one beloved in a particular and special way was to mistreat every other individual. Nygren's logic led him to the dilemma that to love one person would be to fail in appropriate love to all others. Or, for example, to believe that to feed his cat would be to do an injustice to every other hungry cat that he was not feeding. Stump, in contrast, writes:

> On Aquinas's account of love, a person can have an impartial love of all human beings. But Aquinas also supposes that some loves are and ought to be greater than others. A person ought to love all human beings, but not equally. She should love some people more than others in virtue of having certain relationships with them, which ought to make her love for them greater than her love for humanity in general.[24]

The same could be said of other non-human objects of love, such as pets. The door is opened, then, for equal love to treat individuals differently without arbitrary caprice. In a world of creatures with different capacities and different needs, different forms of divine response are needed and appropriate. God can treat the worm and the cheetah and the human differently, respond to them and their suffering differently, in light of their various capacities. I will return to this consideration below.

The particularity of love also impacts how a lover is affected by each beloved. For Vanstone, a sign of the inauthenticity of love is detachment. A lover who is untouched by the trials of the beloved does not actually love. In Stump's appropriation of Thomist theology, God's affected state is shown by the desire for certain outcomes for the beloved. If God has desires for creation which creatures themselves have the power to resist, then God cannot be unaffected by creation. For classical theists, the conclusion of vulnerability is troublesome since it challenges the notion of God's *aseity* and immutability, that is, God's ability to be totally self-existent, self-reliant, and unchanging. If God responds to the world, then the world has the power to affect God, beyond God's own choice.

God's vulnerability is problematic at first glance. It appears as if there is nothing to prevent God from being overwhelmed by suffering just as people often are. One philosopher wrote, "Love takes us hostage to fortune; it binds us to the weal and woe of the beloved in ways we could not have anticipated and cannot reject."[25] But surely God cannot be taken hostage to fortune!

Moltmann suggests a way to avoid the challenge to God's *aseity* by arguing that even God's suffering in response to the world is God's own action on God's self, and is therefore controllable. However, as Paul Fiddes points out, in Moltmann's system, "God seems less the supreme victim than the supreme self-executioner."[26] Fiddes, along with Edwards and Walter Kasper,[27] finds a middle way between refusing God the ability to suffer and refusing the uncontrollable nature of suffering by suggesting instead that God "chooses that suffering should *befall* him, rather than making himself suffer."[28] God chooses to be vulnerable, and chooses to be open to the suffering that love brings. Fiddes's conclusion coheres well with Vanstone's observation that, "Where love is authentic, the lover gives to the object of his love a certain power over himself – a power which would not otherwise be there."[29] Of itself, the creation has no power to affect God: in this sense God is immutable. As an object of love, however, the creation gains that power because God gives God's self to it. Yet, since the ability to suffer is freely chosen by God, God is not ruled or overwhelmed by it. Suffering remains both uncaused by God and voluntary.

Elizabeth O'Donnell Gandolfo has written forcefully to reject the vulnerability of God to suffering, arguing that "divine invulnerability [is] the ground and source of human courage in the face of vulnerability, suffering and violence."[30] Without a God whose love is invulnerable, there is no sure centre, no refuge, from the storms of suffering. Gandolfo critiques those, like Fiddes and Elizabeth Johnson, who argue that God *chooses* to enter into vulnerable relation with creation.[31] For Gandolfo, the act of entering creation in vulnerable relationship is simply *what love does* – there is no choice about it. "The invulnerability of divine love's free self-expression is most fully manifested in creation when it does precisely what it is in love's essence to do – enter into vulnerable relation with the beloved."[32] God could not act in any other way. Stated this way, Gandolfo's work is actually far more like Thomas Oord's notion of essential kenosis. Oord critiques those who take the view that God voluntarily undergoes kenosis in creation. Instead, Oord argues: "kenotic love is an essential attribute of God's eternal nature. God loves necessarily."[33] God's necessary love means necessary vulnerability, necessary precariousness in the outcomes of creation.

In the end, it is hard to see how Gandolfo actually offers a view of divine invulnerability. She admits, like Vanstone previously, "there is a sense in which divine love for creation makes the invulnerable God inherently vulnerable."[34] What she offers, I think, is an emphasis on the unlimited faithfulness of God's love. God's love will never falter or fail regardless of how much suffering it must bear, no matter how hard we cling to it. It will never lessen, never change, never run out.

Thus, it can form the strong bedrock of support needed by those who suffer, but only because harm done to God cannot erode or diminish God's love.

God is affected by the world, and God desires certain outcomes in the world. Because love is a desire *for* something in the state of the beloved, love is either fulfilled or not fulfilled in its desires by the beloved him- or herself. There is, therefore, no way that the lover can be untouched by the choices of the beloved; no way for God to stand apart from the suffering of the world. This is the foundation of the co-suffering argument advanced by theologians such as Ruth Page and Christopher Southgate: no creature suffers alone because God suffers with it, and God takes on the full consequences of the risk of creation.[35] God therefore loves particularly – loves each individual in itself – and God suffers with each, taking their suffering right into the unlimited heart of the divine being.

Does divine responsiveness and vulnerability to creation make God dependent upon creation? In loving the creation, it seems that needs are formed in the divine person that may or may not be satisfied depending upon the response of creation. It is, as Paul Fiddes says, "a dangerous kind of theology [to propose] that a God who creates 'out of love' has needs to be satisfied."[36] Does the concept of divine need overthrow God's self-sufficiency or threaten God's perfection? It might, depending on how it is conceived. Robert Jenson, for example, realises the worst fears of the classical theists when he proposes that through creation God develops a narrative of self-discovery. That is, God's own identity is found through interaction with creation, or as Jenson writes, God "can have no identity except as he meets the temporal end toward which creatures live."[37] God's own character and abilities are tied essentially with creation.

David Bentley Hart rails against Jenson's notion of divine temporality, passibility, and mutability with good reason: namely that it makes evil part of the development of the character of God.[38] Encounter with evil becomes the place where God grows into God's ultimate self by overcoming evil, and thus the fullness of God's goodness becomes dependent upon the existence of evil. As Hart suggests, this cannot be tolerated.

Rather than making God dependent upon evil, I suggest – with Keith Ward – that there is only mutability within certain parts of God's existence, and not within the central attributes of God's character.[39] God can add to the store of divine knowledge by moving through time, for example, but God cannot grow in love or goodness, since God already contains the perfect fullness of these attributes. God can change in act, but not in character. Creation, then, becomes a place where God has room for the manifestation and expression of divine character in dynamic relationship to creation, but creation is not a realm for the development of God's identity. The same is true of divine needs in relation to creation. If the needs aroused by creation were necessary and essential to the being of God, then creation could pose a threat to God. However, the danger can be avoided if the needs are seen as contingent rather than necessary to the essential being of God, although this still constitutes an important change to the classical understanding of divine attributes.

The *choice* of God to humbly take on need in creation – rather than having an intrinsic need that compels God to create – makes all the difference. Fiddes writes:

> God does not 'need' the world in the sense that this is some intrinsic necessity in his nature, binding his free choice (thus far Aquinas is right); but he does need the world in the sense that he has freely chosen to be in need.[40]

The need aroused by creation arises out of the previous free choice to create, and therefore the need is self-chosen by God. Vanstone illustrates the difference between the two types of need with the example of a happy family.[41] All their essential needs are met in relationship within their own members. Yet, out of the fullness of their love, the family chooses to adopt a child. Now, when the family gathers together, if the adopted child is missing, something from the whole of the family is missing as well: the circle is no longer complete without the additional member. A new need has been created by the very act of love, and the fulfilment of the family's needs now rests also in the adoptee's hands. This need was not essential, but contingent upon the previous act of love. In Vanstone's words, "Love has surrendered its own triumphant self-sufficiency and created its own need. This is the supreme illustration of love's self-giving or self-emptying – that it should surrender its fullness and create in itself the emptiness of need."[42] The surrender of fullness and creation of need is expressed in theology as kenosis.

God's self, then, is given freely and vulnerably to the world in creative engagement, and it is this self-giving that brings about the fullness of creaturely existence. Southgate describes God's kenosis by drawing on Hans Urs von Balthasar's concept of "that movement of the inner life of the Trinity that enables us to understand God as the creative, suffering origin of all things."[43] Southgate calls this understanding "deep intraTrinitarian kenosis." Moltmann, too, argues that God's kenotic actions toward creation are a picture of the inner life of the Trinity: marked by self-surrender, self-limitation, and obedience.[44] The origin of the movement of creation begins deep in the personhood of God: in the giving of the Father to the Son through the Spirit – the self-abandoning love that is the template for all creative endeavours. The nature of the Trinity, the nature of love, is toward self-giving union with the other, which extends to creation.[45] Arthur Peacocke writes, "there is a creative self-emptying and self-offering (a *kenosis*) of *God*, a sharing in the suffering of God's creatures, in the very creative, evolutionary process of the world."[46] The creation is based upon the self-giving of one self to another first modelled in love within the being of God, then given into the fullness of all other life. Thus, the world was made in love, through love, and for love.

Love, in its ideal form, must be unconditional and endless. It cannot depend upon a certain response or a certain set of characteristics (though it can respond to certain characteristics). In Stump's definition, the limitlessness of love is derived from the unlimited desire for the good of the beloved. If the lover loves the beloved, then the lover necessarily desires the good of the beloved, and there is no point at which that desire ceases. For Edwards, the limitlessness of love is demonstrated by God's startling patience: God does not force or coerce creation, but waits through the billions-year-long process of star and element formation and then through the long ages of evolutionary development for life to emerge and grow in complexity.[47] In light of such patience for cosmological processes, the patience extended to individual creatures is impossible to exhaust.[48]

Furthermore, if God loves creatures, then regardless of the outcomes or cost, God must commit to the project of creation without hesitation and without calculation. Limitlessness means that God will never turn away from the desires of love for creation. No amount of disvalue, pain, or even of rebellion will turn God away from desiring the creation's good and seeking union with creatures. Because God's desire will not be turned away, the patient action of God (even if only in actively waiting) will never end. God's love is limitless: "it bears all things, believes all things, hopes all things, endures all things."[49] Hope for creation is not grounded in God's ability to unilaterally decide the whole of history, but in the unlimited faithfulness and creativity of divine love.[50]

One more aspect of love needs to be explored in relation to the particularity of love: the sense of shared history.[51] Kolodny proposes: "one's reason for loving a person is one's relationship to her: the on going history that one shares with her."[52] We love because we have historical experience that draws out attachment to a particular individual. Love is not situated only in the attributes of the beloved (which may change) nor solely in the character or intentions of the lover (which ends up being non-responsive to the beloved), but in the relationship between them.[53]

Depending on what is meant by "relationship," the historical position is open to critique: as Stump points out, too narrow a definition of "relationship" may deny the reality of unrequited love.[54] There is no place for Dante's famous love for Beatrice, for example, a love that Dante held for decades (and even after her death), despite only meeting her on two occasions. There was no shared history, and no hope for a future shared history – no relationship (by Kolodny's standards, at any rate) to justify Dante's love. For Kolodny, this simply is not love. As Stump points out:

> On Kolodny's account, we have to say not that there is something defective or deplorable about Dante's love for Beatrice, but just that he did not love her. Dante did not suppose that he had a relationship (in Kolodny's sense of 'relationship') with Beatrice, and so he also did not believe that there was such a relationship between him and Beatrice that rendered his love of her appropriate.[55]

If only requited two-way love is considered a relationship, the implications extended to divine love would be disastrous. It would mean that God could not love those who did not return God's love.[56] The unrequited nature of much of God's love for humanity or for creatures who have no capacity for love would meet Kolodny's criticism that God should (in these cases) "get over it, and move on."[57] Again, Kolodny's conclusion would be that in the light of a profound inequality of positions or without the prospect of reciprocated concern, concern is likely inappropriate and love is simply absent.[58] This is obviously an inappropriate conclusion when it comes to divine love, so whatever one's definition of love, it must include the possibility of one-sided, unrequited love that is still love. The historical qualification can be added even when there is no reciprocal relationship: God's accompaniment of creation reveals a love given where there is no hope of return. It also counters the substitutability of creatures. Where we might see little difference in the hundreds of individual spiders in a single hatch, God relates to each of them individually and has a particular relationship with each of them based on God's accompaniment of each moment of their existence. This will become important in thinking about the scope of redemption, which will be explored in Chapter 6.

Love, then, as the desire for the good of and for union with the beloved, holds together the qualities of the beloved, the relationship of the lover to the beloved, and the volition of the lover into a unified whole. It also allows for unrequited love. Since the desires of love are centred in the lover, in the case of unrequited love the desires will not be fulfilled, accounting for love's painfulness.

Now it is time to move on from the first part of theodicy, "How is God loving?", to the secondary application to the God-world relationship. I will argue that the divine expression of love results in self-limitations that allow for behavioural freedoms that shape evolutionary development even into paths that cause disvalues. I argue that the free actions of creatures in response to environmental and survival pressures are not fallen desires, since they remain inside the broad purposes of God for creation (to create the world "in love, through love, and for love") and are within the specific intentions of God for individual creatures (towards selving and the reception of divine love). Furthermore, the continuation of creaturely selving also leads towards God's aim of developing creatures that can return God's love.[59]

"For God so loved the worms"

The Aquinas/Stump philosophical definition of love is well suited to deal with some common objections to developing an evolutionary theodicy based around love. The first of these is that God cannot or does not love the non-human world. For some definitions of love, the non-human world is not a proper object of divine love. Without the complex brain structures that humans have, worms (for example) are not capable of sentient brain states, and therefore are unable to love God back. From a relational view of love, this would be a fatal objection. For Kolodny and his fellow theorists, the possibility of love for worms is already ruled out. However, for the Aquinas/Stump thesis of love, God's desire for the good of each and every worm *is* plausible, as is God's desire for union with each worm – as long as the caveat is included that the union must be appropriate to the office of love. In the case of worms, the office of love that exists between God and a worm is that of Creator and "wormly creature" respectively. The form the relationship of love takes will also be appropriate to the inherent abilities and limitations of the worm: the love will be "wormish" in nature. I do not mean to say that the worm loves God in a "wormly" way (worms do not, now,[60] have the capacity to love) but that the love of God for the worm will be of a type appropriate to the ability of the worm to receive and enjoy. Just as a newborn baby does not yet have the complex capacity to love, but is a proper object of and can receptively participate in his or her parents' love, so the non-human world can receive and participate in God's love. And since that love will be specific to the beloved creature – it is "wormish" for the worm – the love participated in between God and the beloved need not be perceivable or understandable to any other species.

The Aquinas/Stump definition of love helps solve another objection: that if God loves all creatures, God has to treat all creatures completely equally in every respect. The nature of love *does* require that God desire union with each beloved and desire the good of each beloved. However, since each beloved has unique characteristics, experiences, and potentials that determine the shape of the good and the type of union available to God, there can be variation in *how* God loves each creature. God can love the adult chimpanzee with a different sort of love than God loves the worm, because the adult chimpanzee is sentient, has memory, and experiences suffering. The adult chimpanzee also has the capacity for altruism and aggression. The worm, as far as we know, has none of these things. The good for the chimpanzee and the worm will therefore be different. Although both will ultimately (as with all created things) find their good in union with God, the chimpanzee will have far more specified needs to fulfil than the worm. In fact, as a theodicy with regard to the worm is set out, there is no particular reason that even being trod underfoot should be inimical to the ultimate good of the worm, if one accepts the following:

- The worm does not have the sentient capacity to experience suffering.
- The worm has the ability to participate fully in the divine gift of life.
- The simple stretching out of the worm's life for longer does not necessarily equate to value for the worm because of its lack of sentience.
- The worm shares in the hope of redemption with all of creation and therefore the "self" of the worm is not lost in death.
- The manner of the worm's death and the subsequent outcomes of the worm's death (its feeding a passing bird, for example) may all be reflected back to the glory of the eschatological self of the worm.[61]

Insofar as the worm exists in relationship with God and the world, the worm is pursuing its greatest good with as much intention and capacity as it is able.[62] The death of the worm is a simple result of those relationships having consequential integrity. For the chimpanzee the matter of life and death becomes more complicated, because there is more ability to choose and more ability to suffer. For that highly intelligent primate, *Homo sapiens*, in whom mutual loving relationship with God finds its greatest potential, the considerations become the most complex. Nonetheless, there is no reason that God cannot love the worms, even though they do not (in our current understanding) have the capacity to love God back.[63] Insofar as the existence of worms adds to the fullness of creation, God loves worms out of God's own volitional desire and in response to a worm's ability to be a worm.

Related to the equality of treatment, there is a theodicy-related objection to the conclusion that God loves every creature. Namely, if God loves and knows every sentient creature, then God cannot act in a way to relieve the suffering of one sentient creature without being morally obligated to respond in a similar way to every other sentient creature. To do so would seem to make God morally arbitrary – a point raised by Wesley Wildman.[64] In response, Philip Clayton and Steven Knapp have proposed the "not-even-once" principle: "A benevolent God could not intervene *even once* without incurring the responsibility to intervene in every case where doing so would prevent an instance of innocent suffering."[65] However, the Thomist definition of love gives another option because it does not propose that God's relationship to each creature is equal. Quite the opposite. Every creature has a unique relationship to God based on the "givenness" of its species, abilities, personality, environment, and history. God's love and concern is radically individual: how to promote *this* creature's greatest good. Therefore, God would not be automatically morally obligated to intervene in every other situation of suffering, but only to act in each individual's life in a way that is consistent with its own greatest good. Since every situation is different, each choice of divine action will be uniquely considered under the surrounding circumstances and in light of the particular suffering subject.

To God, who would know the inner experience of each creature, a justification could be made that one creature might be able to bear suffering differently to and better than another creature. Equally, on a macroscale, the increased complexity, power, and skill of diverse species in response to eons of adverse conditions gives more than a hint that there certainly have been responses to suffering that have brought about a glorification rather than a diminution of the selfhood of creatures. In turn, the possibility that glorification through suffering is likely for some and impossible for others in the same circumstances allows for the justification of different treatment of creatures depending on various factors.

The not-even-once principle, on the contrary, assumes that every instance of innocent suffering is problematic in the same sort of way. But there are as many different types and circumstances of suffering as there are instances. Someone stubbing their toe and a seal being eaten alive are both instances of innocent suffering, but they should not be compared: they exist in totally different realms of moral importance. Clayton and Knapp don't agree with this assertion. Although people see differences in suffering, they argue, "God sees no such dichotomy but a vast continuum of suffering far more pervasive, intense, and immediate in its need for relief than we could ever allow ourselves to appreciate."[66]

Let me, for the sake of the argument, run with Clayton and Knapp's idea that there is only a grey-scale of suffering, no black and white. It does not follow that if intensities of suffering exist on a continuous scale in creation, that instances of suffering in an individual's life are likewise scaled. In fact, we often see just the opposite: many instances of suffering help people grow and develop as an individual (in physical even if not in spiritual ways). But some instances of suffering are key turning points in the life of an individual, forever crushing their sense of self. This is most obvious in death, but can exist in other ways as well, such as a crippling accident or serious abuse. That means it is not necessarily the intensity of suffering that is the main concern, but the effect of the suffering. When an innocent creature has their selfhood destroyed by suffering, this makes a different sort of appeal for divine action than the suffering that does not destroy a self. A differentiation can be made, especially by God who will be in the best position to anticipate what sort of impact any one instance of suffering will have.

The observation that God can treat individuals differently in response to their unique needs avoids Wildman's charge that a God who would intervene in some cases and not in others is totally inconsistent without dropping all possibility of physical interaction with the world, as Clayton and Knapp do.[67] In practice, there might be little difference in how God treats a worm, a beetle, and a spider. The lack of difference does not arise out of moral limitations on God, nor out of lack of love, but simply because none of those creatures have specific needs that require particularly different treatment.

A quite different question about divine love for the non-human world is: "How far into creation can God's love extend?" If God can love worms, what about a smallpox virus, a tree, or a mountain? There are no clear-cut, satisfying answers to this question, because it is impossible at some levels to discern what the "entity" is that is to be loved. A tree may be a distinct unit, but how is the mountain to be divided from the tectonic plate below? Should slime mould be considered one organism or an aggregate of organisms? For a process theist, every unit conceivable, down to the components of an atom, are unique entities and therefore recipients of the love of God. However, I contend that something has to have life in order to "have" a good.[68] Anything that can adapt – that is, exhibit behaviour and respond to external stimuli in a way that benefits itself – can have both a definable good (e.g. "reach more sunlight" or "exchange DNA with a fellow bacterium") and some means of pursuing that good (e.g. "grow taller" or "move over there").[69] While the existence of a mountain might *be* good, it has no good of its own to pursue, and no ability to adjust or adapt to a good. Therefore, while a person might have a desire to see or possess something inanimate, and that desire might imitate or echo the desires of love, inanimate objects are not proper objects of love since they have no real good that can be pursued. God can love the smallpox virus, but not the mountain.[70]

Of creaturely freedom and package deals

If one accepts that "God is love" (1 John 4:8) and works from the philosophical definition and theological description of love developed earlier, there are particular outcomes for God's relationship with creation. A God who loves the world according to the preceding definition will not be able to relate to the world in the way the classical tradition has described the Creator-creation relationship – characterised by the expression of omnipotence, omniscience, eternity, and immutability. Some of these attributes are only incompatible with love if they are expressed. Omnipotence, God's ability to do anything that is logically possible, is compatible with love as long as God *does not* do everything; is not occasionalist.

Immutability, however, is simply impossible because there is no difference between its existence and its expression. While God might possess these traits within God's self, God cannot relate to the world with these attributes and maintain the desires of love according to the definition given earlier. Love *requires* vulnerability, precariousness, and making place for the freedom of the other. Even the classical tradition has acknowledged the mutual exclusiveness of some of the classical attributes of God and the love of God as expressed in the Incarnation. Classical theology solves this problem through the distinction between the economic Trinity and the immanent Trinity. God acts in the economic Trinity in ways impossible to the immanent Trinity, allowing for the acts of love to be genuine – at least, at some level.[71]

Central to the thesis of love and its vulnerability is the concern of freedom. The freedom of creation is the freedom for creatures to act with real causative effect on earth history without their behaviour being fully determined by God.[72] If God loves all created beings, God will not wilfully withdraw the "otherness" of those creatures by determining their behaviour; their freedom is part of their status as beloved. The same is true at the larger scale of the pathways of evolutionary development. If God has really made creatures free, then God allows creatures to "create themselves," and does not regulate how evolutionary tactics emerge.

The freedom of creation, thus conceived, offers a response to one of the strongest critiques of God's involvement in evolution. Darwin famously exclaimed to Joseph Hooker, "What a book a Devil's chaplain might write on the clumsy, wasteful, blundering low & horridly cruel works of nature!"[73] From parasitic wasps to the devastating fungal cordyceps, the world is full of survival techniques that inspire horror. If God had specifically designed these mechanisms to function just as they do, Darwin's horror-filled reaction would be justified. However, in a creation established upon the freedom granted by love, the Creator does not choose for the creatures how they must live. Instead, creatures make choices (from whatever range of behaviours lies within their capacity) in order to survive and reproduce, and descendants stand in the genetic and behavioural traditions passed on to them, on which they themselves innovate. There is no singular path set out by God for creatures' development. God works with creation, empowering it,[74] but as Vanstone writes, "the activity of God in creation must be precarious. It must proceed by no assured programme. Its progress, like every progress of love, must be an angular process – in which each step is a precarious step into the unknown."[75] The path of creation is improvised: a dance between God and creatures, and between creatures and their contexts. No creature has complete and unencumbered freedom, including humans.[76] Every creature is limited by its own innate capacity and by environmental factors, but it is free to develop within those constraints, with internal freedom and without a determined end. There is no single path for a creature to tread; rather there are fields of possibility (with boundaries[77]) within which the creature explores. These fields of possibility can include outcomes that inspire our horror, and are not spaces of ideal perfection. This is not the best of all possible worlds in the sense that only the best possible choices, given all relevant circumstances, are ever realised. It is a world where value and disvalue are intermingled, and where value for one creature often comes at the expense of disvalue for another. This freedom is not an end in itself. It exists because it is the outcome of divine love for the creation and the requisite foundation for the possibility of creatures being able to participate in and to return that love. It is the spandrel of the pillars of creative love supporting a physical world.

Of course, the concept of freedom is only useful as an explanation of disvalue if creatures can make choices. If they only have one possible response to a situation, then they have no freedom and the path of their actions would be determined by their environmental circumstances. Instead of creatures exploring an open field of possibilities, there would only be an automatic response to environmental conditions, a tightrope of instinct.

Do non-human animals make real choices? I will adopt a rather broad definition of "choice," meaning only that a creature has more than one behavioural response available in light of environmental stimuli. This sort of choice, or plasticity of response, is commonly observed. Neurobiologist Timothy Goldsmith writes, "Within any major category of behaviour there is a myriad of secondary choices that must be made."[78] He goes on to offer the example of the "broken wing" choice made by the killdeer bird. When a killdeer's open ground nest is in danger of being discovered by a predator, the adult takes up a position away from the nest, and,

> attracts the attention of the predator by feigning injury, usually holding wings as if broken and laboring across the field. If the dog, fox, or other animal fails to follow, the killdeer flies quite normally to a new location and tries the ruse again.[79]

Once the lure has succeeded and the danger is past, the killdeer flies normally again. However, if the nest is threatened by a grazing animal rather than a predator, the killdeer stays close to the nest and makes itself as obvious as possible by spreading its wings and chirping to encourage the sheep or cow to take another route. Thus, the bird is able to appreciate that a threat is imminent, assess the type of threat, and choose (if only by instinct) an appropriate response from at least two different behaviours: the broken wing ruse and the high visibility deterrent.

To have real choice, and thus to have real freedom, creatures do not need a full range of human decision-making abilities. Very simple organisms will have very few freedoms. Complex organisms will have more freedoms. Normally functioning adult humans will exercise complex moral freedoms unknown to the rest of the animal world. For disvalues to arise in evolutionary behaviours, non-human animals only need to have a desire for certain ends (even basic evolutionary desires[80]) and the possibility to pursue those ends in ways that are potentially harmful to others. Even very small choices, multiplied over the countless living beings making countless choices day by day, can cause the evolutionary process as a whole to shift in dramatic ways towards patterns of harmful behaviours that, individually, do not reflect God's loving character, but are still part of a process that is desired by God. The behaviour is still "within the boundaries," still achieving the purpose for which God created, namely to exist within the project of creation that was founded in love and for the sake of developing love. Thus, the Ichneumon wasp developed a parasitic reproductive cycle (laying its eggs in the bodies of living caterpillars) from pursuing its good desires down roads of opportunity that have caused much harm (if not suffering) to caterpillars.

John Polkinghorne has used the term "free process" to refer to the freedom of the evolutionary world, and Sarah Coakley has used the term "evolutionary contingency,"[81] but these terms include non-living processes as well as the choices and behaviours of living creatures. I am interested primarily in the "freedom of choice" that living creatures have within the environments created by non-animate processes. This freedom is not always conscious choice, and not moral, but it is still choice. Small choices contribute to shape an individual's life and go on into the life of the ecosystem, and those ecosystems shape the paths of the evolutionary process as a whole. Thus, "evolution" as a whole is not a process that has any intention of its own (which is why I hesitate to use Polkinghorne's "free process") but it is a description of the change that occurs because of the free and self-directed intentions – such as they are – of every living creature, combined with environmental factors and variations of genetic inheritance.[82]

One of the contested questions in this area is whether the development of biological disvalues, such as predation and parasitism, should be considered a result of evil or fallenness. I have argued that these disvalues are not evil since there is no moral element to them, nor do they stand outside the purposes of God. The non-human world is "unfallen" in this narrow sense. While God did not choose for the tiger to have sharp teeth, a long line of free creaturely actions combined with chance mutations and environmental constraints has led to a tiger that has sharp teeth and an instinct to hunt. The violence in the tiger's hunting reflects God's freedom-giving character, while not reflecting God's own moral character. The tiger's aggressive way of being in the world was not directly planned by God, or caused by God's persuasive call upon the long line of tiger ancestors, but came about through each ancestor pursuing its own good, developing new skills, and surviving long enough to reproduce successfully. The skills and attributes, the desires and the instincts, will come back into the story of creative redemption with the section on Elphinstone later.

Another way to say it is that while God would not directly cause one creature to attack another, God did create a world in which the freedom given to creatures allowed some to develop methods of survival involving a complex enmeshing of values and disvalues. It is interesting, perhaps, to note that the earliest and simplest organisms experienced neither suffering nor harm. It was only as behaviour became increasingly complex, and thus more choice emerged, that living forms either capitalised on disvalues or (much later again) suffered in any meaningful way from those means of survival with the development of complex central nervous systems.[83] God is culpable for setting up a system with such significant freedoms that grave harms may occur, but such a system with real and effective choice is essential to the nature of the love that creates. In love, the desired outcomes cannot be controlled.

Some theologians have suggested that morality and sinfulness should be extended beyond humans, and so the non-human world can and should be considered fallen in moral terms. Nicola Hoggard Creegan writes that in instances such as chimp cannibalism, "something like sin can be pushed further down into the evolutionary tree."[84] Her position is based simply on the analogy that if a human were to perform a cannibalistic act, it would be sinful. However, it is theologically difficult to consider a chimp's actions as sin since they (so far as we know) have no conscious recognition of God's laws, and therefore cannot be held culpable on a moral level, whatever proto-moral concepts of fair and unfair they might have. I contend that a theological definition of sin is uniquely human; that humans alone are fallen. Pannenberg describes the concept of sin in the Hebrew Bible, pointing out that understanding God's law is central to sinfulness:

> the idea of the heart that is intent upon evil and that of the new heart that is in harmony with God's command refer always to our relation to the command of God, whether in the form of breaking it or keeping it.[85]

Without the referent point of the law, what is sin? In the New Testament a text of central importance is Paul's discussion in Romans 7, where he teases out the place of law in relation to sin. He allows that sin was not created by the law (7:7), but that through the law sin becomes active. Paul writes:

> Yet, if it had not been for the law, I would not have known sin. I would not have known what it is to covet if the law had not said, "You shall not covet." But sin, seizing an opportunity in the commandment, produced in me all kinds of covetousness. Apart from the law sin lies dead. I was once alive apart from the law, but when the commandment came, sin revived and I died, and the very commandment that promised life proved to be death to me.[86]

So, as Pannenberg says, "sin expresses itself in desires that are against the commands of God and therefore against the God who issues them."[87] Sin seems to require some knowledge of the moral law to be "alive." If non-human animals are to be ascribed "something like sin," it could – at most – only be the sin that Paul here calls "dead." Hoggard Creegan's argument by analogy to human sin simply does not provide a strong enough case for assuming either sin or a freewill defence for the non-human world.

A much more satisfying account of non-human sin comes from David Clough who contends that: "the primary evidence for the [non-human] fall is that Christ came to effect reconciliation between all things and God."[88] If Christ's reconciling work is for all of creation, as passages such as Romans 8 and Colossians 1 suggest, then there must be something left to reconcile beyond human sin. In what sense can the cosmos be reconciled? I will explore my own response to this question in Chapter 6, proposing how Christ might be a reconciler for those without sin. For Clough, however, the alleged estrangement from God is shown in predator/prey relations and the violence throughout creation. The consequent reconciliation needed is one of creating peaceable relations between predators and prey.[89] However, Clough's foundation for such an argument is open to serious challenge. He draws primarily from prophetic passages anticipating a peaceable nature (Isaiah 11:6–8) as evidence that violence was not intended in the original creation, but these passages are not sufficient evidence for his claim. First, there are contrasting passages where God points to the violent creation with approval and even emphasises God's own part in orchestrating it (Job 38:39–41; Psalm 104:21). Second, although there are certainly prophetic passages that envision the end of predator/prey relationships – most notably that the wolf will lay down with the lamb and the calf and the lion will be bedfellows in Isaiah 11:7, and the lion will eat straw in Isaiah 65:25 – these must be read together with the images in Isaiah 35:9 which state: "no lion will be there, nor any ravenous beast."[90] Should one believe that there will be no lions (or tigers or hyenas etc.) in the new creation, or that there *will* be lions but they are vegetarian?

The contradictions between the passages forbid the literalistic readings that Clough suggests. Rather these passages, highly symbolic as they are, should be understood as exalted imagery. None of the images should be read back into an evaluation of the non-human world and its history. There is no reason to think from these passages that the creation was initially meant to lack predator/prey relations or other types of disvalue.[91] Instead, these pictures image the redemption and reconciliation of all creation in Christ as something that is more than the simple recovery of something once lost, as the gathering up of all of existence into a new creation that is radically different from any past historical reality. I do not assume that because predator/prey (or parasitic) relationships exist, that God necessarily directly wills them in all their present forms. Predator/prey relationships are one of the possibilities of creation's freedom that have been productive of great goods such as complexity, diversity, and a quickening of the evolutionary process, but also productive of great and sometimes needless suffering. As Southgate says, "creation, then, is both 'good' and 'groaning.'"[92]

The temptation to consider evolutionary disvalue a result of "fallenness" or even of non-human sin emerges from a sense that evolution is a process designed and determined by God toward peaceful ends, and that it could not produce anything harmful unless something had gone wrong. In Stephen Webb's endorsement of a fallen world, he voices just such a perspective of God creating through evolution:

> If God designed evolution, then he must endorse it. If it is his tool, then it must fit his hands – if it is his creature, then it must do his bidding – and thus it must say something about what he is.[93]

Behind Webb's statement is an assumption about a type of control. God's "design" of evolution – note well the mechanistic language – means that evolution "must do his [God's] bidding." Yet, that is only true in a world where the creatures that evolve have no significant freedom in their physical or behavioural choices. In a deterministic world, and by "deterministic" I use Wildman's definition, "given that the world is a particular way at one moment, its unfolding thereafter is fixed and inflexible,"[94] the whole of history is determined by the initial conditions of the universe. Like the movement of a good clock, each event in the world is a direct outcome of the state of the world preceding it. If that were the case, Webb's argument that the "tool" of evolution must do God's bidding would be correct. Any other conclusion would mean that God's craftsmanship was terribly flawed.

However, I think Webb uses the wrong sort of analogy to illustrate the God-world relationship. Evolution should use an organic analogy. (An organic analogy is more appropriate since, as I have argued, the relationship between God and creation is one of love, and only living things can be proper objects of love.) Imagine, for a moment, an organic entity in Webb's argument, and it becomes clear how non-intuitive his argument and its outcomes really are. Take a look at Webb's quotation that we saw a moment ago and try to substitute the words "God" and "evolution" for "mother" and "son":[95]

> In other words, if a mother [voluntarily] gives birth to a son, then the mother must endorse him. If he is her tool, then he must fit her hands – if he is her creature, then he must do her bidding – and thus he must say something about what she is.[96]

One can clearly see both the truth and the falsity of Webb's statement. If a mother chooses to bring a child into the world, then she does indeed endorse that child. But that does not mean that the son is her tool, or that he necessarily does her bidding. It is true that the son will tell us something about the mother (at the very least, genetically), but he will not tell us many things and may indeed embody traits quite opposite from his mother, since he is his own creature. It is the same with God and the living creatures who are the offspring of evolution. God chose a creative process with creatures that have self-generative and self-selecting capabilities, which means that they will both reflect and not reflect God.

I am not saying that God cannot hold any purposes in relation to evolution. A mother may well have some purposes in mind, such as having a relationship with her child. Other outcomes will be strongly influenced or even determined by the mother; such as what language the son will initially speak. But having a strong guiding influence, or even determining certain broad parameters within which freedom is at play is a vastly different thing from the sort of control implied in one "doing the bidding" of another. Similarly, the evolutionary process can serve God's purposes without being fully controlled as long as God's outcomes are relational ends.

God and time

There are implications in free relationship for God's experience of time. If God does not determine the future, and outcomes are flexible and relational, it logically requires that the divine experience involve temporal aspects. God cannot stand outside of time, viewing all of time and space as a single instant of experience.

If that were the case, God would know precisely the outcome of each action, and there would be no sense of the precariousness or freedom necessary to love. Instead, love requires that God not have any such timeless vantage point and instead has an experience of temporal progression in order to facilitate responsive relationship with creatures. Polkinghorne conceives this lack of future knowledge as an act of kenosis, but other relational and open theists think that God cannot know the future since it simply does not ontologically exist.[97] I will not repeat the many lengthy arguments that arrive at this conclusion here. In either case, whether kenosis or the non-existence of the future, there is a "present" moment in God's experience, a bright line in the time-space continuum that marks what is happening now.[98] The content of that present moment is created by both creaturely and divine action. God knows the past and present perfectly, but insofar as the future depends on free creaturely action, it is knowable only as varieties of possibilities. God's real engagement with temporality means that God will be able to act in creation in ways that are impossible in the classical tradition: most notably, God can respond to, co-suffer, and act as a cause-amongst-causes in the creation.[99]

Another result of God's temporal experience is that it lends a different perspective to the question of seemingly pointless evil. In 1979 William Rowe famously challenged the theistic world to respond to the question of non-human animal suffering. His example of extreme and unnecessary animal suffering comes from what must have been a reasonably common experience throughout the long ages of evolutionary development:

> Suppose in some distant forest lightning strikes a dead tree, resulting in a forest fire. In the fire a fawn is trapped, horribly burned, and lies in terrible agony for several days before death relieves its suffering. So far as we can see, the fawn's intense suffering is pointless.[100]

The typical theodical response is to say that the fawn's suffering is not at all pointless, but is actually a working out of the essential qualities the world must hold if there is to be nomic regularity. Actions and processes must have reliable consequences for choices to have effective force. If no harmful or ill-intentioned action were effective, choice (especially moral choice) would be cut off. For a person, only good or harmless actions could be carried through, while harmful actions would isolate a person further and further into a world where irregular interventions would cut short the effect of every action he or she tried to take. The worth of all love and altruism would also be completely ruled out because altruistic action would be the only effective choice. Similarly, for the non-human world, any physical skill or action would be made obsolete in a world where feather mattresses appeared every time something fell from a tree, or where a lion cub's claw softened upon touching a brother's ear. No creature could properly "selve" in a world ruled by countless divine interventions that prevented all harm. Package deal and Only Way arguments point out that there is no completely pointless suffering, since all suffering is at least meaningful on the property-consequence level of nomic regularity. Rowe's argument is that the suffering is not always developmental or instrumentally beneficial to the individual who suffers: it is only in this limited sense that the suffering of the fawn is pointless.[101] And this question of individual self-benefit is where the problem of non-human animal suffering is most acute. If a human were present, they would undoubtedly and rightly relieve the suffering of the fawn in whatever way possible. Allowing the deer to continue to suffer seems to lead to no greater good. So why does God allow the animal's suffering to continue? Divine temporalism, I think, helps address this conundrum.

One implication of divine temporalism is that God experiences events at the time of their occurrence. I add the suggestion that even God encounters events without a particular purpose in mind for how the event will fit into the grand scheme of things – without teleology. Events can happen simply due to the chance meeting of natural forces. Disvalues can occur and the harm caused was not something that God particularly intended with the event being necessary in an instrumental or developmental way to some greater future purpose. There need not be an immediate developmental goal or instrumental purpose that God has in mind when God allows a particular disvalue to occur. Divine temporalism means that God does not plan or predestine the individual acts of predation or parasitism, or earthquakes and cancers, that also cause harm and suffering.

How does it help, theologically, to say that evolutionary suffering is not instrumentally intended from God's perspective as well? At the very least, it gets rid of the image of God as an abusive being who actively causes horrendous suffering in order to work out a master plan. The theologian does not have to try and squeeze meaning out of harmful events through logical gymnastics in order to make them seem immediately useful. Second, it allows the theologian to advance co-suffering arguments with greater force: God's experience of the suffering is unmitigated by the knowledge of how the event will one day be re-woven into the new creation's harmony (that remains a future creative act even for God[102]), and so God feels the full brunt of the suffering with the individual. Third, it turns the theologian ever more forcefully toward that creative redemption which can give new meaning to events, a turn I explore in the next two chapters. The only answer to seemingly pointless suffering is the creative and redemptive response of God.

One of the challenges of acknowledging non-instrumental harms and the kenosis of omniscience is that if God does not know what harms might arise out of the evolutionary process, how can one be sure that they will eventually be brought to harmony? How can God be sure that the events are actually redeemable? The response to this challenge must be that trust is placed, not in God's overwhelming power to force every event into the form God wants, but in God's limitless skill and infinite creativity to reshape – rather than coerce – events into redemptive outcomes. Perhaps there are some "rules" or initial constraints in place in the very make-up of the cosmos, so that the possibilities of evil are limited to events that are redeemable, a caveat offered by Vernon White.[103]

When it comes to non-instrumental disvalues, Thomas Merton wrote: "the grace of Christ is constantly working to turn useless suffering to something useful after all."[104] One can say that God did not intend particular instances of suffering to happen, but God can and will redeem all suffering.[105] New meaning is brought to old events in light of new realities; a concept I will discuss further in Chapter 6.

I have explored how one of the necessary outcomes of love is that it allows freedom to the one beloved. The ability of creatures to freely explore the possibilities of life and desire is part of their being the beloved of God. This world, so full of harm and disvalue, is part of what has to be possible if the world is founded in love and not something else – like mere efficiency. Still, the creaturely desires that cause so much of the suffering are not to be considered fallen because they still play a key part in bringing about creatures who are capable of the desires of love, a selving that transcends evolutionary desires altogether. It is this process of transforming beyond evolutionary desires and into the desires of love that will comprise the last section of this chapter. This is also the only argument that directly relies upon human involvement.

Elphinstone's link

The journey toward the desires of love is a long and arduous process. Andrew Elphinstone proposes an elegant link between the development of creation's capacity for self-giving love and the ubiquity of violence and suffering in his book *Freedom, Suffering & Love*.[106] For Elphinstone, the key to understanding disvalue in nature is to pay attention to the whole evolutionary narrative, most of which happened prior to human existence. As opposed to the familiar Garden of Eden narrative where love and wisdom coincide with or even precede pain and suffering, the evolutionary story sees creaturely love as a very new arrival on the world stage. Against the background of evolutionary suffering, Elphinstone writes, "we now see love slowly dawning, a newcomer amid the tougher ingredients of the evolutionary scene. . . . It kindled and struggled to existence when pain had long been indigenous to life."[107] In his view the harm of creatures, the "tougher" aspects, are indeed "ingredients." Pain and aggression in the world are the very components of love in their raw form. By a process Elphinstone calls "divine alchemy," the base materials of selfishness, fear, and aggression are transmuted into the stuff of love.[108] If love is thought of as the interaction of certain desires, this makes quite a coherent picture: selfishness, fear, and aggression can be thought of as desires; desires for safety, security, or power – usually for oneself, perhaps for one's kin. Love, by contrast, is desire focussed on the good of the other. If Elphinstone is right in his theological construction, then a world *with* love and *without* suffering, violence, and aggression can no more exist than a diamond can exist in a world without graphite.[109] The basic building blocks are necessary to the desired end. Similarly, if one wants bread, one has to have wheat, salt, sugar, and yeast. But the basic components themselves are not bread until they have been combined and transformed through human effort. So it is with human love: it is made up of basic evolutionary desires, but those desires have to be transformed by a co-participation of human and divine effort. Here my argument shifts slightly from the path of defence that God's love require that God not control the evolutionary pathways, to a developmental pathway where the goal of cultivating love requires a process that involves harmful desires as component pieces.

There is one place where I would add to Elphinstone's argument: I do not think that it is only the "negative" desires of the evolutionary process that have to be transformed, but the altruistic and generous tendencies as well. Love is different from altruism. This is an important point to make when the two words are so often conflated. A creature can be altruistic without love. Alms-giving, a classic example of altruistic behaviour, is a good example. In 1 Corinthians 13, Paul advises that, "if I give away all my possessions, and if I hand over my body so that I may boast, but do not have love, I gain nothing."[110] Apparently, it was possible to give away all one's possessions and even one's body, but without love. Equally, when Jesus teaches about the way of love in the Sermon on the Mount, he warns his listeners that those who give alms in the synagogues and in the streets so that they can be praised (no doubt encouraging positive social bonding) have been given their altruistic reward. Rather, Jesus tells that giving should be done in secret, where no one will know and where the social bonds of reciprocal behaviour will not be formed. One can give alms without love.

Love and altruism are also defined differently. In a paper on the evolutionary emergence of human altruism, James Van Slyke writes: "One of the central tenets of the Christian tradition is the denial of self for the benefit of another, which is a general definition of altruism."[111] Van Slyke's statement is woefully wrong. The central commandment of the Christian faith is not "deny yourself," it is "Love the Lord your God with all your heart, and all your soul, and with all your strength and with all your mind; and your neighbour as yourself."[112] Love might occasionally involve self-denial, but that is not its essence. Love seeks fulfilment, not denial. Patricia Williams defines altruism as, "behavior that decreases an organism's own chances to survive to reproduce while increasing those of another, helped, animal."[113] Love, however, is not first and foremost defined by behaviour, but by desire. The desire for the good of the beloved may sometimes involve self-denial or the diminishment of reproductive success, but there is no reason that the good of the beloved and the good of the lover should not coincide as well.[114] In such cases, desiring the good of the beloved and desiring one's own good go hand in hand. Similarly, desire for union with the beloved may sometimes lead to self-denial if the beloved is unable to respond appropriately to love. But the deep union of love found in friendship, for example, is a good for both the lover and the beloved, and so the desires of love complement rather than compete with each other.

Love is inherently self-reflexive if not self-seeking. While both the desires of love (for good and for union) may independently have correlates in the non-human world, there are not the complex interactions of desires that are able to function in the robust way human love does. For example, Vanstone's insight that, "the external restraint which love practices is often a mark of its freedom from internal limit"[115] has no correlate in the non-human world. Imagine a mother with a drug-addicted son. After various attempts at interventions, she may – in real and robust love – decide to let him go his own way and live the life he chooses. Such a choice is not due to altruistic motives, nor selfish motives. It emerges from the complex desires of love, where the self-restraint is in the hope of ultimate healing and reconciliation. Complex love like this is not only absent from the non-human world, it is even rare amongst humans. Elphinstone's theological construction differs from the many other theological anthropologies that see love as original or inherent in human nature. Alan Torrance, for example, writes, "The essential nature of humanity, we find, is to love God and thereby to love one's neighbor – to be oriented to the creator and human persons in a manner that corresponds to and participates in God's orientation to his people."[116] According to Elphinstone, love is not essential but rather the potential of human nature. Much of what is seen amongst humans is simply the basic evolutionary desires at play, but where people participate willingly in God's work of transformation, there is the emergence of love.[117] This is the creation come full circle, come into willing participation of love with God, and its glory is such that it contributes to the meaning of every life that came before.

Without launching into a full theological anthropology, I will briefly outline how this picture of emergent love might be sketched onto the concerns of human personhood. How does the possibility of love's transformation emerge? It can be thought of as created by the call of God to respond to and inhabit divine love, and thus to be formed in God's image (*imago Dei*). Joshua Moritz has previously defined the *imago Dei* as a particular calling, or election.[118] Christopher Southgate has associated the *imago Dei* with the human ability to participate in love.[119] Combining these perspectives, I see the call or election of God combined with the graced work of God as creating a unique potential in humans: the potential to transcend beyond all natural evolutionary desires by transforming them into the desires of robust love. Once this call is made, once the new capacity for love is opened, there also opens the possibility of rejection of this new capacity. It is the rejection of this call, and the subsequent use of the desires intended to be transformed into love for other ends that constitutes sin. Acts of sin emerge from acting on the untransformed desires of our evolutionary heritage, rather than accepting the divine invitation and assistance to transform them.

My position differs from a more classic notion of sin, which Anthony Lane articulates as, "God created us with natural desires, but sin has twisted these into inordinate and disordered desires,"[120] because I do not suggest that humans already had all that was needed for a righteous life, and there was a fall from that original and natural state. Rather, I argue that God created us with natural desires that were well suited for evolutionary survival.[121] But those desires were not sufficient to answer the call of divine love. It is the introduction of a new calling, and a new capacity for self-transcendence through the work of God that also introduces the capacity for sin and evil.[122]

Sin, in this view, is the failure to embrace the new, not the twisting and corruption of the old in itself. Sin is not an inherent factor of human self-awareness, as Philip Hefner has argued,[123] but is a result of the self-aware rejection of the human call. Sin is further catalysed by a person's enmeshment in complex societal structures of other people who have also rejected God's invitation and work. When a person rejects the pursuit of love, it leaves the now-transcended evolutionary desires without a proper end. Thus do the natural desires – intended within the human being for transformation into love – sour and fall into corruption, individually and collectively.

Identifying the potential of love with a human calling carries with it several benefits. First, it clearly demarcates human from non-human without resorting solely to a particular capacity. In fact, the expectation is that there would be similar actions and desires across the human/non-human spectrum precisely because humans are acting out of the same basic desires. Second, it gives a stronger reason for denying that moral choice or sinfulness exists beyond human beings, even when non-human creatures act in ways that would be sinful for a human. If a chimpanzee kills and cannibalises a neighbour's offspring, it can be considered only a harmful result of evolutionary desires. If a human does the same, it is a sinful act because the human is called to love that neighbour's offspring in a way that the chimpanzee is not. Non-human acts are amoral,[124] whilst human acts are always engaged within a moral and spiritual[125] process that involves transformed, semi-transformed, and yet-to-be transformed desires. No human action is excluded from this process of transforming love, and so no human action is – strictly speaking – entirely natural.

Elphinstone points out that love's base materials are the evolutionary desires that transform into love through the work of the Spirit and the participation of people. The hope inherent in this picture is that the strength of the often selfish and aggressive evolutionary desires, which cause so much suffering, are directly proportional to the magnitude of love possible once the desires have been transformed.[126] A human can suffer much, sin much, and love much; a worm cannot do very much of any of these. The greater capacity for suffering is in direct correlation to a greater capacity for love.

I have explored the concept that the freedom of creation, given in love, has resulted in the strengths of certain disvalues, certain desires that seem to be at odds with the very love that created it. Elphinstone's contribution links the evolutionary desires that cause harm to the building blocks of the desires of love that can be returned to the Creator.

Conclusion

I have attempted in this chapter to show how divine love can be a strong starting point for an exploration of theodicy, instead of the weigh scales of goods and harms in either an instrumental or developmental way. This approach brings with it a property-consequence GHA, where the primary property is that of divine love. If love is (as Aquinas argues) the result of a desire for the good of the beloved and the desire for union with the beloved, then the freedom of action of the beloved creation is a necessary consequence. The freedom of life, seen in the evolutionary process, can result in methods of survival that do not necessarily reflect God's design or purpose, but are coherent from within a perspective of the freedom extended by divine love. Therefore, God did not design the parasitic Ichneumon wasp to lay eggs within a living host, but God's love created an open field of possibilities in which the Ichneumon would have the freedom to develop that survival technique as it pursued its desires. The love of God, by this definition, means that God can act towards different creatures in different ways, and so the "not-even-once" principle does not apply.

I then explored theological concerns about love's limitlessness, precariousness, and vulnerability, and how these considerations affect traditional notions about the attributes of God. I argued that the nature of love suggests that concepts such as divine need, passibility, and vulnerability are necessary to God's work of creation and are a central component of the God-world relationship. I explored the question of whether God, in taking the risk of love and therefore creating needs that could only be satisfied by creaturely action, created an insurmountable challenge to God's nature. God's unique transcendent character can be reconciled with the vulnerable nature of love through a self-assumed act of kenosis. Finally, I constructed a developmental argument that saw evolutionary desires (both positive and negative) as the component ingredients of love, and therefore necessary to the emergence of creatures who could love God.

One of the trickiest parts of beginning with the nature of love is that the nature of love does not make economic sense. Love does not reach its goals efficiently. It is not always rational, and seldom fair. Think of the parables of the kingdom that Jesus tells. In the parable of the lost sheep the shepherd is willing to leave 99 sheep exposed on the hills to go after the one.[127] In the same way, the parable of the labourers in the vineyard strikes at any sense of fairness.[128] Those who work only one hour are given the same compensation as those who worked throughout the whole day. Neither parable makes economic sense. Yet both, when viewed from the vantage point of love, have a certain logic. The shepherd is unwilling to lose one of his precious sheep, because it is unique and irreplaceable in its particularity. The landowner has compassion on the labourers who could find no work and gives generously to fulfil their daily needs. Love takes extraordinary risks, and its limitless nature does not calculate the costs of its own existence. Therefore, although theologians may construct partial theodicies based on GHA approaches, they will never fully satisfy because the logic of love is not one that lends itself to rational calculation. Any theodicy rooted in love will have to make an account of the seemingly illogical nature of love's endeavour.

In terms of the theodicy I am beginning to explore, four points can be drawn from the contents of this chapter. First, many of the disvalues in the evolutionary process are attributable to the freedom that is a result of divine love for creation. Second, the love of God for each creature is individually particular. God's treatment of each creature is uniquely considered, and each creature is unable to be substituted for another. Third, God is vulnerable to creation in love, which means that God co-suffers with the creation, and thus participates in and accompanies the pain of the non-human world. Finally, both the negative and positive desires developed in evolutionary process are necessary to the aim of love, since they make up love's raw ingredients.

In the next chapter, I will explore how God acts in the world, given the kenotic constraints of love.

Notes

1 See the section on compound theodicies and defences in Chapter 3, 79–80.
2 William Rowe, "The Problem of Evil and Some Varieties of Atheism," *American Philosophical Quarterly* 16:4 (October 1979): 335–341.
3 William Dembski, *The End of Christianity: Finding a Good God in an Evil World* (Nashville, TN: B&H, 2009); Michael A. Corey, *Evolution and the Problem of Natural Evil* (Lanham, MD: University Press of America, 2000).
4 Jules J. Toner, *The Experience of Love* (Washington, DC: Corpus Books, 1968), 8.
5 Eleonore Stump, *Wandering in Darkness: Narrative and the Problem of Suffering* (Oxford: Clarendon Press, 2010), 85–107. Cf. Eleonore Stump, "Love by All Accounts," *Proceedings and Addresses of the American Philosophical Association* 80:2 (November 2006): 25–43.
6 In some circumstances, the truest act of love for the good of the beloved, temporarily, is to hold back from the union that is desired because to pursue that union would be to overwhelm the beloved. However, this would always be done in hope that the beloved (in having their freedom) will develop and grow to the point where the expressions of love would be received and returned. Even the withdrawal of acts of love out of interest for the good of the beloved can be in pursuit of an ultimate union with him or her.
7 W. H. Vanstone, *Love's Endeavour, Love's Expense: The Response of Being to the Love of God* (London: Darton, Longman and Todd, 1977). Vanstone's book has had a significant effect on later thinkers. The 2001 edited volume *The Work of Love: Creation as Kenosis*, which explores the engagement of love and creation, was dedicated to Vanstone. Each chapter begins with a quotation from *Love's Endeavour*. The volume contains essays from many of the foremost scholars in science and religion, including Arthur Peacocke, John Polkinghorne, Sarah Coakley, Holmes Rolston III, Keith Ward, Paul Fiddes, and Jürgen Moltmann.
8 Vanstone, *Love's Endeavour*, 45.
9 Some might think that parental love is a counter example: that parents who let their children do whatever they wish are bad parents, not loving parents. However, there is confusion here between coercive control and loving parenting which involves setting boundaries (whether physical or otherwise) and giving guidance. I argue, in Chapter 5, that God's action does involve setting boundaries and constraints and giving guidance. What God cannot do, if love is genuine, is prevent all harm by wholly controlling the choices of individuals. Neither can good parents decide every outcome of their children's choices. Thomas Jay Oord provides the extreme end of this perspective in the form of "essential kenosis" in *The Uncontrolling Love of God: An Open and Relational Account of Providence* (Downers Grove, IL: IVP Academic, 2015), 167–180.
10 Denis Edwards, *How God Acts: Creation, Redemption, and Special Divine Action* (Minneapolis, MN: Fortress Press, 2010), 51.
11 A person might very well lose their attributes, or even their power of choice, due to an accident, dementia, or other misfortune. This objection only applies if we see love as a current response to attributes. If we continue to love someone for attributes they used to have, it falls under the historical category of love that is developed later.
12 Niko Kolodny, "Love as Valuing a Relationship," *The Philosophical Review* 112:2 (April 2003): 135–189, 135. This argument reaches as far back as Plato, who understood love as a response to beauty.
13 Gabriele Taylor, "Love," *Proceedings of the Aristotelian Society* 76 (1975–76): 147–164, 153.
14 J. David Velleman, "Love as a Moral Emotion," *Ethics* 109:2 (January 1999): 338–378, 360.
15 Harry G. Frankfurt, *The Reasons of Love* (Princeton, NJ: Princeton University Press, 2004), 39.

16 Anders Nygren, *Agape and Eros*, trans. Philip S. Watson (New York, NY: Harper & Row, 1953), 75–77.

17 Nygren, *Agape and Eros*, 75.

18 Stump, *Wandering in Darkness*, 87. Italics original. David Bentley Hart critiques the monopoly of agape love in his own way when he writes of beauty evoking desire. "Here Christian thought learns something, perhaps, of how the trinitarian love of God – and the love God requires of creatures – is eros and agape at once: a desire for the other that delights in the distance of otherness." David Bentley Hart, *The Beauty of the Infinite: The Aesthetics of Christian Truth* (Grand Rapids, MI: Eerdmans, 2003), 20.

19 Arbitrary, and perhaps even unjust. Nygren follows this logic to its end by saying that any real love has to be universal in order to avoid the charge of arbitrariness, and therefore any love that chooses a specific object is not real love. See the discussion of Nygren's cat later, 96.

20 It should be noted here that the first desire of good for the beloved will regulate both the type and the action of union: as mentioned in the note above, it may be that there are cases where the best option for the beloved is not to have significant union with the lover. The self-restraint of love will be explored at greater length later.

21 It should be noted that "union," in this context, is not a euphemism for sexual relations. It means to share oneself, be accepted by the other, and to accept what the other shares of him or herself in return. That sharing could involve conversation, skills, gifts, or any other type of sharing one's self with another.

22 Stump, *Wandering in Darkness*, 98. She uses the term in a similar way to Kraut's definition in Robert Kraut, "Love *De Re*," *Midwest Studies in Philosophy* 10 (1986): 413–430, 425–426.

23 Stump, *Wandering in Darkness*, 99.

24 Stump, *Wandering in Darkness*, 97.

25 Jeanette Kennett, "True and Proper Selves: Velleman on Love," *Ethics* 118:2 (January 2008): 217.

26 Paul S. Fiddes, *The Creative Suffering of God* (Oxford: Clarendon Press, 1988), 137.

27 Edwards, *How God Acts*, 31–32; Walter Kasper, *The God of Jesus Christ: New Edition* (New York, NY: Continuum, 2012), 194–195. Kasper writes, "God's self-emptying, his weakness and his suffering are not the expression of a lack, as they are in finite beings; nor are they expression of a fated necessity. If God suffers, then he suffers in a divine manner, that is, his suffering is an expression of his freedom; suffering does not befall God, therefore, rather he freely allows it to touch him. He does not suffer, as creatures do, from a lack of being; he suffers out of love and by reason of his love, which is the overflow of his being. To predicate becoming, suffering and movement of God does not, therefore, mean that he is turned into a developing God who reaches the fullness of his being only through becoming; such a passage from potency to act is excluded in God. To predicate becoming, suffering and movement of God is to understand God as the fullness of being, as pure actuality, as overflow of life and love. Because God is the omnipotence of love, he can as it were indulge in the weakness of love; he can enter into suffering and death without perishing therein. Only thus can he redeem our death through his own death."

28 Fiddes, *Creative Suffering of God*, 108. Italics original.

29 Vanstone, *Love's Endeavour*, 51.

30 Elizabeth O'Donnell Gandolfo, *The Power and Vulnerability of Love: A Theological Anthropology* (Minneapolis, MN: Fortress Press, 2015), 189.

31 Gandolfo, *Power and Vulnerability*, 223.

32 Gandolfo, *Power and Vulnerability*, 224.

33 Thomas Jay Oord, *The Uncontrolling Love of God: An Open and Relational Account of Providence* (Downer's Grove, IL: IVP Academic, 2015), 161.

34 Gandolfo, *Power and Vulnerability*, 236.
35 Page, *The Web of Creation*, 53–54; Southgate, *Groaning of Creation*, 50–54.
36 Fiddes, "Creation Out of Love," in *The Work of Love: Creation as Kenosis*, ed. John Polkinghorne (Grand Rapids, MI: Eerdmans, 2001), 169.
37 Robert W. Jenson, *Systematic Theology*, Vol. 1, *The Triune God* (Oxford: Oxford University Press, 1997), 65.
38 Hart, *Beauty of the Infinite*, 165. Cf. David Bentley Hart, "No Shadow of Turning: On Divine Impassibility," *Pro Ecclesia* 11:2 (Spring 2002): 184–206, 191.
39 Keith Ward expresses it as: "God possesses both necessary and contingent properties." *Religion and Creation* (Oxford: Oxford University Press, 1996), 190.
40 Fiddes, *Creative Suffering*, 74.
41 Vanstone, *Love's Endeavour*, 69.
42 Vanstone, *Love's Endeavour*, 69. Walter Kasper makes the same point: "The lover allows the other to affect him; he becomes vulnerable precisely in his love. Thus love and suffering go together. The suffering of love is not, however, a passive being-affected, but an active allowing others to affect one." Kasper, *The God of Jesus Christ*, 196.
43 Southgate, *Groaning of Creation*, 58.
44 Jürgen Moltmann, "God's Kenosis in the Creation and Consummation of the World," in *The Work of Love: Creation as Kenosis*, ed. John Polkinghorne (Grand Rapids, MI: Eerdmans, 2001), 137–151, 140.
45 Kasper, *The God of Jesus Christ*, xxiii.
46 Arthur Peacocke, "The Cost of a New Life," in *Work of Love: Creation as Kenosis*, ed. John Polkinghorne (Grand Rapids, MI: Eerdmans, 2001), 21–42, 38. Italics original.
47 Edwards, *How God Acts*, 51.
48 One is reminded, in discussion of God's unlimited patience, of Jesus's answer to the disciples about how many times to forgive someone who sins against you: not seven times in a day, but seventy times seven. Matthew 18:21–22.
49 1 Corinthians 13:7, NRSV.
50 Vanstone, *Love's Endeavour*, 63.
51 Niko Kolodny, Christopher Grau, and Robert Kraut all add a historical dimension to their definition of love. Cf. Kolodny, "Love as Valuing,"; Christopher Grau, "Love and History," *The Southern Journal of Philosophy* 48:3 (September 2010): 246–271; Kraut, "Love *De Re*," 413–430.
52 Kolodny, "Love as Valuing," 135–136. "Why do you love me?" would then be answered with "because I've practiced," which might be the best answer to such a difficult question!
53 There are interesting links here with the Trinitarian theology that considers the Holy Spirit to be the personal emergence of the love bond between the Father and the Son.
54 Stump, *Wandering in Darkness*, 88–90. Kolodny presents shared history as an essential, and not simply an important, component of love. If it was only an important component, Stump's objection would not stand, since one could simply say that Dante's love lacked a component that would make it ideal, rather than non-existent.
55 Stump, *Wandering in Darkness*, 89.
56 In the case of Dante, if one agreed with Kolodny, one could at least appeal to the option that Dante's love was a fantasy completely invented in his own mind. Dante was not so much perverse, as simply misled. Such a defence could not be used of God, because God really is in relationship with every creature at every moment.
57 Kolodny, "Love as Valuing," 171.
58 Kolodny, "Love as Valuing," 170–171.
59 This conclusion is echoed in Lee Barrett's evaluation of Kierkegaard. Cf. Lee C. Barrett, *Eros and Self-Emptying: The intersections of Augustine and Kierkegaard* (Grand Rapids, MI: Eerdmans, 2013), 201.
60 That worms and every other creature may develop that capacity in the new creation is a possibility explored in Chapter 6.

61 Trent Dougherty proposes, along with John Wesley, that in the new creation, non-human creatures will someday have the capacity to love God back in the fullness of the new creation. *The Problem of Animal Pain: A Theodicy for All Creatures Great and Small* (New York, NY: Palgrave Macmillan, 2014). See Chapter 6.

62 The goods I have proposed here are necessarily speculative. What the true good of the worm is (alluded to here as "union with God") is not something I could know without being a worm or being God, as I have no access to the inner content of the divine-worm relationship. Readers may immediately jump to the ethical question of "then is there any way that I can harm the worm by treading it underfoot?" In the case of the worm, I would say "probably not" but in the case of more sentient animals, the answer would be "certainly." In the case of the trod-upon worm, the greatest damage would likely be to the soul of the person, if the person – by cruelty or malice – intentionally set out to destroy another living creature. But there is no room to pursue the ethical treatment of animals here. See Southgate, *Groaning of Creation*, 92–115.

63 C.f. Werner Jeanrond, *A Theology of Love* (London, T & T Clark, 2010), 105–134.

64 Wesley J. Wildman, "Incongruous Goodness, Perilous Beauty, Disconcerting Truth: Ultimate Reality and Suffering in Nature," in *Physics and Cosmology: Scientific Perspectives on the Problem of Natural Evil*, eds. Nancey Murphy, Robert J. Russell, and William R. Stoeger, S. J. (Vatican City and Berkeley, CA: Vatican Observatory, CTNS, 2007), 267–294.

65 Philip Clayton and Steven Knapp, *The Predicament of Belief: Science, Philosophy, Faith* (Oxford: Oxford University Press, 2011), 49. Italics original. Refer to Chapter 3, subsection "Radically Redefining God" for the explanation of Wildman, Clayton, and Knapp's views, 64–70.

66 Clayton and Knapp, *Predicament of Belief*, 51.

67 More on the possibilities of divine interaction in the world will follow in Chapter 5.

68 Cf. Holmes Rolston, "Naturalizing and Systematizing Evil," in *Is Nature Ever Evil? Religion, Science and Value*, ed. Willem B. Drees (New York, NY: Routledge, 2003), 67–86, 70–71, 76–80. This does not solve the problem what is an "individual," however, if love entails redemption, and redemption continues shared relationships, the question may not matter very much.

69 Of course, there are times when life itself is fairly ambiguous. A virus outside of a host does not act like a living organism. Some might consider inanimate objects to have a "good" as well, for example, the "good" of a river to reach the sea. But we can only be speaking metaphorically if we speak of the river's "good" in this way. The water in the river is not harmed by being dammed up or otherwise prevented from achieving this "good." However, living creatures are harmed, even destroyed, if they are prevented from achieving their various goods.

70 On this definition, a human cannot love the mountain either. While we might use the language of love in regard to inanimate objects, we can only mean it metaphorically.

71 Traditionally, there is a great deal of theological strain around the concept of the immutability of God in light of the Incarnation. Bulgakov, for example, held that Christ's divine nature was not impassible in Jesus, but that the immanent Trinity was untouched by the kenosis of the Incarnation. How the Incarnation should have failed to touch the inner being of God is problematic. See Gilles Emery, "The Immutability of the God of Love and the Problem of Language Concerning the 'Suffering of God'," in *Divine Impassibility and the Mystery of Human Suffering*, trans. Thomas J. White and eds. James F. Keating and Thomas J. White, O. P. (Grand Rapids, MI: Eerdmans, 2009), 46–47. C.f. "Rahner's rule."

72 That is not to say that there is no providence at work in creation. I think there is, in the ways I will describe in Chapter 5. However, that providence does not determine earth history. It only guides, and perhaps sometimes protectively constrains.

73 Charles R. Darwin to Joseph D. Hooker, "Letter 1924," 13 July 1856. Accessed 19 October 2013. Online: www.darwinproject.ac.uk/letter/entry-1924.

74 God's work of empowering rather than causing/determining is a particular emphasis of Sarah Coakley's work on kenosis. Sarah Coakley, "Kenosis: Theological Meanings and Gender Connotations," in *The Work of Love*, ed. John Polkinghorne (Grand Rapids, MI: Eerdmans, 2001), 202–206.

75 Vanstone, *Love's Endeavour*, 62–63.

76 God's intention, then, is not to simply maximise freedom, which might be done in various others ways, from increasing intelligence to providing unlimited resources to each creature. God's intention is to live in free relationship with self-developing creatures in community.

77 See the discussion of the constraints on initial conditions in divine action in Chapter 5.

78 Timothy Goldsmith, *Biological Roots of Human Nature* (New York, NY: Oxford University Press, 1991), 113. I was made aware of Goldsmith's work and the choice of the killdeer by Patricia A. Williams, "Sociobiology and Original Sin," *Zygon* 35:4 (December 2000): 783–812.

79 Goldsmith, *Biological Roots*, 113.

80 Basic evolutionary desires are sometimes known as the four F's: feeding, fleeing, fighting and . . . reproduction. These were originally set out by Karl Pribram. He did not call them "the Four F's," although the appellation has become common enough to merit its own Wikipedia page and wide recognition. Karl Pribram, "A Review of Theory in Physiological Psychology," *Annual Review of Psychology* 111:1 (1960): 1–40.

81 John Polkinghorne, *Science and Providence: God's Interaction with the World* (London: SPCK, 1989, 2005), 77; Sarah Coakley, "Evolution, Cooperation, and Divine Providence," in *Evolution, Games, and God: Principles of Cooperation*, eds. Martin A. Nowak and Sarah Coakley (Cambridge, MA: Harvard University Press, 2013), 378. See also Sarah Coakley, "God and Evolution: A New Solution," *Harvard Divinity Bulletin* 35:2–3 (Spring/Summer 2007): 8–13.

82 Behavioural impact on evolutionary pathways is increasingly important in contemporary biology, even when these transmissions are not "active or automatic or intentional." See Eva Jablonka and Marion J. Lamb, *Evolution in Four Dimensions: Genetic, Epigenetic, Behavioral, and Symbolic Variation in the History of Life*, revised ed. (Cambridge, MA: MIT Press, 2014), Chapter 5, 156. Jablonka, Lamb and Zeligowski also emphasise that in more advanced behavioural transmissions, whether by direct teaching or imitation, "in no sense is the origin of the new variation random or blind" (p. 169).

83 The earliest forms of large predation emerges 550mya, while microbial evidence points to defensive strategies evolving 740mya. Yet, both of these are small portions of life's 3.5 billion year history. And even if the simulations suggesting predation emerged in the very earliest stages of cellular life, these would not have caused anything like suffering. Silvester de Nooijer, Barbara R. Holland, David Penny, "The Emergence of Predators in Early Life: There Was No Garden of Eden," *PLoS ONE* 4:6 (2009). Open Access. Online: http://journals.plos.org/plosone/article?id=10.1371/journal.pone.0005507.

84 Nicola Hoggard Creegan, *Animal Suffering & the Problem of Evil* (Oxford: Oxford University Press, 2013), 77.

85 Wolfhart Pannenberg, *Systematic Theology*, Vol.2, trans. Geoffrey W. Bromiley (Edinburgh: T & T Clark, 1994), 239.

86 Romans 7:7b-10, NRSV.

87 Pannenberg, *Systematic Theology*, 240.

88 David Clough, *On Animals*, Vol. 1 of *Systematic Theology* (Edinburgh: T & T Clark, 2012), 125.

89 Clough, *On Animals*, 127.

90 Another similar issue is raised with Revelation 21:1 and the vision that "there will be no sea." Are we to think that the existence of the sea itself is a result of the mysterious fallenness of creation and contrary to the will of God? Surely not.

91 Indeed, the inclusion the great sea monsters (Genesis 1:21) in the original creation suggests just the opposite.

92 Southgate, *Groaning of Creation*, 15.

93 Stephen H. Webb, *The Dome of Eden: A New Solution to the Problem of Creation and Evolution* (Eugene, OR: Cascade, 2010), 104.

94 Wesley J. Wildman, "The Divine Action Project, 1998–2003," *Theology and Science* 2:1 (2004): 39.

95 If the reader is concerned about the personification of "evolution" here, let him or her be reminded that evolution is a process that describes the change of countless living beings. If those beings are not God's "tools," then the process that describes their changes cannot be God's tool either.

96 The original quotation, here adapted by exchanging "mother and son" for "God and evolution", is from Webb, *The Dome of Eden*, 104.

97 John Polkinghorne, "Kenotic Creation and Divine Action," in *The Work of Love: Creation as Kenosis*, ed. John Polkinghorne (Grand Rapids, MI: Eerdmans, 2001), 90–106, 103–104. Peter Geach, "The Future," *New Blackfriars* 54:636 (May 1973): 208–218; Clark Pinnock, "Systematic Theology," in *The Openness of God: A Biblical Challenge to the Traditional Understanding of God* (Downer's Grove, IL: InterVarsity, 1994), 121.

98 For a philosophical treatment of how this bright line could exist in light of the Minkowski interpretation of Special Theory of Relativity, which would seem to make such a line meaningless, see David M. Woodruff, "Presentism and the Problem of Special Relativity," in *God in an Open Universe: Science, Metaphysics, and Open Theism*, eds. William Hasker, Thomas Jay Oord, and Dean Zimmerman (Eugene, OR: Pickwick, 2011), 94–124.

99 See Chapter 5 for more on divine action in creation.

100 William Rowe, "The Problem of Evil and Some Varieties of Atheism," *American Philosophical Quarterly* 16:4 (October 1979): 335–341, 337.

101 The word "gratuitous" is often used to indicate this sort of pointless event; "instances of evil which neither serve as means for bringing about a greater good, nor for preventing a greater evil." William Hasker, *Providence, Evil and the Openness of God* (London: Routledge, 2004), 42. Hasker, in particular has argued for what he calls the "necessity of gratuitous evil." However, Hasker's argument deals primarily with moral evil, and where it deals with natural evil it does so with an unapologetically anthropocentric bias: to prevent gratuitous natural evil, he says, would be to either diminish the goods that natural evils produce in humans, such as promoting foresight and courage, or to perpetrate a "disinformation campaign" by seeming to allow natural evil without actually allowing it. (see "The Necessity of Gratuitous Evil," in *Providence, Evil and the Openness of God*, 58–79).

102 See the fractal mosaic analogy in Chapter 6.

103 Vernon White, *The Fall of a Sparrow: The Concept of Special Divine Action* (Exeter: Paternoster, 1985), 144. The very fact that all life is inevitably mortal may be one such constraint. Nothing suffers forever, and nothing can cause suffering forever. Christopher Southgate also suggests that the "only way" argument might equally be applied to redemption: "that the sort of world we live in is the only sort of world that could make possible that redemption to which the Christian gospel testifies – reconciliation to God through the incarnation, death, and resurrection of the divine Son." in "Does God's Care Make Any Difference? Theological Reflection on the Suffering of God's Creatures," in *Christian Faith and the Earth: Current Paths and Emerging Horizons in Ecotheology*, eds. Ernst M. Conradie, Sigurd Bergmann, Celia Deane-Drummond, and Denis Edwards (London: T & T Clark, 2014), 97–114, 110.

104 Thomas Merton, *No Man Is an Island* (Tunbridge Wells: Burns & Oats, 1955), 80.

105 It is a very different thing to create a world where there is the possibility, even the inevitable possibility, of suffering from willing a specific instance of suffering. If someday I choose to bring a child into the world, for example, I could only do so

knowing that the child will experience suffering. That is very different from willing them to experience suffering.

106 Andrew Elphinstone, *Freedom, Suffering & Love* (London: SCM Press, 1976).

107 Elphinstone, *Freedom, Suffering & Love*, 30.

108 There are parallels here to Augustine's view of how desires must be transformed. "According to Augustine's critique of the Stoic view, the task of the individual is to redirect desires toward their proper object. Desire is not to be uprooted, but is rather to be carefully cultivated, channeled, and aimed in the correct direction. . . . Cupiditas must be transmuted into caritas." Barrett, *Eros and Self-Emptying*, 74.

109 Desire itself being, in this case, the carbon atoms that make up both diamonds and graphite.

110 1 Cor 13:3, NRSV.

111 James A. van Slyke, "Cognitive and Evolutionary Factors in the Emergence of Human Altruism," *Zygon* 45:4 (December 2010): 841–859, 841.

112 Luke 10:27, NRSV. C.f. Matthew 22:37, Mark 12:30.

113 Williams "Sociobiology and Original Sin," *Zygon* (2000): 788.

114 Indeed, love has even been known – on rare occasion – to contribute to reproductive success. . . . I jest, but the point still stands.

115 Vanstone, *Love's Endeavour*, 44.

116 Alan Torrance, "Is There a Distinctive Human Nature? Approaching the Question from a Christian Epistemic Base," *Zygon* 47:4 (December 2012): 903–917, 908.

117 This can occur, I think, in anyone who desires to love well, and is not limited to a particular religious affiliation. The grace of God is not absent from those who do not recognise the source of that grace.

118 Joshua Moritz, "Evolution, the End of Human Uniqueness, and the Election of the Imago Dei," *Theology & Science* 9:3 (2011): 307–339.

119 Christopher Southgate, "New Thought on Humans Created in the Image and Likeness of God," ISSR Conference presentation, Vienna 27–29 August 2015. This is a development on the thought of "Re-Reading Genesis, John, and Job: A Christian Response to Darwinism," *Zygon* 46:2 (June 2011): 370–395, wherein he writes "if the image and likeness of God is understood as being the imago Trinitatis, then it can be understood not as the capacity for such perfect self-giving, for that is uniquely the character of the life of God in Godself, but as the capacity to respond with self-giving to an initiative of self-giving love." (375)

120 Anthony N. S. Lane, "Lust: The Human Person as Affected by Disordered Desires," *Evangelical Quarterly* 78:1 (2006): 21–35, 33.

121 I think of Ruth Page's sense of "Teleology Now!" – Each creature develops its desires and thereby achieves its good and proper end. It is not simply playing a part in a larger narrative in which it has no personal fulfilment. Ruth Page, *God and the Web of Creation* (London: SCM Press, 1996), 63ff.

122 Self-transcendence is a primary theme in Christopher Southgate's work, *The Groaning of Creation: God, Evolution and the Problem of Evil* (Louisville, KY: Westminster John Knox, 2008).

123 Philip Hefner, "Biological Perspectives on Fall and Original Sin," *Zygon* 28:1 (March 1993): 77–101, 95.

124 I agree here with Holmes Rolston, who calls the morality of non-human animals a "category mistake." Holmes Rolston III, "Naturalizing and Systematizing Evil," in *Is Nature Ever Evil? Religion, Science and Value*, ed. Willem B. Drees (London: Routledge, 2003), 67–86, 67. The morality of animals is an ongoing debate, as discussed in Chapter 3, 68–69.

125 By "spiritual" here, I mean "conducted by the Spirit of God."

126 More will be said about the nature of redemption emerging from this understanding of love in Chapter 6.

127 Matthew 18:10–14.

128 Matthew 20:1–16.

5   Special divine action

Special divine action

If love informs the basic freedoms of the world, then it is necessary to explore how God can be active amongst those freedoms. In the last chapter, I made a case that the starting place for theodicy is in the nature of divine love. Love was described as vulnerable, limitless, and freedom bestowing. How then does God, characterised by such love, act in the world? Does the freedom given to creation preclude God acting at all?[1] Does God act? Vanstone notes "We know that, if the love of God is authentic, God is not 'detached' from His creation." [2] Love cannot be detached from creation. Love demands both involvement and vulnerability. Working out how that might be true of God's acts in creation is the purpose of this chapter.

To begin, I will lay out some categories through which the action of God has been discussed in recent scholarship. This brief survey is offered in order to contrast how the majority of science and religion scholarship has conducted conversations on divine action – with its focus on the mechanism of God's action – with my own approach, which Sarah Lane Ritchie classifies as the "theological turn" in divine action theories.[3] My emphasis is on the character, not the mechanism, of divine action. I am less interested in how God acts than why or when God acts; less interested in the mechanism of action than the outcome of the action. I will propose that various models of special divine action can work alongside each other in complementary ways.[4] No one model should bear all the theological weight as "the way" God acts in the world. In particular, I will explore how the gift of being, God's presence, divine lure, and divine participation can be primary ways to understand the special divine acts of God towards all living creatures in light of the respect of love for the "otherness" of the other.

Models of special divine action in science and religion

Prior scholarship relating to God's action has traditionally been divided into two different categories: general divine action (GDA) and special divine action (SDA). I will use the definitions offered by Nicholas Saunders:

> General Divine Action (GDA): Those actions of God that pertain to the whole of creation universally and simultaneously. These include actions such as the

initial creation and the maintenance of scientific regularity and the laws of nature by God.

Special Divine Action (SDA): Those actions of God that pertain to a *particular* time and place in creation as distinct from another. This is a broad category and includes the traditional understanding of 'miracles,' the notion of particular providence, responses to intercessionary prayer, God's personal actions, and some forms of religious experience.[5]

These two categories are not always clearly distinguishable, and sometimes disappear into one another as emphasis on one is exaggerated to the exclusion of the other. Sometimes nothing is considered SDA and others consider that every event is SDA.

There is no special divine action

The work of Maurice Wiles provides one example where SDA disappears into GDA.[6] Wiles writes, "the proposal that I want to make is that the primary usage for the idea of divine action should be in relation to the world as a whole rather than to particular occurrences within it."[7]

Wiles borrows an analogy from John Lucas about Solomon building the temple.[8] While a person might say, "Solomon built the temple," they do not mean that Solomon placed every stone, or wove every curtain. Instead, Solomon had an intention and a goal that a temple should be built. He made provision for others to carry out the actual building of the temple, without micromanaging the workmen's strokes. In fact, the temple building did not even require Solomon's direct presence, despite the building being attributed to his action. In saying "Solomon built the temple" one unified act is indicated, which in practice was made up of many other actions by many other agents. In the same way, the whole world and its history is, for Wiles, a single act of God.

Gordon Kaufman, who inspired Wiles, makes a similar distinction between master-acts of God and sub-acts.[9] All of history is one master-act of God with a set purpose and goal, while the first instantiation of any new events toward that goal (whether it be the creation of stars or the emergence of life) are sub-acts of God.[10] Therefore, these scholars see no reason to say that God acts further in "special divine acts" since to do so would raise the paradox of God intervening in or deviating from what is already God's action. Instead, God's primary action allows all other actions to be and directs them toward the ultimate goals of history. Creatures are free to act and their actions are made more intelligible in light of higher realms of meaning.

Wiles does not recognise any particular or special divine interaction within creation, such as answers to prayer, or any sort of directive agency. All such notions of divine action are "to be firmly rejected"[11] because, according to Wiles, they propose a trivial and inconsistent view of divine action and, crucially, they seem to oppose the consistency with which science describes the world. Instead, if all divine action is conceived as one act, there is room for *interpreting* portions of that act as special acts of God. There may be moments where one part of the divine act *seems* to become especially significant, but it is not to be distinguished from the original act of creation.[12]

If creation is one act, then there is no special response to evil or suffering; no special care of the suffering creature. In Kaufman's blunt words: "This is no God who 'walks with me and talks with me' in close interpersonal communion . . . this is the Lord of heaven and earth, whose purposes we cannot fully fathom and whose ways are past finding out."[13] Redemption, so far as it exists, is tied up with the initial action of creation. "Evil was part of the risk taken by God in bringing a world into being out of the triviality of the pre-existing chaos,"[14] writes Wiles, and the process of overcoming evil is part of the overall movement of creation. There is no divine response, and therefore no divine comforting, or relating to the pain or suffering of creatures. Wiles claims that any response of God to human prayer is highly unsatisfactory because: "the picture follows too closely the analogy of one human person's relation with another."[15] This is a confusing objection, since Wiles also puts a great deal of emphasis on the character of God as personal – as defined by love. In the end, although Wiles describes his view as being founded on the nature of the love of God, his conclusions end up denying the very love he first espouses.

In Wiles's final description of divine action, to go back to the temple analogy, Solomon may only order the temple to be built, but can no longer pick up a hammer and a chisel or talk to the workers. This view of providence ends up losing any sense of engagement or divine response to the creation – notions that are central to the type of love I argued for in the previous chapter.

Everything is special divine action

On the other side of the theological spectrum, Denis Edwards and Niels Gregersen collapse the category of GDA altogether into the category of SDA.[16] Instead of seeing God's action as something that is always and everywhere acted without variation, they argue that each event should be considered as a particular divine act, which – because of the consistency of God's character – has many similarities with all the other particular acts of God. What people have taken to be GDA in its universal and simultaneous regularity is in fact multiple instances of SDA reflecting God's faithfulness: there is no ontological difference.

While preferable to Wiles and Kaufman's collapse of SDA into GDA, the collapse of GDA into SDA raises serious problems for theodicy. Every occurrence in history becomes something brought into being by the special willed act of God. When this includes destructive and horrific suffering, it raises further questions about the goodness of God. If, as Gregersen insists, occasionalism is not being argued for by this position,[17] then the question becomes: "is the suffering of creatures intended by God? And if not, how does it come about?"

All the attempts of Wiles, Kaufman, Edwards, and Gregersen share at least one similarity: they are the result of an attempt to avoid the language of "intervention." Why is avoiding divine intervention such a strong motivation? What is wrong with a good old-fashioned "miracle"?

Reasons to avoid interventionism

Contemporary discussions about miracles cannot avoid the shadow of David Hume. For Hume, emerging out of the mechanistic worldview of the eighteenth century, a miracle (or SDA in general) meant a violation of the laws of nature.[18] Hume's definition has become the layperson's definition both of miracle and SDA: a divine intervention that contradicts the regular working of the natural in order to produce a desired result. Paul Davies, for example, defines intervention as those times when "God acts like a physical force in the world. God moves atoms and other microscopic objects about, but to do so, God must violate the physical laws studied by science."[19] Scholars of science and religion usually reject this interventionist-type of miracle.[20]

There are various reasons scientists and theologians do not find the concept of interventions in the world order appealing.[21] A violation of natural laws is problematic on at least two counts. First, science cannot investigate such action since it lies outside the ability of science to study.[22] Science can only study natural causes. If something has a supernatural cause, as the case would be with an intervention, it is beyond the scope of science.[23] Second, interventions raise questions about the character of a God who would set up natural laws and then violate them. These can be classified as the scientific and theological objections, or the mechanistic and the moral.

The claim that interventions are anti-scientific[24] – that they cannot be explained or studied by science – is less problematic than the second objection. If interventions happen at all, they would be expected to be extremely rare. One should not expect scientists to find them, or be able to study them, in any sort of systematic way because they do not fall under the regular operations of the world. Yet, while interventions would not be able to be studied by science, that does not mean that they could not occur.[25] They would simply have to be studied by other disciplines, or through other means. Perhaps scientists would evaluate the effect of a miracle rather than try to figure out how it happened or whether and when it might happen again. The scientist (or scientific theologian), then, can have little to say about the occurrence of intervention except to warn that the reliable predictions that science often makes may discourage one from making the claim that interventionistic miracles are common.

The second theological reason scholars do not want to countenance an intervening God is for moral reasons: it strikes at God's character. Interventions create a contradiction in the understanding of God's faithfulness: why would a God who creates and sustains the laws of nature then flout them?[26] Intervention-type action would also challenge traditional notions of God's omnipotence, perfection, immutability, and atemporality. An omnipotent and perfect God would not create a world with such obvious flaws that God had to intervene to correct them. God's impassibility and immutability would mean that God could not be affected or changed by worldly occurrences and, therefore, there would be no motivation to intervene. Finally, for an atemporal God, no intervention would be possible because it would be impossible for God to relate to the world in time-bound ways;

impossible to choose one moment over another in which to intervene. For classical theists, an intervention of Paul Davies's type where "God acts like a physical force in the world" would also make God one cause among others in creation rather than the source of all being – something they see as a serious diminution of God's being.[27]

A third theological argument is raised by Clayton and Knapp's already explored "Not-even-once" principle, which argues that if God intervened even once to save a creature from innocent suffering, God would be morally obliged to do so in every case, leading to the collapse of the regularities of our world.[28] All these reasons, scientific and theological, contribute to interventionist divine action being rejected by theologians.[29] Indeed, it is so out of favour that it does not even appear as a possible model of divine action in one introductory textbook.[30] Instead scientists and theologians have developed various models of non-interventionist divine action that propose how God can be objectively active in the world without the need for overruling natural laws.[31] These models – three mechanistic models and one non-mechanistic model – provide options for how God could act toward suffering creatures.

Influence through initial conditions

If God cannot intervene once the world system is set up, God can at least influence the state of affairs by carefully arranging the initial conditions from which they emerge. Even in a world of spontaneity and randomness, if the initial conditions of creation could be carefully ordered, it would have a marked effect on the outcome of later natural processes. By constraining, ordering, and sustaining certain initial conditions God could create a universe that would substantially create itself toward certain ends through chance, law, and creaturely agency. The definite outcomes need not be precise, but the propensity for life to emerge could be overwhelmingly probable. Paul Davies advocates that the initial action of creation can be sustained by uniformitarian divine action and still result in a complex and emergent world. For him, God continues to be involved in the world through sustaining action, but God is not involved in any ways that were not inherent in natural laws instilled in the original moment of creation. The laws of creation are of such a particular sort that "though nature's complexity gives every appearance of intentional design and purpose, it is entirely the result of natural processes."[32] Davies likens the natural world to a chess game: the rules are set by God to encourage some sorts of action, discourage others, and limit some altogether, in order to facilitate rich and varied play by the free agents or "chess pieces" of creation.[33] In one way, this view seems to ease the theological burden of suffering, since God is not directly to blame for any suffering: any particular form of disvalue in nature is the outcome of chance or freewill. Nor is God responsible for alleviating suffering, for God does not generally have any direct engagement with the world. Yet, God is still culpable for setting up the system in such a way that suffering would be an inevitable outcome. The cost paid for the advantages of Davies's system is very dear: any hope of eschatological redemption is lost since

God has no direct contact with the world, and there is no personal aspect of God's direct relationship with creatures.

In a different way, Christopher Knight also advocates for an "influence through initial conditions" view, while maintaining the appearance of SDA.[34] He uses the analogy of children appealing to their parents for money while away at school, and gives three options of parental action. First, a parent could set up regular standing orders that would give a certain amount of money at certain times: roughly equivalent to GDA. Second, a parent might occasionally deposit money in the child's account because of a special appeal: likened to SDA. Third, a parent might set up a trust fund that gives regular payments, but can also have stipulations in which, under particular situations, extra money will be deposited. This third option has the non-interventionist reality of the first option, with the appearance of responsive or interventionist engagement of the second. Thus, Knight can defend a non-interventionist approach while maintaining that experience might sometimes point toward what seem like interventions. Knight is insistent that there is no real-time divine response to creation: regarding prayer he writes that theistic naturalists cannot "see intercessory prayer as having any purpose – other, perhaps, than that of refining the religious sensibilities of those who indulge in it."[35] All divine action has been set from eternity into the initial conditions of the world.

While this model is appealing if one wants to defend an unchanging, untouched Aristotelian God, it has little appeal for those who see vibrant relationship at the heart of being. To take Knight's analogy into the human world: would it be a good parent who simply sets up a watertight trust fund and does not actually interact with their child? What does this tell us about the nature of the parent? What of the parent's love? As with the models of Kaufman and Wiles, God remains a distant figure, far removed from the suffering creation. In attempting to draw the problematic thorn of suffering from the neck of theology, these theologians have decapitated their theology instead. Their solutions do, in one sense, solve the problem: the thorn of suffering can be extracted without difficulty. But living forms of theology die when too great a chasm is made between the intimately personal God seen in Christ and the theological abstractions theologians create in response to philosophical quandaries.

Special divine action in quantum indeterminacy

In pursuit of a model of SDA with more traction, several theologians have attempted to find ways for God to be involved in the world in objective physical but non-interventionist ways, commonly known as NIODA.[36] Nancey Murphy, Robert Russell, Thomas Tracy, George Ellis, and Keith Ward are all examples of scientist-theologians who have searched for a "causal joint," a mechanism, in creation that would allow for SDA to engage with and change the nature of physical events without intervening in such a way as to overthrow the integrity of the natural world processes or natural law.[37]

For Murphy, Russell, Tracy, and Ellis, God is thought to be able to influence the outcome of indeterminate quantum events to bring about desired physical outcomes through the causal openness of certain chance processes. There is disagreement over how involved God is: whether God controls all quantum events (Murphy), some (Tracy), or even only those events that would affect non-sentient beings (Russell).[38]

Two major problems have emerged from the line of enquiry on divine action in quantum realms. The first is outlined by Nicholas Saunders: the "basis of quantum theory is a paradigm deterministic theory. . . [therefore] incompatibilist SDA is not possible in a non-interventionist sense."[39] There might be uncertainty in quantum events, but the outcomes of any group of events are still deterministic. Saunders shows convincingly that for God to determine purposeful outcomes toward a desired end in the macroscale world would, in the Copenhagen interpretation, involve just as much intervention as a direct macroscale act of intervention.[40] Even if it was possible for God to act in the underdetermined systems of quantum states, the outcome of indeterministic systems at quantum levels of scale do not generally have macroscopic effects.[41] Therefore, the outcome of these quantum events do not have the desired theological importance, since there are very limited ways these effects can be amplified into macroscopic events.[42] Saunders states his final conclusion bluntly: "on the terms of our current understanding of quantum theory, incompatibilist non-interventionist quantum SDA is not theoretically possible."[43]

Special divine action in complex systems

To avoid the difficulties of bridging quantum and non-quantum worlds, John Polkinghorne has pursued the idea that God could act in non-interventionist ways through macroscopic complex or chaotic systems.[44] Captured by Polkinghorne's formula that "epistemology models ontology," he holds that the unpredictability of complex systems speaks to an "emergent property of flexible process, even within the world of classical physics."[45] God could be at work within this flexibility without overturning natural law. However, chaotic systems are still deterministic even if they are unpredictable. It is unclear, therefore, how God could affect these systems toward desired outcomes without intervention, unless (as suggested by Tracy[46]) the highly sensitive initial conditions were involved with the uncertainty in quantum systems and amplified through the chaotic system.[47] In the end we are still left with an unsatisfactory model that is highly limited in its outcomes. It is not clear that God could act to alleviate the suffering of individual creatures or prevent the emergence of predatory violence through these models.

All of these non-interventionist models still advance a mechanism for divine action, whether natural law, or various open processes in nature. There is another model of divine action that eschews a causal joint altogether, while maintaining a distinct sense of objective divine action.

Primary and secondary causation

The model of primary and secondary causation held by neo-Thomists, including Denis Edwards, William Stoeger, Elizabeth Johnson, and David Burrell,[48] maintains that God never works with any "causal joint" or through any mechanism. Based on the Aristotelian division of primary and secondary causation, neo-Thomists recognise God as the primary cause of events in the world, while creatures are the secondary cause. The advantage to this approach is that it does not see God as one cause amongst others – thus maintaining God's distinction from creation – and it maintains a clear view of divine action without intervention. Denis Edwards argues that it upholds "both God's transcendence and creaturely autonomy."[49] A disadvantage is that there is no way to tell how or if God is at work in the world. The work of God will never be able to have any sort of scientific explanation since the (secondary) causes are already evident.[50] It also means that divine work is impossible to "find" since it is perfectly hidden in the secondary causes. John Polkinghorne, who finds this apparent paradox unsatisfactory, calls Austin Farrer's version of secondary causation, known as double agency, a kind of "theological doublespeak."[51]

Another critique of the model of secondary causation comes directly out of the problem of suffering. If God works in and through secondary causes, is God the primary cause of harmful or evil events as well? Some defenders say "yes," and hold that in every evil event there is some deeper good to be found. Vernon White attempts theodicy from this perspective.[52] White does not accept that some events are only permitted as instrumental to other goods. For White every event and therefore every activity of God in every event has a self-contained meaning. Nothing is reduced to being a means to an end.[53] Nicholas Saunders objects that if this is true, there can be no distinction in importance between various divine acts: "The problem is that not only are the falling rain or any other natural events and the resurrection similar accounts of God's action, but they must be given an equal status in our theological understanding."[54] Any categorisation, when all actions are equally caused by God, become instances of special pleading.[55] This is especially problematic when it comes to evil. White tries to evade the issue by saying that evil events should not follow the rule of being events in themselves, but need to be understood in their wider context where they lose ontological reality.[56] White writes: "Evil only exists in a certain configuration of events which can always be seen from a different perspective, and as such may never have an ultimate hold on reality."[57] If this is true, then either there is no reason for God's redemptive action because there is no ontological reality of evil to be redeemed (one need only wait to see apparent evil resolved), or the model becomes absolutely tied to an atemporal understanding of God, meaning, and history, where the resolution of the wider context is eternally real.[58] However, since my concept of love and freewill is tied to responsive and temporal understandings of God, I cannot accept this solution.

Other defenders of the secondary causation model will not accept the unpalatable notion that White is willing to engage, and would say, "No, God does not cause evil." It is unclear how they can defend themselves without ending up in various difficulties. They might say that God is the primary cause behind only good events, which leaves evil events without a primary cause, or sets up a dualism of some sort to cause the evil events. Both solutions end up with problems:

dualism with its attendant problems, or an incoherent world where evil actions are without a cause.

Edwards tries to avoid these problems by saying that God's primary causation, God's will and intention in creation, is limited by the creaturely agents who act as secondary causes. God accepts creaturely limits, and those creaturely limits are the source of natural disvalues.[59] The problem with this (and other *privatio boni* arguments) is that those very same disvalues are often deeply productive, and Edwards would want to ascribe that productivity to God. It seems an inescapable fact that disvalues are necessary for the emergence of biological goods. If the cougar's carnivorousness is a result of creaturely limitation, then so is the skill and agility of the fleet-footed deer. Taken to the extreme, very little in the world would be attributable to God's creation. With secondary causation either not enough is attributable to God and much of the beauty of creation is ascribable to creaturely limitation, or too much is attributed to God and God is the direct cause of all suffering. The only other option is to diminish the effectiveness of God's work. Astronomer and theologian William Stoeger upholds the freedom of creation to act as an agent and argues for a model of double agency, yet does so at the expense of saying that God only works "metaphorically" in and through the laws of nature.[60] Stoeger explains, "When we refer to God or God's action we can do so only 'symbolically' or 'analogically.'"[61] Ultimately, the differentiation between GDA and SDA is lost.[62] In which case, we may call God's creative action "special," but really it is only redefining semantics and no longer talking about particular acts. No act is special precisely because every act is.

I do not mean to write off the model of secondary causation in the world. It is an elegant way of conceiving of diving action and should not be discarded. But alone, it cannot shoulder the entire burden of describing divine action.[63]

Character of special divine action

My proposal is that divine action should not be reduced to just one type or level of action, but instead recognise SDA through multiple models, in various ways. Brian Hebblethwaite writes: "It will be apparent that God's action in relation to any one human being at any one time will be a multi-faceted and multi-level business."[64] The same is true of divine action in relation to any particular non-human animal, and by a different scale of measure, to evolutionary history as a whole. To do justice to the complexity of divine action, I want to avoid the temptation of saying that God is always and everywhere doing one and the same thing.[65] God constraining the possibilities of physical existence is not inconsistent with God using secondary causes. However, none of the models explored previously get to the heart of the question: they do not tell us the purpose or outcome of God's action for suffering creatures. I will, therefore, frame my work in terms of the character, rather than the mechanism or efficient cause of divine action.[66] I propose four different ways of understanding SDA, which, together, form a robust whole: SDA as the gift of being, as divine presence, as divine lure and invitation, and as participation in creation.

Gift of being

The gift of being is perhaps the least obvious category to be listed as "special" divine action, since traditionally the provision of being would have been labelled as GDA – along with the upholding, sustaining, and empowering of creation. I argue that the gift of being – that is, the gift of allowing something to be rather than letting it fall into non-existence – becomes an act of SDA in the case of living beings. The continued existence of rocks and stars do not require SDA, only general divine sustaining action. The gift of being to an individual creature (whether human or non-human) involves – to borrow language from Southgate – the gifts of the Logos and of the Spirit: form and particularity.[67] As each creature participates in life, of which God is the source, it is a particular instance of special divine action for that creature to be and to have the room to be what it is.[68] There are two gifts here: the first allows a creature to exist (the ontological sustaining of being); the second gives it the power to act according to its own agency. It is this latter aspect of giving the agential power that makes living beings unique recipients of SDA. A rock does not have any independent agency – it accesses only the first gift. Elizabeth Johnson uses similar imagery in her panentheistic vision of creation:

> To be imaginative for a moment, it is as if at the Big Bang the Spirit gave the natural world a push saying, 'Go, have an adventure, see what you can become. And I will be with you every step of the way.' In more classical language, the Giver of life not only creates and conserves all things, holding them in existence over the abyss of nothingness, but is also the dynamic ground of their becoming, empowering from within their emergence into new complex forms.[69]

General providence sets the ordering of the initial cosmos in place, and continues to sustain and uphold it, while a particular type of SDA gives uniqueness and relational freedom to every living individual.[70]

Viewing being as a gift is problematic for those creatures whose particular circumstances necessarily mean that there will be no chance of their flourishing. Imagine a leopard born with deformed legs that will never walk, never hunt, and therefore never act as a leopard in the full sense. The leopard may seem a tragedy, but the argument could be turned on its head by pointing out that God does not give the gift of being generously only to those who embody the regular or successful forms of life, but instead abundantly bestows life upon all sorts of unlikely candidates. There is a super-fecundity of being that lies at the foundation of the universe, reflecting the abundance of divine generosity. Instead of only choosing desired outcomes and then driving natural forces to promote those outcomes, God gives abundantly to as many lives as there are possibilities for taking form.

In terms of the non-human animal creation this means that it is through the superabundant provision of life that the moment of novelty is created. If only the creatures that could most perfectly benefit from life received it, there would be little change to life forms. It is the abundant variation amongst creatures that provides the source for evolutionary development. Syndactyly, for example, is a genetic disorder in humans where connective tissues between the digits remain fused. Yet, in flying squirrels, this type of genetic anomaly has been developed to expand the surface area of the patagium – the flap of tissue between wrists and the hind limbs.[71] If the environmental circumstances are right, and an abnormal feature is favoured, it may become the beginning of some new element of flourishing. If, as is often the case, the creature is not favoured either by a mutation or by conditions – and does not survive to reproduce and pass on a new way of living – then God will redeem its life in ways explored in the next chapter, as well as comfort and accompany it in its suffering.

Co-presence

A second type of divine action is found in the co-presence of God with the creature. Distinct from the gift of being, which creates the possibilities of life, co-presence dispels notions of deism and envisions God as living with the created world. Ruth Page proposes the term "pansyntheism" to describe this special divine presence, drawing from the Heideggerian concept of *Mitsein*, or "with being."[72] It is utterly impossible for creatures to live independently of a complex web of relationships: with other creatures of the same species, with the creatures they eat and are eaten by, with the air (or water) around them, and with the ground beneath them. Always and everywhere, all beings live in relationship. God, in creating, freely chooses to enter into relationships as well. God's co-presence, or co-experience, can be thought of as a continual act of kenosis that God undertakes to maintain loving, responsive relationship with creation. Co-presence is the special divine act of continual re-commitment to the project of creation, the continual divine humbling, in the form of not exercising divine power, knowledge, and eternity to their full extent. It is not a necessary commitment for God, but one entered into from the fullness of love.[73]

Divine co-presence is therefore closely linked to divine co-suffering. Because God is with creation, God also co-experiences the suffering of creation. Too often, theologians have understood God as distant. Holmes Rolston famously said: "if God watches the sparrow fall, God must do so from a great distance."[74] Completely transcendent, God watches the cosmic drama from the heavens, while creatures are left to whatever fate might befall. If the work on love developed in Chapter 4 is correct, and love requires the desire of union, then Rolston's God cannot be one of love.

The 2001 movie *Shrek* brilliantly depicts the dangers of a distant ruler in Lord Farquaad.[75] At one point, as Farquaad stands on a balcony far above a group of gathered knights below, he tells the knights that they will be sent to embark on a perilous journey to rescue the Princess Fiona so that Farquaad can marry her. "Some of you may die" he says as the audience murmurs in sadness and worry, "but it's a sacrifice *I* am willing to make." Rapturous applause breaks out.

The picture is not very far from what some theologies have suggested is the purpose of the suffering of non-human creatures. God, standing aloof from the danger and hurt of creation, voices plans that the universe should produce life, which would one day include human beings whom God would take as an eschatological bride. Just as Lord Farquaad sends others into peril to rescue Fiona, so God sacrifices numberless creatures in the pursuit of the realisation of humans with free moral choice.[76] To glorify God for such a creation is morally repugnant, as absurd as the crowd's applause at Lord Farquaad's declaration. But if God is instead *with* the creation, accompanying it and co-suffering with it, the objection fades.

Does divine co-presence or co-suffering actually *do* anything for the suffering creation? David Clough challenges the co-suffering claim:

> The pain inflicted on an individual by a surgeon, for example, may or may not be judged to be justified on the basis of benefit to the patient or to others, but if the surgeon decided to inflict the same pain on themselves, it would not materially alter the judgement one way or another.[77]

For humans, God's co-suffering has often brought a great deal of comfort to those who suffer. The notion that they are not alone, but that God has suffered and now suffers with them, can alleviate some of the mental suffering they experience.[78] We do not know if the same is true of the non-human animal creation. Christopher Southgate, drawing on the work of Jay McDaniel, reflects on this eloquently:

> When I consider the starving pelican chick, or the impala hobbled by a mother cheetah so that her cubs can learn to pull a prey animal down, I cannot pretend that God's presence as the 'heart' of the world takes the pain of the experience away; I cannot pretend that the suffering may not destroy the creature's consciousness before death claims it. That is the power of suffering, that it can destroy selves.
>
> I can only suppose that God's suffering presence is just that, presence, of the most profoundly attentive and loving sort, a solidarity that at some deep level takes away the aloneness of the suffering creature's experience.[79]

If God's presence changes a non-human animal's experience of suffering and death, it will do so in a way that is inaccessible to humans. Having said that, I do not imagine that the presence has to be consciously acknowledged to be effective: babies respond to, and are comforted by, a mother's presence long before they can grasp abstract concepts like "self" and "mother" and "love." Perhaps the most important thing is that the concept of divine co-presence and co-suffering radically alters one's understanding of the type of world we live in. It is not a world in which creatures are left alone to struggle through whatever mayhem may come, like *Lord of the Flies* made large. It is instead a world where perilous journeys must be undertaken, but in which God is accompanying the creation every step of the way. Rather than Lord Farquaad, we might imagine God as a historical doctor or midwife attending creation's labour pains.[80] Before anaesthetics, the person assisting a birth could not take away the pain of the mother, nor even significantly lessen it, but instead she accompanied, encouraged, embraced, and sat in solidarity with the suffering (and sometimes dying) mother. Therefore, in the venture of theodicy, God's presence in creation – quite apart from any causality – goes a long way toward understanding a beloved creation that suffers through to new life, even if God's presence does not necessarily alleviate creation's pain or brutality.

Lure

Another type of SDA is present in the divine lure. This lure can be parsed in several different ways. First, it is described in the lure toward the good and harmonious that is so central to process thought. Ian Barbour, John Cobb, David Ray Griffin, John Haught, and Jay McDaniel are the major recent representatives of this approach to divine action.[81] God does not coerce creation into pre-formed plans. Instead, God lures every entity of creation toward greater inter-relational harmonies and goods, and every entity of creation has the power to either accept or reject this divine lure. Insofar as the creation is self-determining and holds creative autonomy, entities may diverge from the divine invitation of order and novelty. The great strength of process thought is that it explains harms in the world as those moments when entities resist the divine lure toward the good, and so explains disvalues without creating a dualism or leaving disvalues without any explanation. Another strength is that process theology is rooted in the concept of God's unfailing love for each and every part of creation.[82]

A major challenge posed for process theology by classical theology is that process theology offers no guarantee of good triumphing over evil, no certain defeat of evil.[83] God can never decisively destroy evil, nor (if the track-record of the world is any evidence) is there a guarantee that creatures will one day respond positively toward divine suggestion. There exists only the long, slow, uncertain lure toward the good that may or may not result in harmony and goodness.

How far does this lure extend? For process theists who adhere to the concept of panpsychism, the divine lure extends to every conceivable "entity" of creation: to quarks and electrons just as much as to humans and hippos. I do not follow them in this reasoning, and would argue that the extent of lure is similar to the extent of love.[84] Lure is an idea loaded with personal concepts such as desire and fulfilment. As such, I would restrict the objects of divine lure to living beings.[85] One might object that personal categories are just as inappropriate when applied to bacteria as to stone. From a human perspective, that would be true: since I cannot know a bacterium, there can be no appropriate union with it in the sense of the desires of love. God, however, can know a bacterium intimately: can know its range of responses and what constitutes its good, can share a history with it, and can share an office of love with it – at the very least – as Creator and creature. Therefore, the concept of lure can also presumably apply, although it would not be lure towards a choice of moral good (as it would be for humans) but simply a lure toward actions for its own selving.

The process paradigm also highlights one of the paradigmatic paradoxes of evolution: the violence one might wish to reject is also the seed of admired novelty. On the one hand, there is a temptation to say that the Ichneumon's parasitic eggs planted within caterpillars are an evil use of the gift of life that God did not design and does not intend. Their survival tactic is allowed, tolerated, rather than rejoiced in. On the other hand, the life style of the wasp demonstrates skill, complexity, and ingenuity. Their reproduction can be a saving grace for the trees and shrubs that the caterpillars would otherwise destroy. It is a constant temptation to put the "peaceable elements" – the bunny rabbits, the swallows, and the autotrophic life – in one category of "God approved" evolutionary developments, and snakes, lions, and parasites into another camp of "not approved, violent" developments. But this is too simple. The "peaceful" species rely upon the violent species for their own flourishing, and the "peaceful" species only exist because they have entered into competition in their own ways with other species. Even autotrophic organisms compete with those around them for resources, squeezing out other organisms in the race for space and sunlight. Therefore, instead of having two categories in our minds of "violent" and "peaceful" creation (*pace* Messer), or even "wheat" and "tares" (*pace* Hoggard Creegan), the creation must be seen as one community. As a whole, it stands as God's very good creation, including its components of violence and suffering. Creation is, as Southgate reminds, "*both* good *and* groaning."[86] The wheat, *as wheat*, inflicts its own forms of violence on the organisms that surround and relate to it. Therefore, if God is the God of all of creation, then violence too must be part of God's creation.[87] Until humans emerge and moral decision-making becomes a reality (some would argue this is also present to some degree in some of the other most complex forms of life) the only category of creation is the "very good." So I argue that while the divine lure may indeed be toward the good, one cannot characterise that good as being exclusively the harmonious or the peaceful, as process theists do, and thus blame every instance of violence on resistance to the divine lure.[88] Nor does an attempt like Sarah Coakley's to point to inter-species cooperation as evidence of particular goodness and altruism in evolution succeed.[89] It is like talking about the coordination of gang members as evidence of human altruism: cooperation happens because it leads to greater strength as a unit, which then competes against other units, usually violently. Instances of true altruism are surpassingly rare in the non-human realm, if evidenced at all.[90]

A second type of lure is the model advanced by Philip Clayton and Steven Knapp that revolves around the non-law-like nature of mental events. The model depends entirely on Donald Davidson's concept of "anomalous monism,"[91] which allows Clayton and Knapp to categorise mental events as a form of emergent complexity. According to them, the underlying laws of physics and chemistry no longer determine the outcome of events in these highly complex processes.[92] Instead, mental events are open to divine interaction because they do not rely directly upon the physical processes that make them possible. Despite this being a very limited model of divine action on its own, Clayton and Knapp insist it is necessary – from a mechanistic perspective – because scientific understandings now give such complete explanations of the universe's interactions that God could not undertake SDA without overthrowing those interactions.

Clayton and Knapp also argue from a moral perspective that such a limited view of divine action is necessary, based on the premise that if a good and benevolent God could have averted such profoundly harmful events as the Indonesian tsunami of 2004 or the Holocaust, God would have done so. Since God did not avert them, God must therefore not be able to intervene in the physical world.

Clayton and Knapp's argument presupposes there is a certain type of response to evil that God "ought" to do. Yet, God's ways of defeating evil are rarely transparent and rarely avoid suffering. In the Incarnation, for example, God's action was seldom obvious or predictable, despite being physical and (in some sense) "interventionist." Jesus's way of responding to evil, most notably in the cross, did not at all meet expectations of how people thought the coming Messiah should overcome their oppressions. So there is room to question Clayton and Knapp's assumption that God would necessarily avert evil in straightforward ways.

According to Clayton and Knapp, God can only interact with the world through the mental states of creatures, although those messages can be resisted or ignored. "What God cannot do," they write

> if the problem of evil is answerable, is to give us thoughts or feelings that compel an automatic or reflexive response, because if that was the way God acted in the world, God would have an obligation to prevent or correct our mistakes and other failures whenever they might occur.[93]

But it seems from their position that God does not even need to make it clear to the recipient of this divine action that anything out of the ordinary is taking place, since they say these messages of lure can take place on a subconscious level.[94] If it is subconscious, the divine action is neither accepted nor rejected by the agent and has no way of being discerned by the agent themselves. This is a point that Clayton and Knapp acknowledge: "There is no reliable way, then, to separate the divine from the human contributions to any particular instance of divine-human interaction."[95] Nor can God impart information directly, in this view, but can only introduce axiological lures or a sense of divine presence, for the direct impartation of information would override creaturely freedom and introduce a moral dilemma.[96]

Problematic from a *scientific* perspective, Clayton and Knapp's view is founded upon the assumption that mental events are not reducible to physical brain events, a step which has come under criticism.[97] Ultimately, it leaves the theologian with one more possible place where further scientific discovery might edge God out of the picture if further neuropsychological study should find that minds do in fact work on nomological principles.

Problematic from a *theological* perspective, the model leaves no clear distinction between divine and creaturely action, and allows only a very limited sphere for divine action. The outcomes of Clayton and Knapp's approach may resonate more or less with the divine values of love, but it does so at great cost. The most troubling aspect of this line of thought is that the Incarnation itself, as classically understood, would be ruled out as a possible distinctive divine action, and with it, all the theodicies built on Christological foundations.[98]

A better proposal than the process lure toward harmonious relationships comes from Christopher Southgate who speaks of the divine invitation to self-transcendence.[99] This self-transcendence in humans involves the call to altruism and to robust love, but in the non-human realm self-transcendence is the Spirit's work helping the individual in "growing to maturity in the form of its species, and in the sense of its possible explorations of new behaviours, going beyond what was previously the character of that species."[100] In neither of these instances is self-transcendence linked to what might be considered the "good" or "pleasant" aspects of creation. The parasitic wasp growing to maturity is just as much the work of the Spirit as the bunny rabbit. The work of the Spirit is active in the moment when the wasp stretches its wings to fly for the first time, when it wrestles an insect and feeds, or when it explores new territory. In each moment the Spirit lures the wasp toward self-transcendence, toward its own characteristic "selving," and toward playing its role in the unfolding history of life. Creation is not divided up into the "good" and the "evil." All creatures are invited to self-transcendence. Sometimes, Southgate notes, the answer to this invitation does result in cooperation and symbiosis, but is not limited to those outcomes.[101] The basis of the ability for creatures to explore is found in "deep intratrinitarian kenosis" where a creature "is conforming to the pattern offered by the divine Word, and begotten in the Spirit out of the perfect self-abandoning love of the Father."[102] In this sense, the lure of God is also intrinsically linked to God creating the possibilities of action, or in other words, creating the fabric of the fitness landscape the creature explores.

One way I would differ from Southgate's suggestion is to stress the particularity of the form offered to the individual over species norms. Creatures are not invited to conform to a species ideal, but to the particular form offered out of God's love for that particular creature. Just as God's love for each creature is highly particular, so is the form of the invitation to self-transcendence.

A different sort of proposal of divine lure altogether comes from Robert Farrar Capon. Instead of assuming that the divine lure is something situated in the action of God, as if God were trying to actively lead creation down certain paths, Capon proposes that desire for God is intrinsic in creation. Capon writes colourfully:

> What [God] does to the world, he does subtly; his effect on creation is like what a stunning woman does to a man. . . . She doesn't touch his freedom, and she doesn't muck about with the constitution of his being by installing some trick nisus that makes Harry love Martha.[103]

Creation is not led along fortuitous paths like a donkey lured by a carrot and coaxing words, rather the very stuff of creation is attracted to the divine being the same way the earth is attracted to the sun, or (in Capon's personal example) a man is attracted to a beautiful woman. Both the sun and the woman simply exist, and are attractive. No further action is necessary, and there is no need to search for the particularity of how God lures. Divine goodness is its own explanation for why creation pursues it. And the effect on creation is marked: it is drawn toward God-likeness, most evidently in humans. The explorations of creation – the bio-diversity and increase of complexity – can all be seen as creaturely attempts to pursue the satisfaction of that elusive attraction.

Each of these models of divine lure, particularly those of Southgate and Capon, provide helpful paths to explore the directionality of evolutionary pathways with-out looking for intervention. They also include robust accounts of God working in and with the non-human creation in ways that extend well beyond simply sustain-ing action.

Participation

Finally, I offer SDA as participation. In an important way, all the other forms of divine action investigated so far are also participation in as much as they are descriptions of God at work in the world. The gift of being, the divine accompani-ment of creation, and the divine lure are all types of action that place one firmly in the camp of theism. However, in using the word participation, I want to bring attention to at least two ways in which God acts that are not covered by these other ways of thinking: embodiment and the shaping of meaning.

Participation: embodiment

God's action of embodiment in creation is primarily evidenced in the Incarna-tion. This stands in contrast to the proposals of Sallie McFague or Grace Jantzen that the world can regularly be thought of as God's body, with God's spirit as the body's mind.[104] In the Incarnation, God was significantly present – uniquely united to the world – in one man, Jesus Christ.

Denis Edwards has worked a great deal on the impact the character of the Incar-nation has for reflecting on how God acts. Edwards draws from several different sources for his model: from the parables of the Kingdom, Jesus's acts of healing, his keeping an open table, and the character of his community. Edwards concludes that God's love leads to divine action with a "radically participatory character"[105] characterised by two central aspects. First, God actively and lovingly waits upon creation, and second, that God's love results in divine vulnerability.[106]

According to Edwards, in the death of Jesus, God awaits creaturely response and does not overwhelm creaturely action even when it means crucifixion. In the forgiveness and resurrection of Jesus, it becomes apparent that God can achieve the divine purpose in, through, and with creaturely choices, even when those choices are harmful.[107] Although God remains unchanging in constant love and faithfulness, God can still suffer and is vulnerable to creaturely action, as exem-plified in the cross. God is not left at the mercy of creatures, however, because God can always "bring all things to their promised fulfilment."[108] Edwards writes, "the true nature of divine power is revealed in the vulnerability of the crucified – and in the resurrection of the crucified."[109] It is both God's ability to suffer, and God's ability to redeem suffering (especially, perhaps, the suffering caused by moral evil), that reveals the full extent of divine power.

Edwards's reflections on the Incarnation resonate with my own explorations of the philosophical nature of love found in Chapter 4. In addition, reflection on the surprising physicality of the Incarnation gives a strong reason to maintain that SDA is something very different from GDA, and that divine participation is more involved than one might otherwise believe, even to the point of God becoming one cause amongst others in the physical world. I disagree with Edwards, who reflected earlier so helpfully on the Incarnation, when he states: "God is never found as a cause among other causes in the universe."[110] David Burrell also rejects the possibility of God becoming one agent amongst others. Burrell writes, commenting on Aquinas's metaphysical assertion that God is the *cause* of being rather than *a* being: "it would be idolatry to think one could speak of the creator bereft of so powerful a metaphysics, for it would then become one being among others, however large or powerful."[111]

In GDA, I agree that God does not act as a cause among causes: God sustains all creation and is the cause of all other causes. However, the scandal of the Incarnation is that God became just one person amongst others; that God fully participated in the joys and constraints of humanity by becoming fully human.[112] If the Incarnation is the prime exemplar of SDA, then God is seen joining creation, becoming a causal agent within creation, while not overriding it.[113] Jesus did not compel those around him to listen or obey; he simply and seamlessly joined the world of causal agents. Even beyond the Incarnation itself, I do not see any compelling reason why God could not act in other times and places in similar participatory ways.

Is such an assertion open to the critiques of intervention outlined previously? Certainly embodied participation is not the type of divine action that could be predicted, nor could it be investigated by science, and so it would not be open to the mechanistic critique. Though God acted decisively in the Incarnation, most people missed it. I do not think it is open to the moral critique either. The moral critique, as described earlier, was that intervention would show an inconsistency in God's character to interrupt or overrule the very regularities that God put in place. But the Incarnation is not an example of God overruling creation, but *joining* creation. It a creative act that actualises a whole new possibility of divine activity, not simply a change of certain causal chains to ensure a desired outcome. Insofar as participation is a different mode of divine experience and action altogether, it does not pose a moral contradiction for God to act in this way. Participation in embodiment is not God deciding that there was something wrong with how the world was created; it is an entirely new way of creating possibilities in the world. There was no option of writing participation of an incarnational sort into the initial laws of nature.

In the Incarnation, other forms of SDA become the principles or character of God's embodied acts. Take divine lure, for example. Ruth Page, in exploring Jesus's action as a type of *concursus*, speaks of how

> the power exercised in relationship is that of attraction, of drawing the attention and concern of the other without extinguishing that other's

freedom. . . [Jesus] was there among the people; his words and actions were there for any who would hear or see.[114]

Jesus's type of lure in preaching on hilltops is qualitatively different from the sort of lure that God might be making in the invitation to self-transcendence. Yet, they both reflect the same character because they are both rooted in the nature of God's love.

My interest in embodied forms of divine action is not motivated by the claim that there are numerous instances of divine embodiment: indeed, I think it likely that such instances are exceedingly rare. At the same time, it is necessary to acknowledge all possible exceptions in order to allow for as full an account of SDA as possible. If God is able to become one human being amongst millions of others in the Incarnation, then the objection to God ever being considered as one agent amongst others in creation must be problematic. If the door is open to God being one agent amongst others in creation (even once) through participatory human embodiment, then perhaps God is able to engage with creation through other forms of embodiment as well.

The Hebrew Bible theophanies that visualise God's presence as pillars of cloud and fire (Exodus 13:21), then, become something more than simple imagery, and may be seen as instances of God actually participating in the world in physical ways.[115] In other passages God is equally described as having physical forms, such as Moses being able to see God's backside (Exodus 33:17–23), Jacob wrestling with God at the ford of the Jabbok (Genesis 32:22–32), and God appearing to Abraham as the three strangers (Genesis 18:1–2). I will not speculate long on how God might participate in these ways, since to do so would involve a much longer discussion of the historical and theological reliability of these texts in light of critical methods of reading.[116] If I were to speculate at all, I might imagine God taking up – embodying – the molecules in a particular place to suit the action that God wishes to take. After all, in Jesus, God did embody carbon, and nitrogen, and all the other assorted atoms that make up the human body.[117]

The mechanism of God's action is less important than its nature. The action must be reminiscent of God's gracious action in incarnating the divine form in human form, bearing the stamp of love. God, in this view, can interact physically and particularly in history in the same physical sense that the second person of the Trinity did by becoming Jesus. The embodied view of God's work opens the door to interaction with the world in a way that is more than just sustaining or concurrent.

In some ways, advocating that God can participate in the world in physically embodied – and thus physically causative ways – opens up many more problems than it solves in regard to theodicy. For God to have the ability to participate in an embodied way that could conceivably change the fortunes of a creature caught in innocent suffering, and for God to rescue in some cases and not in others, does raise a serious charge of either inconsistency or neglect. A response emerges directly from the discussion of the nature of love that was explored in Chapter 4. Emerging out of a Thomist view of love, I concluded that love is necessarily particular, historical, and unique to the office of love shared between the lover and the beloved. As such, the action taken in each case need not be identical.

With the perspective that love does not have to treat all beloved creatures in exactly the same way in order to still be equally loving to all, the possibility opens that God could prevent one instance of suffering without being morally required to do so in another case. For example, God would not be morally required to prevent an instance of suffering that did *not* lead to the destruction of a self, if in another case, God did prevent an equivalent amount of suffering. Why, then, does God not observably end the many instances of innocent suffering of creatures, if God has the capacity to do so?

The question has to take one more step back and ask if the office of love of Creator to a particular creature ever ought to mean that God should prevent such suffering. When Austin Farrer asks the question of why, if we are moved to put severely injured animals out of their misery, God is not moved to do likewise, he answers,

> the question is amiable, but it is confused. God loves his animal creatures by being God to them, that is, by natural providence and creative power; not by being a brother creature to them, as he does for mankind in the unique miracle of his incarnation.[118]

For Farrer, God's lack of prevention of suffering in the non-human creation is not because of issues of fair play in moral responsibility, but because the office of love between God and the non-human creation is not the type that would call for it. Miracles, in Farrer's mind, do not happen simply to relieve suffering, but serve as signposts indicating the coming Kingdom of God, which are totally unable to be interpreted by the non-human world.[119]

For God to act to alleviate the suffering of a God-conscious human being is perhaps to give them an opportunity to grow closer to God, to build faith, or to reconstitute their personhood.[120] These goods would not be available to a non-human who had their suffering alleviated. The arguments that the goods of nomic regularity, the integrity of ecosystems, and the process of evolution itself are greater goods than what would be achieved by relieving the individual creature of pain are well rehearsed.[121] However, the discussion does lead to one important and oft-overlooked factor: the issue is not always what happens, as much as it is the meaning of what happened. Thus, it is necessary to discuss a second type of participation that is rather more abstract.

Participation: shaping of meaning

The second type of participation I want to highlight is that God is active in shaping the meaning of events. This is radically different from God's embodied work of participation since it does not involve any sort of change in the actual events of history. Rather, it recognises that the meaning of past events is not fixed or isolated, and that depending on new events that occur, the meanings of past events also change.

Think about how people interpret various events in their lives. It is apparent that the intuitive meaning ascribed to – and the interpretation of – one event can become closely tied to events that may be quite distant from the original occurrence in time or place. People sometimes radically revise the meaning of an experience: what seemed like a fortuitous event at one time becomes a tragic turning point at another distant time, and vice versa. This sense of the fluidity of meaning is perhaps most famously illustrated in the story of the Taoist Farmer:

> There once was an old man and his son who owned a horse, which provided their only source of income. One night the horse ran away. The next day, all the villagers trotted out to the old farmer's and said: "Oh no! This is the worst thing that could have happened to you."
>
> The old farmer quietly answered, "It's too early to tell."
>
> Soon thereafter the horse returned with five others. The next morning all the villagers trotted out to the farmer and said, "Congratulations! This is the best thing that could ever happen to you."
>
> But the old farmer quietly said, "It's too soon to tell."
>
> Shortly thereafter, his son tried to ride one of the new horses. The horse was wild, and threw him into the corral fence. He was left with a permanent limp. The next morning the villagers came again and said, "This is the worst tragedy that could ever happen to you."
>
> But the farmer said quietly, "It's too soon to tell."
>
> A year later, the army came through the village to take all the healthy young men off to war. The old farmer's son was of no use to them and was left behind. None of the other young men ever returned.[122]

No doubt most people have similar stories where they have jumped, like the villagers, at the meaning of an event only to find that with the passage of time, it has come to mean something else entirely. Meaning is not inherent in an event: it changes as people change and see events from different perspectives.

Traditionally, Christianity has not held such a view of the meaning of events because it was assumed that, from God's eternal vantage point, there was an objective point of view that could perfectly interpret all events in light of both past and future. However, if the nature of love demands true creaturely freedom, and if the possibility of that sort of freewill demands (at the least) a kenotic descent into time for God,[123] so that God does not know all that will happen, then I cannot imagine that there is any such objective viewpoint from which to determine the meaning of events. God, with perfect knowledge of the past and the present, will certainly be best placed to understand events as they occur, but even to God the meaning of events is not fixed. Therefore, God can have an active hand in crafting and shaping the meaning of events by interpreting them with other events in time and evoking unforeseen conclusions from them.[124] One might, poetically speaking, say that God is telling and re-telling the narrative of creation. As the history of the world unfolds, there is no limit to the creativity that God can bring to the unfolding process. The profound suffering of creatures caught up in the evolutionary tale has not yet been told for the final time.

The advantage to thinking of suffering from this perspective is that God does not ordain events of disvalue to happen, nor do they have any "hidden meaning" at the time they happen, but God can redeem disvalues within the scope of history as well as beyond it. There is no one corridor down which God must force events for them to find redemption, but rather God can creatively bring about good in a variety of ways. How this works in terms of redemption will be explored in a more explicit way in the next chapter.

Primacy of biological telos?

Before considering redemption, it is vital to have a sense of what a creature is redeemed from and what redemption it is headed toward. Where does a creature's life find meaning? What is its final end? In Darwinian terms, the meaning of a creature's life is found in survival and reproduction. If it passes on its genes, its life has been successful. Thus, for many creatures – spiders and praying mantises, but also octopi and salmon – one or both parents die in the act of reproduction. Reproduction is the grand finale after a life of winning the odds in a battle for survival. But ought it to be assumed that this type of biological flourishing is the only worthwhile end, the only – or even the primary – creaturely *telos*?

For humans, it is clear that this is not the case. Human life has many other good and worthwhile ends. One does not have to look farther than Jesus to see that this is true. As the paradigmatic human being, Jesus demonstrated what it means to be fully human. Yet, Jesus had no children,[125] nor did he live to a grand old age. He lived to maybe a third of what a regular human body can ultimately sustain. Biologically speaking, Jesus was a failure.[126] Yet, he was the one who perfectly fulfilled the human vocation.

The questions of creaturely value and the meaning of life become even more poignant when considered in light of serious illness. John Swinton, for example, writes about dementia and the loss of a person's memories.[127] He chastises theologians for having "hyper-cognitive theological assumptions" of what it means to be human, where dementia is seen as the loss of personhood entirely, rather than only the loss of memories. Swinton rejects outright the usual practice of adopting medical and societal evaluations of the worth of a person's existence rather than rooting the person's worth in theological considerations. He writes:

> At a very basic level, well-being within Christianity is not gauged by the presence or absence of illness or distress. . . . Theologically speaking, well-being has nothing to do with the absence or reduction of anything. It has to do with the presence of something: the presence of God-in-relationship.[128]

If there is the presence of God-in-relationship, then there is the presence of worth and well-being. For humans, at least, reflections on Jesus's life and on the lives of those who suffer severe illness reveal that there is far more to life than Darwinian success.[129]

Can that framework legitimately be extended beyond humans into the non-human realm? From a theological perspective, I think it is reasonable to put forward other reasons for being: to live in relationship with others and to participate in the divine gift of life. All creatures are necessarily in relationship with those around them: being sustained by and sustaining others. Ruth Page insists that relationship provides a different *telos*: "Fellowship, concurrence or relationship among creatures and between creatures and God is the greatest good of creation. The possibility of such relationships is what creation is about."[130] For Page, relationship is not simply a great good, but the greatest good. If a creature has participated in relationship, then it has achieved a meaningful life. Having a meaningful life does not mean that a creature has participated in every possible creaturely good.

As previously explored with the argument on divine shaping of the meaning of history, the question is less about the events of a creature's life and more about what they mean. By redefining what is meant by a purposeful life, the number of creatures who fulfil that category can be extended, and thus lessen the burden that the theodicist carries. I once watched a documentary about a penguin chick that spent 13 months being nurtured by doting parents and congregating with other young. The chick was then killed within a matter of moments of entering the ocean for the first time by a leopard seal. While the narrator of the documentary emphasised the tragic nature of the lost life, it did not strike me as nearly the hardest case for the theodicist to think about. The chick had experienced rich relationship, even if only briefly. The much more difficult case is that of the second pelican chick who is denied primary relationships with sibling and parents and the majority of its life experience involves the suffering of starvation. Even that chick, however, is involved in a complex ecosystem of relationships, and it is not denied a relationship with God, and it will (as I will argue in the next chapter) receive the gift of redemption in the new life. As the burden of my argument begins to hint more heavily toward themes of redemption, it is perhaps time to move onto those subjects in a more straightforward way.

Conclusion

In the first half of this chapter I set out some of the categories of thought surrounding divine action. Working with a distinction between SDA and GDA, I outlined how they are not always considered distinct categories of action, and I identified the question of divine intervention as one of the primary concerns for how the debate over divine action has proceeded. Particularly, models that avoid interventionism have been proposed with God working through the openness of nature, especially in quantum and chaotic systems. However, I have chosen to focus on the character of divine action rather than the mechanism.

In the second half of the chapter, I argued that divine action is a multi-faceted phenomenon, ranging from divine presence and the gift of being to physical embodiment. Instead of embracing a divine uniformitarianism where God is always thought to be doing the same thing in the same way, I proposed that there are multiple ways in which God can be understood to be acting, and that each of these different acts have various implications for the issues of theodicy.

The gift of being implies that God creates the possibility of possibilities and allows creatures to explore the paths of being that they choose. The result is a free process characterised by significant freedoms and a superabundance of diverse forms of being given the chance of life. The co-presence of God ensures that no creature dies alone, separated from God's consolation and co-suffering. The concept of divine lure can be seen as either an invitation to self-transcendence, or as creaturely attraction to the divine. The second in particular begins to offer some explanation for how one can have teleology without control; desired outcomes without preordained paths. Finally, two types of participation round out my picture of special divine action. The concept of embodiment allows for the mighty acts of salvation history and the Incarnation in a human context without necessarily widening the sphere of this special involvement to all creatures. The shaping of meaning, to be explored further in the next chapter, provides another non-interventionist way to speak about divine action from a narrative perspective. Most of these positions do not envision any sort of intervention on the part of God, except the embodied form of participation. The gift of being, the co-presence of God, the divine lure, and the shaping of meaning all work in and through natural means, or (in the case of shaping meaning) beyond the physical realm, on a metaphysical plane. Embodiment allows an avenue for how God might be more directly active, even intervening, and the particularity and purpose of such acts may offer a reason for why God would intervene in one case and not another. Woven throughout all these concepts of divine action lies the central act of redemption which deserves a chapter all of its own.

Notes

1 A proposal advanced in a recent work by Thomas Jay Oord suggests that God has extremely limited capacity to act due to a primary nature of love. *The Uncontrolling Love of God* (Downer's Grove, IL: InterVarsity Press, 2016).
2 W. H. Vanstone, *Love's Endeavour, Love's Expense: The Response of Being to the Love of God* (London: Dartman, Longman and Todd, 1977), 67.
3 Sarah Lane Ritchie, "Dancing Around the Causal Joint: Challenging the Theological Turn in Divine Action Theories," *Zygon* 53:2 (June 2017): 361–379.
4 I use "God" and "divine" synonymously in this chapter. The literature in this area tends to use the term "divine action" to simply mean: "how God acts." Another concern pointed out to me is the lack of Trinitarian articulation of God's action in much of this chapter and the worry that "divine action" is too hegemonic a term for the nuanced action of a Trinitarian God. For the purposes of this chapter, I primarily use the less nuanced language of "divine action" to be able to stay in dialogue with the majority of the relevant literature, but note that further work could flesh out any of the models below in full and more nuanced Trinitarian terms, as is being done in much of the pneumatological work by Amos Yong and James K. A. Smith. Much of the second half of the chapter uses more Trinitarian language. See Amos Yong, *The Spirit of Creation: Modern Science and Divine Action in the Pentecostal- Charismatic Imagination*

(Grand Rapids, MI: Eerdmans, 2011); James K. A. Smith, "Is the Universe Open for Surprise? Pentecostal Ontology and the Spirit of Naturalism," *Zygon* 43 (2008): 879–896. My thanks to Sarah Williams for raising these issues.

5 Nicholas Saunders, *Divine Action & Modern Science* (Cambridge: Cambridge University Press, 2002), 21. Italics original.

6 Maurice Wiles, *God's Action in the World* (London: SCM Press, 1986), 28–30.

7 Wiles, *God's Action*, 28.

8 Wiles, *God's Action*, 61–62.

9 Gordon D. Kaufman, "On the Meaning of 'Act of God'," *Harvard Theological Review* 61 (1968): 175–201.

10 Kaufman, "On the Meaning of 'Act of God'," 197. Kaufman avoids talking about whether these sub-acts were determined by previous events and were inevitable or if some other history might have emerged if God had acted differently.

11 Wiles, *God's Action*, 100.

12 Wiles gives the example of redemption history as a place where the one act of God in creation-redemption becomes specially significant. *God's Action*, 93.

13 Kaufman, "On the Meaning of 'Act of God'," 200.

14 Wiles, *God's Action*, 45.

15 Wiles, *God's Action*, 101.

16 Niels Gregersen, "Special Divine Action and the Quilt of Laws: Why the Distinction between Special and General Divine Action Cannot Be Maintained," in *Scientific Perspectives on Divine Action: Twenty Years of Challenge and Progress*, eds. Robert J. Russell, Nancey Murphy, and William R. Stoeger, S. J. (Vatican City and Berkeley, CA: Vatican Observatory, CTNS, 2008), 179–199; Denis Edwards, *How God Acts: Creation, Redemption, and Special Divine Action* (Minneapolis, MN: Fortress Press, 2010), 37–39.

17 Gregersen, "Special Divine Action and the Quilt of Laws," 194.

18 For a discussion of Hume's critique of miracles, see Christopher Southgate, "A Test Case: Divine Action," in *God, Humanity and the Cosmos*, ed. Christopher Southgate, 3rd ed. (London: T & T Clark, 2011), 293–294.

19 Paul Davies, "Teleology Without Teleology: Purpose Through Emergent Complexity," in *Evolutionary and Molecular Biology: Scientific Perspective on Divine Action*, eds. Robert J. Russell, William R. Stoeger, S. J., and Francisco J. Ayala (Vatican City and Berkeley, CA: Vatican Observatory, CTNS, 1998), 152.

20 There are other possibilities for the definition of miracle: see Alan G. Padgett, "God and Miracle in An Age of Science," in *The Blackwell Companion to Science and Christianity*, ed. J. B. Stump and Alan G. Padgett (Oxford: Wiley-Blackwell, 2012), 533–542. See also Southgate's definition of miracle: "an extremely unusual event, unfamiliar in terms of naturalistic explanation, which a worshipping community takes to be specially revelatory, by dint of the blessing or healing it conveys, of the divine grace." Southgate, "A test case: divine action," 294. For a much longer discussion of various definitions of intervention (depending as it does on one's conception of natural laws), see Saunders, *Divine Action*, 48–60.

21 See Arthur Peacocke's discussion in *Theology for a Scientific Age: Being and Becoming – Natural, Divine, and Human*, enlarged ed. (London: SCM Press, 1990, 1993), 141–143.

22 See Ritchie, "Dancing Around," 363–364.

23 One might be able to study the effects of miraculous action, but not the cause, since the cause is outside the realm of nature.

24 This is a claim repeated by: Kaufman, "On the Meaning of 'Act of God'," 175–201; John Polkinghorne, *Science & Theology: An Introduction* (London: SPCK, 1998), 92; Robert J. Russell, "Does 'The God Who Acts' Really Act? New Approaches to Divine Action in Light of Science," *Theology Today* 54:1 (April 1997): 49–51; Peacocke, *Theology for a Scientific Age*, 139–142; Southgate, "A Test Case: Divine Action," 279.

25 John Polkinghorne writes, "strictly speaking, science cannot exclude the one-off, though the more it discerns a regular world, the more problematic become the claims for such unique occurrences." *Science & Theology*, 92.

26 Polkinghorne, *Science & Theology: An Introduction* (London: SPCK, 1998), 92; Peacocke, *Theology for a Scientific Age*, 142.

27 Davies, "Teleology Without Teleology," 152; Elizabeth Johnson, *Ask the Beasts: Darwin and the God of Love* (London: Bloomsbury, 2014), 168; Denis Edwards, *How God Acts: Creation, Redemption, and Special Divine Action* (Minneapolis, MN: Fortress Press, 2010), 63; David B. Burrell C. S. C., and Isabelle Moulin, "Albert, Aquinas and Dionysius," *Modern Theology* 24:4 (October 2008): 642.

28 Philip Clayton and Steven Knapp, *The Predicament of Belief: Science, Philosophy, Faith* (Oxford: Oxford University Press, 2011), 44–52; Wesley J. Wildman, "Incongruous Goodness, Perilous Beauty, Disconcerting Truth: Ultimate Reality and Suffering in Nature," in *Physics and Cosmology: Scientific Perspectives on the Problem of Natural Evil*, eds. Nancey Murphy, Robert Russell, and William Stoeger, S. J. (Vatican City and Berkeley, CA: Vatican Observatory, CTNS, 2007), 267–275.

29 Polkinghorne, *Science & Theology*, 93. Peacocke, *Theology for a Scientific Age*, 142. Southgate, "A Test Case: Divine Action," 294.

30 Alister E. McGrath, *Science & Religion: A New Introduction*, 2nd ed. (Oxford: Wiley-Blackwell, 2010), 93–101.

31 Robert J. Russell, "Does 'The God Who Acts' Really Act? New Approaches to Divine Action in Light of Science," *Theology Today* 54:1 (1997): 43–65; John Polkinghorne, "Physical Process, Quantum Events, and Divine Agency," in *Quantum Mechanics: Scientific Perspectives on Divine Action*, eds. Robert Russell, Philip Clayton, Kirk Wegter-McNelly, and John Polkinghorne (Vatican City and Berkeley, CA: Vatican Observatory, CTNS, 2001), 51; Southgate, "A Test Case: Divine Action," 285. The most important research programme in this regard was the 20-year CTNS/Vatican Observatory cooperative project that produced five volumes subtitled *Scientific Perspectives on Divine Action*, ed. Robert J. Russell, et al.

32 Davies, "Teleology Without Teleology," 151.

33 Davies, "Teleology Without Teleology," 155.

34 Christopher Knight, "Divine Action: A Neo-Byzantine Model," *International Journal for Philosophy of Religion* 58 (2005): 181–199. Knight identifies his own position as "theistic naturalism" and sometimes speaks in the language of secondary causes (see the next section below). Yet, since he closely associates with eighteenth-century deism and eschews the concept of "special providence," he does not belong in the same camp as the neo-Thomists. Knight's views actually show remarkable similarity to those of the liberal Anglican and author of the Ninth Bridgewater Treatise, Charles Babbage, who likewise argued that natural laws could be responsible for apparent miracles. Babbage argued this from a trick programmed into his calculating machine. It would generate a steady series of natural numbers, only to jump unexpectedly out of sequence, even though the jump was programmed. Michael Ruse, "The Relationship between Science and Religion in Britain, 1830–1870," *Church History* 44:4 (December 1975): 505–522, 510–511.

35 Knight, "Divine Action," 185.

36 Non-Interventionist Objective Divine Action.

37 The term "causal joint" was first used, pejoratively, by Austin Farrer in *Faith and Speculation: An Essay in Philosophical Theology* (London: Adam & Charles Black, 1967), 65.

38 Nancey Murphy, "Divine Action in the Natural Order: Buridan's Ass and Schrödinger's Cat," in *Chaos and Complexity: Scientific Perspectives on Divine Action*, eds. Robert Russell, Nancey Murphy, and Arthur Peacocke (Vatican City and Berkeley, CA: Vatican Observatory, CTNS, 1995), 325–358; Thomas F. Tracy, "Particular Providence

and the God of the Gaps," in *Chaos and Complexity: Scientific Perspectives on Divine Action*, eds. Robert Russell, Nancey Murphy, and Arthur Peacocke (Vatican City and Berkeley, CA: Vatican Observatory, CTNS, 1995), 289–324; Thomas F. Tracy, "Creation, Providence, and Quantum Chance," in *Quantum Mechanics: Scientific Perspectives on Divine Action*, eds. Robert Russell, Philip Clayton, Kirk Wegter-McNelly, and John Polkinghorne (Vatican City and Berkeley, CA: Vatican Observatory, CTNS, 2001), 235–258; Russell, "Does 'The God Who Acts' Really Act?" 58; Robert J. Russell, "Natural Theodicy in Evolutionary Context: The Need for an Eschatology of New Creation," in *Theodicy and Eschatology*, eds. Bruce Barber and David Neville (Hindmarsh, Australia: ATF, 2005), 126; Robert J. Russell, "Divine Action and Quantum Mechanics: A Fresh Assessment," in *Quantum Mechanics: Scientific Perspectives on Divine Action*, eds. Robert Russell, Philip Clayton, Kirk Wegter-McNelly, and John Polkinghorne (Vatican City and Berkeley, CA: Vatican Observatory, CTNS, 2001), 314–316.

39 Saunders, *Divine Action*, 132.
40 Saunders, *Divine Action*, 144–156.
41 See Jeffrey Koperski, "God, Chaos, and the Quantum Dice," *Zygon* 35:3 (September 2000): 545–559; Arthur Peacocke, "Some Reflections on 'Scientific Perspectives on Divine Action'," in *Scientific Perspectives on Divine Action: Twenty Years of Challenge and Progress*, eds. Robert J. Russell, Nancey Murphy, and William R. Stoeger, S. J. (Vatican City and Berkeley, CA: Vatican Observatory, CTNS, 2008), 216–217; Polkinghorne, "Physical Process, Quantum Events, and Divine Agency," 182.
42 One good example of this kind of critique is Timothy Sansbury, "The False Promise of Quantum Mechanics," *Zygon* 42:1 (March 2007): 111–121. Defence of the influence of microlevel events on macrolevel structures (that it can be amplified up in meaningful ways) is found in George F. R. Ellis, "Quantum Theory and the Macroscopic World," in *Quantum Mechanics: Scientific Perspectives on Divine Action*, eds. Robert Russell, Philip Clayton, Kirk Wegter-McNelly, and John Polkinghorne (Vatican City and Berkeley, CA: Vatican Observatory, CTNS, 2001), 259–291.
43 Saunders, *Divine Action*, 172. Italics original.
44 Polkinghorne, "Physical Process, Quantum Events, and Divine Agency," 181–190.
45 Polkinghorne, *Science and Providence*, 35.
46 Tracy, "Creation, Providence, and Quantum Chance," 255–257.
47 Keith Ward does not choose between the quantum and chaotic systems, but allows both to be places where God can interact with the world, through non-deterministic systems. Keith Ward, *Divine Action* (London: Collins, 1990), 74–102.
48 Edwards, *How God Acts*, 62–66; William R. Stoeger, S. J., "Conceiving Divine Action in a Dynamic Universe," in *Scientific Perspectives on Divine Action: Twenty Years of Challenge and Progress*, eds. Robert J. Russell, Nancey Murphy, and William R. Stoeger, S. J. (Vatican City and Berkeley, CA: Vatican Observatory, CTNS, 2008), 225–247; Johnson, *Ask the Beasts*, 154–180; Burrell and Moulin, "Albert, Aquinas and Dionysius," 642; David B. Burrell C. S. C., "Creation, Metaphysics, and Ethics," *Faith and Philosophy* 18:2 (April 2001): 204–221.
49 Edwards, *How God Acts*, 62.
50 As noted earlier, I do not find this a strong argument in itself, nor a reason not to hold this model, but it is problematic if it is used to ignore science altogether. See Ritchie, "Dancing Around," 368–371.
51 John Polkinghorne, *Science and Christian Belief: Theological Reflections of a Bottom-Up Thinker* (London: SPCK, 1994), 81–82.
52 Vernon White, *The Fall of a Sparrow: The Concept of Special Divine Action* (Exeter: Paternoster, 1985), 125–142; particularly 134–136.
53 White, *Fall of a Sparrow*, 128–132.
54 Saunders, *Divine Action*, 31.

55 White's attempt to make these distinctions is found in *Fall of a Sparrow*, 139–142.
56 White, *Fall of a Sparrow*, 133–136.
57 White, *Fall of a Sparrow*, 136.
58 A point White acknowledges. *Fall of a Sparrow*, 144.
59 Edwards, *How God Acts*, 63.
60 William R. Stoeger, S. J., "The Big Bang, Quantum Cosmology and creatio ex nihilo," in *Creation and the God of Abraham*, eds. David B. Burrell, Carlo Cogliati, Janet M. Soskice, and William R. Stoeger, S. J. (Cambridge: Cambridge University Press, 2010), 173.
61 Stoeger, "The Big Bang, Quantum Cosmology and creatio ex nihilo," 174.
62 This loss is admitted by Stoeger who continues to view some events through secondary causes as specially revelatory of God's work largely because they are the result of self-choosing individuals or communities who intuit God's purposes and actively pursue them. This does not, therefore, apply to the non-human world. Stoeger, "Conceiving Divine Action in a Dynamic Universe," 245.
63 For a further critique of this position, see Bethany Sollereder, "A Modest Objection: Neo-Thomism and God as a Cause Among Causes," *Theology & Science* 13:3 (2015): 345–353.
64 Brian L. Hebblethwaite, "Providence and Divine Action," *Religious Studies* 14:2 (June 1978), 231.
65 See Gregersen on the problem of uniformitarianism in divine action: "Special Divine Action and the Quilt of Laws," 183–84. Southgate warns: "It is best not to limit God's action to a particular locus – or indeed to focus on efficient causation as the sole way of thinking of God's acting." Southgate, "A Test Case: Divine Action," 299. In the same place, Southgate quotes Thomas Tracy's opinion that "what is needed is not so much a theory of divine action as an array of coherent possibilities that can be called upon as needed to articulate the claims of a particular religious tradition." I hope to present such an array of coherent possibilities later.
66 Christopher Southgate observes, "the divine action debate is ever more markedly being framed not in terms of mechanism but morality" in "A Test Case: Divine Action," 299.
67 Southgate, *Groaning of Creation*, 62. I am not assuming the idea of form relates to the species of the individual as Southgate does. Instead, it may relate to the best form of flourishing that individual can attain.
68 In similar ways, John Haught and Jürgen Moltmann also both speak of the letting-be of creation, but they do so by advocating for the absence or self-restricting of God in creation. Haught calls this kenotic withdrawal, and Moltmann advocates for the kabbalistic notion of simsum. Jürgen Moltmann, *God in Creation: A New Theology of Creation and the Spirit of God*, trans. Margaret Kohl (Minneapolis, MN: Fortress Press, 1993), 88–89; John Haught, *God after Darwin: A Theology of Evolution* (Boulder, CO: Westview, 2000), 47–56. See also the discussion of Ruth Page and *Gelassenheit* in Chapter 3, 73–74.
69 Johnson, *Ask the Beasts*, 150.
70 Precisely what constitutes an individual can sometimes be ambiguous (as in the case with slime mould), but it is not really an important question until a creature has a sense of self, at which point the definition of an individual is usually clear. It is also true that one could conceivably classify the giving of free process/free agency as a general rather than a special divine act. However, since I see it as a particular act of love from God toward the individual, it is better classified as SDA even though something very similar could be conceived under the rubric of GDA, where creatures automatically have this sort of freedom.
71 The patagium itself was likely a genetic anomaly at one point. Humans are sometimes born with similar connective tissues attaching the arms to the body.

72 Ruth Page, *God and the Web of Creation* (London: SCM Press, 1996), 42.
73 Here I diverge from process theism and Thomas Jay Oord's proposals that God is essentially bound to creation.
74 Holmes Rolston III, *Science and Religion: A Critical Survey*, 2nd ed. (West Conshohocken, PA: Templeton Foundation Press, 1987/2006), 140.
75 *Shrek*, DVD, Directed by Andrew Adamson & Vicky Jenson (Glendale, CA: Dream Works, 2001).
76 This is precisely what Michael A. Corey proposes, reviewed in Chapter 3, 51.
77 David Clough, *On Animals*, Vol. 1 of *Systematic Theology* (Edinburgh: T & T Clark, 2012), 124.
78 A classic example of this is found in the life of Julian of Norwich, whose visions of the crucified Christ comfort her in her own physical suffering, and turn her illness into an experience of God's love.
79 Southgate, *Groaning of Creation*, 52. See also Southgate's newer analysis on presence and encouragement in "Does God's Care Make Any Difference? Theological Reflections on the Suffering of God's Creatures," in *Christian Faith and the Earth: Current Paths and Emerging Horizons in Ecotheology*, eds. Ernst M. Conradie, Sigurd Bermann, Celia Deane-Drummond, and Denis Edwards (London: Bloomsbury, T & T Clark, 2014), 110–112.
80 Note the birthing imagery in Romans 8:22.
81 Ian Barbour, *Religion and Science: Historical and Contemporary Issues* (San Francisco: HarperCollins, 1997), 284–300; Barbour, *Religion in an Age of Science: The Gifford Lectures 1989–1991* (London: SCM Press, 1990), 232–234; John B. Cobb, Jr., *God and the World* (Philadelphia: Westminster, 1969); John B. Cobb Jr. and David Ray Griffin, *Process Theology: An Introductory Exposition* (Louisville, TN: Westminster John Knox, 1976), 48–54; McDaniel, *Of God and Pelicans*, 38–39. Haught, *God after Darwin*, 165–184. Historical defenders of this position include Alfred North Whitehead and Charles Hartshorne.
82 McDaniel, *Of God and Pelicans*, 35–41.
83 Barbour, *Religion and Science*, 326.
84 See Chapter 4, 104.
85 Ian Barbour notes that not all aggregates of creation would be considered entities in Whitehead's thought. So an atom could in principle be an entity, but not necessarily a stone. *Religion in an Age of Science*, 224–225.
86 Southgate, *Groaning of Creation*, 2. Italics original.
87 C.f. Neil Messer, "Natural Evil after Darwin," in *Theology after Darwin*, eds. Michael S. Northcott and R. J. Berry (Milton Keynes: Paternoster, 2009), 139–154.
88 In Chapter 6 I will expand on one sense of what this "good" might entail in the form of redemptive eschatological patterns.
89 A longer discussion of altruistic views is found in Chapter 3, 54.
90 See Christopher Southgate's critique along the same lines in "Does God's Care Make Any Difference?" 107–108. Southgate (in this same place) also acknowledges with Coakley that there may be a "natural praeparatio in the process of selection for the potential later heights of saintly human self-sacrifice."
91 Clayton and Knapp, *Predicament of Belief*, 54.
92 Clayton and Knapp, *Predicament of Belief*, 53–54.
93 Clayton and Knapp, *Predicament of Belief*, 62.
94 Clayton and Knapp, *Predicament of Belief*, 63.
95 Clayton and Knapp, *Predicament of Belief*, 63.
96 Clayton and Knapp, *Predicament of Belief*, 61.
97 See the critique in Christopher Southgate's review of *The Predicament of Belief* in *Religious Studies* 49:1 (March 2013): 127.
98 Though a Schleiermacher-type incarnation model could still be held.

99 Southgate, *Groaning of Creation*, 61–62.
100 Southgate, *Groaning of Creation*, 62.
101 Southgate, *Groaning of Creation*, 161.
102 Southgate, *Groaning of Creation*, 63.
103 Robert Farrer Capon, *The Third Peacock: The Problem of God and Evil* In *The Romance of the Word* (Grand Rapids, MI: Eerdmans, 1995), 201.
104 Sallie McFague, *The Body of God: An Ecological Theology* (London: SCM Press, 1993); Grace M. Jantzen, *God's World, God's Body* (London: Darton, Longman and Todd, 1984).
105 Edwards, *How God Acts*, 24.
106 Edwards, *How God Acts*, 26.
107 Edwards, *How God Acts*, 29.
108 Edwards, *How God Acts*, 30.
109 Edwards, *How God Acts*, 31.
110 Edwards, *How God Acts*, 47. It is unclear in Edwards's approach how this coincides with his view that in the Christ-event God is "acting in Jesus, in his words and deeds, in his death and resurrection in a way that is special, specific, and historical." *How God Acts*, 37. Edwards roots his approach to divine action in Christ, yet does not allow the Christ-event as a particular action of God to influence what he later says about how God could act creatively. Niels Gregersen also advocates for this approach, writing "On the view taken here, God cannot act as one factor among others at the level of secondary causes." "Special Divine Action and the Quilt of Laws," 195.
111 Burrell and Moulin, "Albert, Aquinas and Dionysius," 642.
112 I hold here, as do Edwards and Johnson, to an orthodox model of the Incarnation, as advanced in Nicene and Chalcedonian Creeds.
113 I realise that not every aspect of the Incarnation is necessarily representative of divine action. I would not want to assume, for example, that God's action has to be male or Jewish because the particularities of the Incarnation included those aspects of Jesus's life. Embodiment, however, is the main action that is undertaken. How that embodiment took place is of lesser importance than the fact of it happening at all. Therefore, in the Incarnation the embodiment is central, whereas the particularities of that embodiment were contingent. See Wendy Farley, *The Healing and Wounding of Desire: Weaving Heaven and Earth* (Louisville, KY: Westminster John Knox, 2005), 102.
114 Page, *Web of Creation*, 60.
115 Benjamin D. Sommer, *The Bodies of God and the World of Ancient Israel* (Cambridge: Cambridge University Press, 2009).
116 For more, see Terence Fretheim, "The God Who Acts: An Old Testament Perspective," *Theology Today* 54:1 (1997): 6–18; and Nicholas Saunders, *Divine Action and Modern Science*, 1–12.
117 God's incarnation of diverse molecules is pointed out in particular by the advocates of "Deep Incarnation": Niels Gregersen, "Cross of Christ in an Evolutionary World," *dialog* 40:3 (Fall 2001): 192–207, 205; Celia Deane-Drummond, "Who on Earth Is Jesus Christ? Plumbing the Depths of Deep Incarnation," in *Christian Faith and the Earth: Current Paths and Emerging Horizons in Ecotheology*, eds. Ernst M. Conradie, Sigurd Bergmann, Celia Deane-Drummond, and Denis Edwards (London: T & T Clark, 2014), 31–50.
118 Austin Farrer, *Love Almighty and Ills Unlimited* (London: HarperCollins, 1966), 104. Of course, the concept of "Deep Incarnation" would challenge this by pointing out that God did in fact become a brother creature to all of creation.

119 This stands in line with the usual contemporary definition of miracle: a wonder-inspiring occurrence that points to the Kingdom of God, rather than an overthrow of the laws of nature. Padgett, "God and Miracle in An Age of Science," 533–542.

120 See Eleonore Stump's argument concerning human suffering to this effect in *Wandering in Darkness* (Oxford: Clarendon Press, 2010).

121 See Murray, *Nature Red in Tooth and Claw*, 130–192 and the property-consequence GHAs in Chapter 3, 48–50.

122 This is the story as taught by Lao Tzu. Retold by Kenneth Kramer in *World Scriptures: An Introduction to Comparative Religions* (Mahwah, NJ: Paulist, 1986), 118.

123 See the argument about God and time in Chapter 4.

124 An example is that the death of a dinosaur could be directly responsible (in a very long line of causes) for the composition of one of Mozart's symphonies. Without the dinosaur's death, Mozart would not have been born. Therefore, the dinosaur's death has new meaning in light of the beauty and significance of *The Violin Concerto #3*. This will be explored at greater length in Chapter 6.

125 At least, as far as historical records attest.

126 Niels Gregersen, "Cross of Christ in an Evolutionary World," 203.

127 John Swinton, *Dementia: Living in the Memories of God* (Grand Rapids, MI: Eerdmans, 2012), 1–15.

128 Swinton, *Dementia*, 7. Italics original.

129 Similar conclusions have been reached by parents of children with severe illnesses. See Andrew Solomon, *Far from the Tree: A Dozen Kinds of Love* (London: Chatto & Windus, 2013), 167–217; Sarah C. Williams, *The Shaming of the Strong: The Challenge of an Unborn Life* (Vancouver, BC: Regent College, 2007); Frances M. Young, *Face to Face: A Narrative Essay in the Theology of Suffering* (Edinburgh: T & T Clark, 1990).

130 Page, *Web of Creation*, 105.

6 Redemption

Possibilities of redemption

In the last chapter, the themes of divine action moved ever more strongly toward the necessity of redemption for a comprehensive account of theodicy. Without redemption, without the completion of God's work, creation stands without coherence: the story remains unfinished. Nor can the suffering of creation find final resolution without redemption.

The status of non-human animals in the act of redemption has a long history of conflicting views. Scripture gives only a few hints and those are often far from straightforward.[1] Various guesses have also been made in the works of later thinkers. Thomas Aquinas did not think that non-human animals had the aptitude for resurrection because they did not have immortal rational souls.[2] John Wesley, to the contrary, not only thought that non-human animals would be included in the general resurrection, but that their capacities would increase so that they would have the ability to be able to understand the full implications of the gift they would be given:

> May I be permitted to mention here a conjecture concerning the brute creation? What, if it should then please the all-wise, the all-gracious Creator to raise them higher in the scale of beings? What, if it should please him, when he makes us 'equal to angels,' to make them what we are now, – creatures capable of God; capable of knowing and loving and enjoying the Author of their being?[3]

Yet, there has been far less reflection in the tradition on the fate of the non-human world than might be expected or desired. More recently, there has been an increase of speculation on the scope of non-human redemption. In the first part of this chapter, I will explore four contemporary concepts of redemption by analysing the content of redemption (what redemption will look like), the scope of redemption (what creatures will be redeemed), and the motivation of redemption (why those who are redeemed will be redeemed).

What is redemption? Jay McDaniel lays out four possible meanings:

> It can mean (1) freedom from the consequences of sin, in which case it applies almost exclusively to humans. But it can also mean (2) freedom from

what distresses or harms, (3) contribution to lives beyond one's own, and (4) transformation into an improved state of existence.[4]

All of the categories of redemption which follow will exclude definition (1) since it applies (I have argued) only to humans,[5] and all of them will include (2). However, (2) alone is not sufficient. If a creature dies, it is indeed freed from the circumstances that distress or harm it, but it could hardly be considered redeemed. One must not only be *freed from* but also *redeemed to* some reality in which some sort of benefit is seen in the redemption. My focus in this chapter will therefore be primarily on definitions (3) and (4). I will argue that redemption can be parsed along several different complementary lines, but my proposal is that each creature is individually redeemed in relationship to everything else, creating a mosaic of eschatological meaning. The second pelican chick will be given a new life that not only gives it a chance to flourish, but that also creates meaning in the lives of those to whom it is in relationship.

The content of redemption can be divided up into two categories: this-worldly and other-worldly. These can be further divided into four sub-categories: in this-worldly, as immanent or ecological; in other-worldly, as objective or classical.

Immanent redemption

This-worldly redemption, as the name implies, refuses to see the redemption of suffering as occurring in some distant time or place, or in another dimension or world order altogether. Its proponents do not think that redemption is an eschatological category, but a present one. Ruth Page is a paradigmatic example of the first sub-category, immanent redemption. Page finds redemption in the present moment, a notion she calls "Teleology Now!" Page writes:

> Neither the purposes of God nor the judgment and apotheosis of creation have to wait for some end-time when the books will be balanced. Rather, they are continually happening now, from moment to moment, and from possibility to possibility . . . when God is believed to be present, then every moment becomes eschatological.[6]

Like a song or a dance, the meaning of the activity is found in the doing of it, not in arriving at its end.[7] Once a song is finished, there is no further scope for redemption – no way in which early faults can be made up. It is finished. However, while a song is still being played, there may be scope for redemption within the song itself. Imagine a jazz trio composed of a master musician and two novices. As they play, the novices make outright mistakes, interrupting the flow and progression of the music with discordant, unintended notes made worse by bad timing. In response, the master musician improvises so that these mistakes become intentional thematic foci later in the song. The maestro wraps the mistakes into resolutions and appropriate timings so that what was an unintentional mistake becomes part of the necessary structure of the song. For Page, the content of redemption is in the immediate possibilities of relationship offered by the creative, dynamic nature of the world. "As far as creation is concerned," she writes, "the Kingdom of God is the synthesis of those moments where freedom and love become actual, while the achievement of these purposes of God for the world are always among current possibilities."[8] The scope of immanent redemption is broad: all things in relationship are offered redemption simply by their participation in life, so no creature is left out.

One problem is that Page's view does not actually guarantee any of McDaniel's four definitions of redemption, and so one might ask whether she is advancing a view of redemption at all. Her thought leans toward the idea that redemption is always offered in new moment-to-moment possibilities, but is not always realised. The unscripted ending of creaturely narratives always offers the chance of redemption, and where that possibility is seized, it becomes a moment of immediate redemptive power, as well as a place where future redemption can be reaped. When this happens that moment becomes a place where love is actualised and freedom from harms and distress are realised.

Page does not hold entirely to a this-worldly view, as she links the concept of redemption with an eternal "harvest of creation" in the joy of God. Present redemptive moments are caught up into God's very being and are preserved. Acts of selfishness are judged as evil by falling into oblivion. In this way, Page holds two views on redemption: her immanent redemption and a form of objective immortality. Together, they gather everything into the scope of redemption except for those instances "where there is no concurrence, or where there is no renunciation of consuming selfishness, [because] there is nothing to harvest."[9] The motivation of Page's scheme is clear: "A distant teleology goes with belief in a distant God who will sort everything out in the end."[10] Immanent redemption is found in the logic of a radically immanent God, even if this is sometimes at the cost of the individual.

There is much to be admired in Page's view. The insistence that redemption should not be relegated only to some hoped-for future centres on the Kingdom of God as a present in-breaking reality.[11] It opens up ways in which God is currently at work, and helps picture a God who is immanent, and therefore can co-suffer with creation. Still, Page's immanent redemption alone eliminates the chance of any future hope for those whose lives have held little but suffering and neglect, where relationships were perhaps forged, but not given time to be fruitful. Even with the addition of her objective "harvest of creation," the whole of creation is not redeemed. Evil is not redeemed in the senses of definitions (3) and (4) – it is not transformed into something of benefit – it is only forgotten or made *nihil*. But the story of Jesus is not that the passion of the cross is forgotten, but that the tragedy of the event is transformed by the glory of the resurrection. Page's view of redemption does not help one understand how this happens.

Ecological redemption

Ecological redemption, the other category in this-worldly redemption, is a view described in the work of Holmes Rolston III. He suggests that while there may be no redemption for particular individuals who die in ways full of pain and suffering, their lives will be redeemed in the ongoing fruitfulness and creativity of the evolutionary process.[12] For example, the second white pelican chick lives a short life full of neglect, but, because it does, white pelicans as a species continue to exist since they are almost always able to raise a chick into adulthood. More than that, the body of the chick who dies is not wasted: it is eaten by a passing predator, or decomposed by a variety of insects and microorganisms that then go on to feed other organisms. Its death allows the evolutionary process to continue. When translated into theological terms, the evils are redeemed by the ongoing story of evolution.[13] Since all life participates in the evolutionary process, the scope of this redemption is perfectly universal. Unlike Page's system, there is no unredeemed act lost in judgement or excluded from the harvest of creation, no wasted life, because every event ripples into the far distant future where it finds redemption in the evolutionary narrative. Rolston's view of redemption is motivated by the fact that it can be equally affirmed by both theologians and biologists: one need do nothing more than to look at the history of evolutionary development to see the blueprint of redemption. The model does not depend on any future act of God being different from what God has already historically done in the creative process of evolution.

Rolston, like Page, does not rule out the possibility of other-worldly redemption, but does not think other-worldly models are the primary loci of redemption. Where Page chooses an objective immortality model, Rolston speculates instead about classic redemption: "Perhaps there is some eschatological sense in which there will, in the further future, come an ultimate redemption of both heaven and earth, of culture and of nature. I am not sure I know what that means."[14] His preference seems to be for a more metaphorical interpretation of the biblical language: "If we place Paul's image [of the body as a seed of resurrection] on an evolutionary scale, you can plant a protozoan and get, a billion years later, a person. If we plant persons, and wait a million years, what might we get?"[15]

There is a great deal of value in Rolston's approach, but it does not give much hope of redemption for the suffering individuals themselves. They are part of a bigger scheme, but they do not find any personal redemption. This is a critique raised by Christopher Southgate and Jay McDaniel.[16] However, it is rebutted by Lisa Sideris who considers their concern for the individual anthropocentric – projecting on to non-human animals the sort of justice we would wish to see in human communities.[17] I disagree with Sideris because I think she, ironically, falls into her own trap of anthropomorphism. Neither Southgate nor McDaniel ever raise the complaint that the suffering of individuals in the evolutionary process is a matter of "injustice." Instead, they point out the difficulty of reconciling the care of God for these creatures in their suffering with God's power and apparent ability to alleviate their pain. They do not defend that non-human animals have a right to not suffer, they only point out that God's benevolence and omnipotence are called into question by the tragedy of sentient suffering and the untimely death of so many.

Rolston's approach also raises the question of what kind of redemption would be available if the ongoing story were to end quite suddenly. If we plant persons, and they plant enough hydrogen bombs or release enough carbon dioxide, it may be that in a million years we only get a completely desolate planet devoid of life. What hope is there then for ecological redemption? It seems that if redemption is God's work, it must have a reality that cannot be trumped by cosmic accident or human stupidity and greed.

Objective immortality

Moving on to other-worldly redemption, John Haught represents the category of objective immortality.[18] Usually advanced by process theists, rooted in the work of Charles Hartshorne,[19] Haught's proposal is that while the individual creature does not experience a new life, "everything whosoever that occurs in evolution – all the suffering and tragedy as well as the emergence of new life and intense beauty – is 'saved' by being taken eternally into God's own feeling of the world."[20] In another place, he likens God to a foundational registry upon which all things that occur – all things that have truth – are written and therefore preserved.[21] The scope of this redemption is universal, but, as with the other forms of redemption, it does not do much for the individual. Haught, contrary to other supporters of objective immortality, acknowledges that a fulfilment of human striving, at the least, would entail that "beyond our own deaths the pursuit of meaning, truth, goodness and beauty that orients our specifically human lives would be open to a conscious, experiential fulfilment."[22] However, the rest of his writing seems to say that this conscious, experiential fulfilment does not belong to the individual but to God. It is God who experiences the bringing together of all things into a harmonious whole: "In God's assimilation of the events that make up our personal lives, biological evolution and cosmic process, things that appear irredeemable from our narrow perspective may contribute to the limitless depth and breadth of God's own life."[23]

Haught's motivation is to find a hope beyond death, but he argues that where Christianity has traditionally anticipated "personal, subjective survival beyond death . . . in an age of science, it has become more difficult than ever to believe in such a prospect."[24] Haught finds a solution that acknowledges and soothes human existential angst while maintaining the scientific predictions of the end of life in the universe. Haught's goal stands in stark contrast with the interest in God's goodness to non-human creatures themselves that is found amongst thinkers like Southgate and McDaniel.

Ernst Conradie presents a slightly modified version of objective immortality, which he calls "material inscription."[25] In this model, every act throughout history is being inscribed into the multidimensional material reality of the cosmos. Like writing in a book, the story of creation is being written – not in a book with words – but on the three dimensions of space and the added dimension of time. God, from the supra-time/space dimension of eternity, encapsulates and holds these dimensions (and thus everything in them) in existence and they can be retrieved in the eschaton.[26] Evil events can be judged and put forever away, while good events can be brought forward and celebrated. Since these are inscribed in four dimensions (the same number of dimensions they initially took place in, rather than a two-dimensional video), the "retrieval of these events would be as real and concrete as the original lived experiences."[27]

Insofar as Conradie's proposal involves the re-telling of the world's narrative in redemptive terms, it has similarities to my own proposal. In addition, Conradie allows for a subjective experience of life for those who are redeemed: the re-playing of the celebrated parts of life will be just as real as they are now. While Conradie does not dwell on non-human resurrection, if everything that has ever happened is inscribed as outlined earlier, then one can safely assume that every non-human being is also present in this redemptive form. What is not clear in Conradie's picture is how healing can be extended to those who only experience neglect and suffering. The insurance pelican chick, for example, would not have many, if any, moments worthy of being recalled since it has had no experience of care, contentment, or peace. Conradie indicates that for humans, through the "mediation of our own embodied human consciousness,"[28] there is scope for healing in those instances of "unfinished business" on earth. It is unclear how this can be the case – even for humans – without novel experiences that go beyond objective immortality: how can business be wrapped up by endlessly re-experiencing the same event? It is even more unclear how this sort of resolution could be achieved for the non-human animal creation. What is missing from the pelican chick's redeemed life on the Conradie model is precisely the experience of flourishing that was alien to its earthly life. The new life ought to include some sort of possibility for extending to it a fully flourishing life.

Haught's views also struggle with explaining how the evil of events can be transformed. If only all that is good, true, and beautiful is registered into the life of God, there is no concept of what happens to the evil. Redemption seems to be little more than a sort of universal divine nostalgia.[29] The second pelican chick, whose life consists of neglect, starvation, and death does not seem to have much worth saving, while the life of the successful older chick, who has already had the joyful experiences of care and growth, would have much more to contribute into God's life. The lack of flourishing in the second pelican's life is not solved by objective immortality: it is enshrined eternally.

Classical resurrection

The fourth model is the classical view of redemption: the resurrection of the body. This view holds that there will be a subjective experience of harmony, peace, and new life by individuals after death. It has been developed most prominently by Jay McDaniel, Christopher Southgate, and Trent Dougherty, but is held to various degrees by others as well.[30] It is not traditional that this form of redemption – physical resurrection – should extend to the non-human creation. Here, perhaps more than in the other three categories, the scope of redemption is closely linked to the theologian's motivations for redemption.

For Paul Griffiths, for example, non-human animals might be present in the new creation only because they are a benefit to human well-being, and not because they have any place there on their own merit.[31] Therefore, it is not necessary for all creatures to be resurrected, but only those needed for human enrichment. For C. S. Lewis and John Polkinghorne, the motivation for non-human resurrection is that some creatures (particularly those we tame) have been "humanised" by interaction with people.[32] Therefore, non-human animals are involved in the resurrection by merit of their link to personhood in and through humanity. I am tempted to call this option the "Velveteen Rabbit" model of redemption.[33] What about all the non-human animals not loved by humans into being "real"? Lewis only confesses ignorance as to the fate of those who do not have this happy link with humanity, while Polkinghorne speculates that perhaps there will be representatives of other species there as well, either for human or divine benefit.[34] Polkinghorne has argued that in terms of resurrection, with the exception of pets, "animals are indeed to be valued, but more in the type than in the token. . . . I think it likely, therefore, that there will be horses in the world to come, but not every horse that has ever lived."[35]

For Christopher Southgate, the motivation for a renewed life is threefold:

> specific scriptural texts, a general sense that human life at its richest will be set in the context of relationship with other creatures, and the need to marry a sense of the goodness of God with the evident lack of blessedness in the lives of many creatures.[36]

Since the scriptural texts give little detail of the new life, the second two concerns are the primary informants. Southgate argues that the human need for relationship does not require that all creatures be included in the redeemed life, and that the goodness of God can be satisfied with the redemption of all the creatures that consciously suffered. Therefore, Southgate concedes that simple organisms, those that possess "little distinctive individual experience or agency" might only be represented in the eschaton by a type.[37] However, he goes on to warn against such an attitude towards all non-human creatures, especially the higher animals that are centres of consciousness. Of these higher animals, redemption is most urgently needed for those who have not experienced any flourishing.[38] In cases where there is little suffering and much flourishing, Southgate advises a position of bold generosity and trust that there will be, in God's grace, abundant provision for all.[39]

Trent Dougherty takes the question of classical resurrection one step farther: not only will suffering creatures experience new subjective life, but they will experience a transition from sentience to personhood in such a way that they will be able to consciously and willingly embrace their own part in the history of the world, even in their suffering. Dougherty writes: "the whole edifice of exclusion of animals from the Irenaean understanding is founded upon the *current* lack of meaning-making properties [in non-human animals]. But of course what import this has in the long run depends on what happens in the long run."[40] While non-human animals cannot make meaning of their suffering now, Dougherty proposes that in the afterlife all creatures will be given the chance to develop the cognitive capacities that allow for a soul-making theodicy. To use John Wesley's words quoted previously, non-human animals will be raised "higher in the scale of beings," and this will allow them to willingly embrace the suffering they underwent and accept the part they played in the evolutionary drama. Dougherty goes on to suggest a helpful analogy between non-human animals and human babies. Babies experience various types of pain that they cannot explain at the time, but could later be grateful for (Dougherty offers the example of male circumcision, I offer vaccination shots). However, babies need to grow into their potential cognitive capacity in order to make sense of the pain. Dougherty's point is that their later capacity for understanding and embracing the pain they went through as a child offers a way to defeat the experience of suffering in the life of the individual. It is the same individual who suffered who also has the possibility of making meaning from that suffering. Dougherty does not clearly state the scope of redemption, but his arguments are primarily about those non-human animals that have enough sentience to suffer.

The advantage of Southgate and Dougherty's approaches, as opposed to the positions of Griffiths, Polkinghorne, and Lewis, is that they finally address the question of the suffering non-human individual. There is full redemption for those that suffer innocently. But I wonder if it goes far enough?

From my perspective, the scope of redemption is not shaped by compensation, or by anthropocentric concerns, or even from the concern for defeating suffering and evil, but by the motivation of God's love. The scope of redemption is universal because a universal redemption is required by the ubiquitous love of God. If what I have argued in Chapter 4 about the irreplaceability of the beloved has any traction, then the main issue at stake is simply "Does God love each creature?" If God does love each creature individually, then a creature cannot be adequately represented by a token or a type, no matter how little distinction lies between it and another individual of the same species. God's interest with *that* individual includes a unique history and a unique relationship in time and space that cannot be held by any other. Therefore, I propose that not only will non-human animals exist in the resurrection, but that every individual of every species will be included, because of God's great love for each. I am led toward Moltmann's position, that "true hope must be universal, because its healing future embraces every individual and the whole universe. If we were to surrender hope for as much as one single creature, for us God would not be God," for God would not be the lover of every being.[41]

One of the regular objections to conjecturing that every creature will be raised is that it might seem redundant. "Surely," it is thought, "there could not be any use for every bacteria, or every beetle, that has ever lived to be raised?" John Wesley once addressed this very question:

> If it be objected to all this, (as very probably it will,) "But of what use will those creatures be in that future state?" I answer this by another question, What use are they of now? If there be (as has commonly been supposed)

eight thousand species of insects, who is able to inform us of what use seven thousand of them are? If there are four thousand species of fishes, who can tell us of what use are more than three thousand of them? If there are six hundred sorts of birds, who can tell of what use five hundred of those species are? If there be four hundred sorts of beasts, to what use do three hundred of them serve? Consider this; consider how little we know of even the present designs of God; and then you will not wonder that we know still less of what he designs to do in the new heavens and the new earth.[42]

The thousands of species of Wesley's day have been expanded to the tens of millions today.[43] There is also a better answer for the use of such diversity: they exist because of the evolutionary process. However, Wesley makes a useful admonition that one should not be too quick to evaluate a creature's worth to God by reference to its use to humans. The new life will be theocentric, not anthropocentric, and so the theological imagination should be shaped by the abundance of God's love and the (already evident) surprising scope of God's creativity. Nor (to meet another common objection), in a world without death or decay, can there be a lack of space or resources for those numberless creatures. There is no reason to think that all should have to co-exist within the present terrestrial boundaries, nor that the present laws of physics which enforce those boundaries will apply.[44]

I want to offer one cautionary note about whether or not the new life offered to creatures is understood as compensation for suffering. Southgate implies that, to some extent, redemption is to be thought of as compensation, since it is meant to answer the question of the goodness of God in light of a suffering world.[45] He suggests that redemption is most important in the lives of those creatures who experienced little or no flourishing, and leaves it an open question as to whether or not such creatures might fade away after a period of heavenly flourishing "if the new life is only a compensation for previous lack of fulfilment."[46] McDaniel also holds that the new life is offered so "that they [unfulfilled creatures] live until they enjoy a fulfilment of their needs as creatures."[47] Yet, biblically at least, redemption (whether earthly or heavenly) is always seen as a gift of grace, not as compensation. To suggest that God owes a certain quality of life, and then has to make up for what was not received (as the concept of "compensation" implies) is to mistake the gift of being for an entitlement. In contrast, seeing redemption as the free gift of God is to avoid schemes of recompense while still answering the objection about the goodness of God. I agree with Dougherty that: "justice is not enough for a *loving* God . . . what is needed is the *defeat* of animal suffering."[48] Redemption is far more than compensation, and the one who receives redemption will be more than compensated for their sufferings. But it would be a grave mistake to see redemption as a mere balancing of the scales of justice. That would be to turn gift into transaction; love into economics.

I have explored four models of redemption: immanent, ecological, objective, and classical. Many of the proposals that have been described do not belong entirely to one sort or another. Both Rolston and Haught speculated about the possibility of classical redemption. Denis Edwards, who writes movingly on redemption, also combines several different views. His model, which he calls "inscription in the life-giving Spirit of God" (in contrast to Conradie's material inscription) has five points:

1   *The future of creation remains obscure and shrouded in mystery.* The promise does not give a clear view of the future.[49]
2   *Individual creatures are inscribed in the eternal divine life through the Holy Spirit.* The Spirit's current embrace of all creatures is the promise and the means of their inclusion in the divine life.[50]
3   *Individual Creatures find Healing and Fulfilment in Christ.* The judgement of Christ assures us that no good thing will be lost, but all will be redeemed in Christ. The scope is universal.[51]
4   *Redemption in Christ will be specific to each kind of creature.* With McDaniel and Southgate, Edwards affirms that in redemption "God relates to each creature on its own terms."[52]
5   *Some individual creatures may find redemption in the living memory and the eternal life of the Trinity and the Communion of Saints.* Some creatures may share in physical resurrection, while others may be simply remembered by God and the Communion of Saints and find a sort of resurrection in that way.[53]

Edwards combines elements of immanent redemption (the present embrace of the Spirit), with objective immortality (being held in the memory, or inscribed into the divine life), and classical redemption (that some may be physically resurrected). These models are not mutually exclusive, and can be pieced together – nested – into resonant images of the profound mystery of redemption. The next section will explore my own proposal for how various models of redemption can form a compound whole.

The fractal mosaic of redemption

I want to suggest a picture of how three of these different models of redemption can work together to give a richer picture of God's final work. Immanent, ecological, and classical resurrection models can be combined in the image of a fractal mosaic.[54] Most people are familiar with photo mosaics: those computer-generated images where each pixel of a large photograph is actually another whole photograph. Together, hundreds or thousands of pictures combine into a greater picture, which may or may not be related to the component parts. The photo mosaic preserves meaning on different levels, and one level is not diminished by being part of another.

It is, perhaps, helpful to compare this picture to another classic eschatological picture: the tapestry. According to the tapestry image, all events and all creatures are like threads in a giant tapestry that God is weaving. While everything is a mess of knots now, God will one day flip over the carpet and reveal the fabulous design that was being woven the whole time.[56] The problem is that a thread is

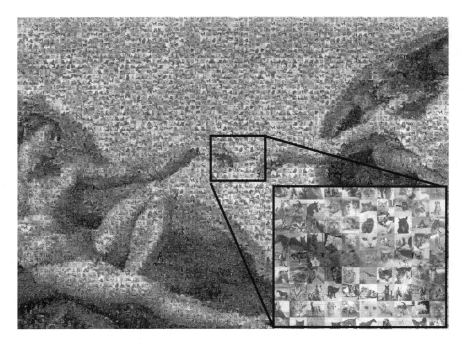

Figure 6.1 A photographic mosaic[55]

not worth very much, nor is one thread very different from another. In the photo mosaic, each pixel is a whole in itself, and has a unique meaning, composition, subject, and so on. Each is a valuable whole in itself. It likewise contributes to part of a greater whole once it has been suitably arranged, but is not reducible to that. Another advantage of the photo mosaic is that it is not limited to two levels. Each pixel could itself be a mosaic, or the larger picture could also form a pixel of a yet greater mosaic. Numerous levels of meaning all operate at once. A third difference is that the tapestry model assumes that the final "picture," the final meaning, is already inherent in events as they unfold: if a person could flip over the tapestry now, they would see the pattern being woven. The photo mosaic model does not assume that the final meaning is somehow present in the disparate events of history, but allows future events to create new meaning. Meaning is not present until the mosaic is assembled. As Ted Peters and Martinez Hewlett write: "It is the divine act of redemption that determines what creation will have meant, and this can be determined only eschatologically." [57]

Three levels of redemption combine in the fractal mosaic. All creatures, during their lives, are creating a picture, from the greatest human to the humblest bacterium. This is the first level of redemption, Page's immanent level: each creature standing in relationship with others, creating overlapping narratives that influence one another. Zoom out far enough, and one begins to see Rolston's level of ecological redemption emerge from the complex interaction of these first relationships. The individual life of each creature contributes to the beauty and wholeness of the ecological mosaic and the still larger mosaic of evolutionary development itself. At the end of time, these mosaics are disassembled. Yet, out of these former identities – these former pictures – God resurrects all creatures and assembles them into a final picture of harmonious life: the peaceable kingdom of eternity. This is the level of classical resurrection. Each creature that died will have a new, personally experienced life restored to it in a new body, in community with a whole new creation. It is the general resurrection on a cosmic scale.

Throughout earthly history, God's continual work of redemption is to arrange each higher level out of the components of the lower levels in such a way that each higher level shows a picture of redemption. The suffering of the individual does contribute to ecological meanings, and ecological meanings give to the overall narrative of evolution. In this fashion, each upward level carries the self-similar signature of God's redemptive purposes, and the whole image becomes a fractal of grace.[58] At the end of history, the level of eschatological creation is remade, and it takes apart and remakes the mosaic entirely. So, everything is old: it is still composed of the same pictures that have been forming meaning all the way along, and incorporates the higher-level images that were themselves mosaics during history. Yet, everything is new: every picture, every creature, every ecosystem, every relationship, is placed in a new arrangement that faithfully captures, redeems, and completes their experience. This redemption, this participation in the peaceable kingdom, is fully experienced by each creature.

How will creatures live in this new community? Will the lion lay down with the lamb? Or will there be, as Southgate suggests, an eternal ecosystem "involving an experience for the redeemed prey-animal that delights in the beauty and flourishing of the predator, and vice versa?"[59] Southgate suggests that the lion may still pursue the gazelle, yet the hunt will not involve terror or pain. Or, perhaps the lion will stalk and pounce, but without the use of claws, so that the lethal hunt becomes a game of play. Perhaps the gazelle, equally redeemed, will be perfectly able to avoid the lion, and so the hunt and flight will simply go on forever in a chase of play. Clough rejects these possibilities entirely and insists that the new creation must involve the loss of those attributes that bring harm to others.[60] I suggest (playfully) a middle way: predators keep the same skills and the same instincts, thus ensuring continuity of essential aspects of identity, but the object of them changes. No longer are other creatures the victims of these instincts, but the instincts are fulfilled in other activities. An analogy could be human sports: the same teamwork, strength, skill and planning that once went into hunting trips are now used in sports activities where the intent is no longer to kill for survival, but to enjoy. In fact, having watched Simone Biles's gravity-defying gymnastics routines in the Rio 2016 Olympics, it is fair to say that sport can allow a far greater expression of human capacity than hunting ever did or could have.

Lions playing sports with gazelles may seem a stretch of the imagination, but it is no more a stretch than resurrection itself, and rather less a stretch than straw-eating lions. Perhaps all the skills, instincts, and strength of all creatures will be focussed entirely on the pursuit and praise of God, who cannot be harmed by claw or fang. However one might want to marry the continuities and discontinuities of the redeemed life, the fractal mosaic image addresses important questions about how each life is related to the models of its own redemption.

For objective immortality, the future existence is completely discontinuous from the present life. The picture mosaic shows how the classical redemption incorporates the present reality, as the "picture" of the creature's life now is used to create the new creation. In objective immortality, the creature does not retain a body or have any centre of self any longer. There is no continuity between the creature and its redemptive form. Similarly, an ecological approach to redemption cuts ties between the present self-conscious experience of a creature and the redemption that they find in ecological harmonies in later evolutionary development. Those later harmonies may share some genetic material with the creature that died, or molecules of their body, but no experiential link is maintained. Therefore, although the life is not wasted in an ecological model, there is no experience of redemption for the individual itself.

The picture mosaic tries to illustrate how each life, past and present, is actually a primary building block of ecological harmonies and of the new life to come. God could not have created the larger mosaics without all the previous compositions. So the suffering of all creatures contributes directly to those redemptive outcomes, and each life has a greater meaning than is apparent from seeing the life in isolation. A creature's death has more meaning when it is understood in the context of evolutionary development. The process re-contextualises the suffering so that senseless loss is not, after all, wasted. It is a picture of glory directly related to what came before.

Because each greater level of meaning is directly dependent on the levels below, the glories of the whole are reflected back, are directly attributable, to each component as well. Every hurt, every broken life, every life cut short by a predator or a natural disaster will be used to create this new kingdom, and each creature will find their suffering a source of glorification, just as the wounds of Christ become marks of honour in the resurrection. I imagine that the loving attention of God to each individual in the resurrected life will communicate peace, love, and joy to them, in whatever capacity is appropriate to each. Each creature will directly and subjectively participate in the new picture of the peaceable kingdom that they themselves helped to create. So, the suffering of the individual is not only instrumental to the wider relationships of ecology and history, but has a direct feedback into the life of the one who suffered. I share a great deal of sympathy here with Trent Dougherty, whose system of theodicy relies upon individual creatures defeating the evil in their life by a personal reconciliation with their part in the suffering of life.[61] He does not assert meticulous providence, where each disvalue has a particular justification, but rather defends:

> The global good God aims at did not require that particular evil to have occurred, but it entailed or made likely that something relevantly similar would occur. Still, that very pain of that very creature – assuming we

have personal identity established – will be considered, on my view, by the creature who suffered it as to whether it – and the whole of which it is a constituent – is something they ultimately accept as an integral part of a very good life.[62]

I agree that particular disvalues do not often occur for the particular good of the one who suffers, but are instrumental for the whole of which it is a constituent. Where my model is slightly different from Dougherty's is that the meaning of a very good life is a gift given by God in an act of eschatological creativity.

The image of a photo mosaic may also be conceived in dynamic terms, as a video mosaic.[63] Each creature's life is a video that, combined with others, makes a large-scale video. Of course, in real life, creatures' life narratives are not carefully acted and scripted pieces, but are rather dynamic real-time improvisations. They are narratives that are being built, not simply pictures taken at one point in time. The course of each individual video, as well as the large-scale videos, are created as each of the actors explores his or her own freedom and response to divine lure in his or her own capacity. God works with the texture and reality of each of these individual narratives and works them into the larger scale ecosystem video which is influenced (but not determined) by each pixel of its make-up, and so on, up through history and the various levels of meaning we can imagine. God interacts at each level of the mosaic,[64] luring and creating relationships between disparate narratives to bring about God's purposes at every level in redemptive form.

The picture of redemption as a dynamic video mosaic depicts, in imaginative terms, how small stories could build up into a meta-narrative without sacrificing the individual uniqueness and worth of each story. It imagines how this-worldly and other-worldly models of redemption can be held together. A single creature's narrative – a centre of worth in itself – contributes up into an ecological narrative. That ecological narrative is one smaller part of the world history narrative, which forms its own mosaic. Each of these levels contributes to God's ultimate composition of the new creation.[65]

Ernst Conradie recognises the ongoing and interactive nature of our life narratives:

> My own life story is not completed with my death. My story continues as long as my life is still honored in the memory of subsequent generations and as long as the material impact of my work is still evident. . . . However, even then the story has not reached its narrative conclusion. My story forms part of the larger (hi)story of the particular genealogy, culture, species, planet, and galaxy in which I participate. My history will in this sense be completed only when the history of the cosmos comes to an end.[66]

Conradie points out that individual stories are not complete on their own. Instead, stories can gain new meaning with the occurrence of new events. Stories of suffering are transformed by subsequent stories into narratives of God's love and power. The example of the cross is central here: the innocent suffering of Jesus on the cross is tragic. Yet, within the context of salvation history and the resurrection, the event of the cross becomes the focal point of heavenly worship:

> 'You [Jesus] are worthy to take the scroll
> and to open its seals,
> for you were slaughtered and by your blood you ransomed for God
> saints from every tribe and language and people and nation;
> you have made them to be a kingdom and priests serving our God,
> and they will reign on earth.' . . .
> 'Worthy is the Lamb that was slaughtered
> to receive power and wealth and wisdom and might
> and honour and glory and blessing!'[67]

If, as Rolston says, the creation is "cruciform,"[68] then it is cruciform in this sense: the stories of the innocent suffering of creatures will be transfigured into narratives of glory, and these narratives will be reflected back on the individual by being honoured through God's love, attention, and communication, just as Jesus's suffering was transfigured in the resurrection and honoured by the Father's glorification of the Son. I could, to use poetic imagination, say that God will tell the redemptive narrative of creation to each creature in light of its life, thus honouring it and bringing it glory.

The result of this type of perspective is that the individual and the "greater whole" are not set against each other competitively, as is so often the case in reasoning about suffering and redemption. The suffering of the individual is not brushed aside in light of the "greater good" or justified by merely pointing to some eschatological order that will make sense of it all. Some good is found directly in the life of the creature itself: its participation in life and in surrounding relationships. The individual pixel – that is, the narrative of the here and now of each creature – is kept in sharp focus as a centre of worth. All its complexity and meaning is maintained. At the same time, a view of ongoing, ever-building, mosaic narratives allows a glimpse into the possibilities of what impact a life might have ontologically, as its actions ripple through the course of history.

The relationship of the present earthly existence to the future new creation existence is one of continuity. We are physical now, we shall be physical then. We exist in relationship now, we shall exist in relationship then. The new creation reality is precisely the present reality extended and transformed into that future reality in such a way that a different reality is created. In Chapter 5, I explored how one way of understanding God's participation in the world is through the shaping of meaning. The new creation mosaic is the final outworking of God's shaping of meaning. God brings new and different meaning to events by placing them within the context of other events. By arranging the pixels of individual creaturely narratives into a larger picture with other narratives, a whole new meaning is created that is not inherent in the lower level of photos. It is because of God's work at various levels that new meanings that emerge are ones of heavenly glory rather than of hellish despair.

In short, as each narrative joins other narratives, the composite meaning of what is seen can change. In a photo mosaic, one pixel may be a picture of a cat. Yet, in the larger scale picture, it forms part of a human finger. In yet another larger scale, the human finger forms part of an icon of the Trinity. Each level forms a whole that contains its own meaning. The meaning of the arrangement, colour, and shade of each image changes depending on the scale. Similarly, God takes the multi-levelled world narratives of tragedy and triumph and arranges them into ever-redemptive forms, changing their meaning. No suffering, then, is left unredeemed, and each individual's experience in the larger whole becomes an experience of redemption. These upper levels of meaning are not automatically generated from the lower levels: God carefully constructs them. One could use the same set of photographs to create a mosaic of Raphael's "The Transfiguration" or one of Heironymous Bosch's disturbing images of hell. It is God's eschatological work that creates one instead of the other.

An example

What would a concrete historical example look like? Some 65 million years ago, dinosaurs were the dominant species on earth. Each creature had its relationships, its narratives of flourishing or suffering. At Page's level, each creature made its own contribution to the make-up of the earth. At the end of the Cretaceous period, a meteorite hit the Yucatan peninsula causing climate change and wide-spread environmental disruption.[69] Dinosaurs could not survive the changes and were wiped out, while mammals, which until that time had been minor players in earth's history, suddenly flourished in the new environments without the competition of the dinosaurs. When dinosaurs went extinct, their absence caused gaping holes in the ecological level of the mosaic. Other creatures filled those holes, and the ecological narrative continued through the narratives of mammals and birds, building into Rolston's level of redemption.

The meteorite was a major plot turn in the narratives. The plot of the second-level ecological mosaic took a turn toward the diversification of mammals, which eventually ended up in the emergence of *Homo sapiens* and, centrally, in the incarnation of God in the person of Jesus Christ. In one sense, then, the event of Christ taking on human flesh is attributable in part to the extinction of the dinosaurs that allowed for the emergence of mammals – an attribution that it is only possible to make in retrospect. The story of Christ is tied up with the meaning of the life of a long-extinct dinosaur.

The essential point to grasp is that the meaning of an individual dinosaur's life was not fixed when it died. All that finished was the composition of its own small narrative pixel. How that pixel would then contribute to other levels of meaning is something still under development. Its life holds new meaning with every passing day. As human stories continue its story, there is an added providential twist, because in each act of divine lure in the present – and in the choices that are made today – the open possibilities of new meaning in the life of a now long-dead dinosaur are either realised or closed. The wonder of human architecture, the transcendence of music, or the capacity of human love are all bound up with the meaning of the death of past creatures we never knew.

The concept can also be expressed as a counterfactual: had the dinosaurs not gone extinct, Bach might never have been born. The world would never have experienced his transcendent music. Instead, because of the extinction of the dinosaurs creating the foundation for contemporary stories (the birth of Bach), present stories expand upon and enrich the outcomes of the dinosaurs' stories (they lived in a world that eventually produced Bach's music). Each story serves the others, and while living creatures benefit now from their contributions, the dinosaurs will experience the fullness of life they contributed to in the new life. By merit of the dinosaurs' extinction humans are here, and our retrospective vision allows us to interpret their deaths as having been meaningful in a way that did not exist at that time. Other equally meaningful and fruitful possibilities of redemption along the road of time were, no doubt, *not* explored in order that the human road might be.

God's work of redemption is to continually interact with the world in order to see that good is realised. As a moment occurs, the narrative lines leading up to it converge and are either enriched with new meaning or diminished by tragedy in the passing event. God's present action is constantly working to redeem the lives of the past by leading creation toward ends that will reflect back greater glory on the individuals now passed away; a glory that they will experience (in whatever way is most appropriate to them) in the new creation.

An analogy to this ongoing sense of redemption may be drawn from the end of Hebrews 11. After the long line of heroes of the faith is listed, the author states: "Yet all these, though they were commended for their faith, did not receive what was promised, since God had provided something better so that they would not, without us, be made perfect."[70] The passage goes straight on from this statement into the paraenetic portion of the epistle, beginning with, "Therefore, since we are surrounded by such a great cloud of witnesses let us," followed by instructions on how to live.[71] The saints of the Hebrew Bible recounted in the chapter had lived and died long before, but the author of Hebrews seems to think that they cannot be made perfect without the actions and faith of current believers. Although the saints are long since dead, part of the promise of their lives is realised in the present; a possibility of fulfilment that would not come to fruition if present believers chose not to "lay aside every weight and the sin that clings so closely."[72]

Another example might be how the legacy of Abraham is enriched by the later reality of Christ. The Church does not consider Abraham as a simple means to an end, but rather as a man who had an important part to play in the story of God's relationship with the world. Abraham's obedient actions (as well as his numerous disobedient actions) are wrapped into the narrative of salvation, and his life is given a greater glory, a greater meaning, because of the subsequent history that followed in Christ. I imagine that the resurrected Abraham would rejoice at this, sharing in some sense in the glory of Christ.[73]

For a human it is at least plausible that conscious involvement in the large-scale narratives of redemption could indeed be a personal experience of redemption as well. Is it plausible for the non-human animal creation? I first have to acknowledge the vast amount of speculation involved. If one accepts the already fuzzy notion of non-human redemption, one must also accept that the form of redemption for other creatures will probably not be fully understandable to humans. If, for humans, conscious recognition is what is needed, then that is presumably what they will receive. It may be that for other creatures redemption looks entirely different. Jay McDaniel insists upon this point:

> Let us be clear about this hope. The hope is not that all creatures share in the same kind of fulfillment beyond death. Rather it is that all creatures share in that kind of fulfillment appropriate to their own interests and needs. What a pelican chick might know as a fulfillment of needs would have its own kind of harmony and intensity, one quite different from what we humans might know. If there is a pelican heaven, it is a *pelican* heaven.[74]

Add to the complication of speculation that a pelican with a new resurrected body might have quite different needs from the needs it has now in a this-worldly body (as 1 Corinthians 15:35–44 strongly implies), and there are very few clues as to what the needs of the pelican chick might be. Nor does anyone know what the new capacities of the chick might be. If they do have new capacities post mortem, the proposal I have given earlier – that recognition of one's place in the greater narrative is itself a form of personal redemption – would by no means be absurd.

The fractal mosaic idea of redemption, while being a highly speculative and highly imaginative account, contributes to a narrative of the goodness of God in light of evolutionary suffering as it helps one to see how the necessary harms of the evolutionary process could be redeemed in both a this-worldly and an otherworldly sense, without the loss of meaning in either place. The key point is that the redemptive meaning is not necessarily present immediately after a disvalue has occurred. Indeed, if what I have said about God creating new meaning in far distant events is true, some disvalues will have no better meaning and remain unredeemed for a long time after they happen, since the context for their redemption has not yet been created.

Why not create heaven first?

The possibility of redemption necessarily raises the question of why God did not simply create the new world first? If an existence without suffering is possible, and it retains the goods of embodiment and relationships, God would seem at fault for not creating that world first. Wesley J. Wildman, in particular, claims that to articulate a "coherent eschatology would only be theological disaster" since "God would be flagrantly morally inconsistent" in creating this world when that idealised world was possible all along.[75] Southgate meets this challenge by reasoning that just as he argues that the evolutionary process is the "only way" to "give rise to creaturely selves" in this world, it is perhaps also the only way to create selves which could populate heaven. He writes: "Our guess must be that though heaven can eternally preserve those selves, subsisting in suffering-free relationship, it could not give rise to them in the first place."[76]

I think there is plausibility in what Southgate argues. Given the nearly unlimited possibilities of life, how would God choose which specific creatures to make? God would have had to make every creature that was logically possible. But then, many of the realities of creaturely existence would not make sense if God were to create them *de novo* in heaven. Would God have created humans with an appendix? Or our vertical spinal columns that so regularly fail us? Yet, divested of these and all the rest of my evolutionary inheritances, to what extent would I still be me? Given the near-infinite possibilities of life forms, how would God choose me? It would make sense to conjecture that God used the autonomy of creaturely development in evolution to decide which theoretically possible selves would become actual.

In addition to producing selves, I would add to Southgate's response that there are certain values that are present in this world that no one ever imagines will be part of the new world. Southgate, who creatively explores possibilities of the new life, speculates that there may still be hunting and predator/prey relations, though stripped of their pain, terror, and destruction.[77] Yet, he does not include, nor does anyone else include, reproduction as a possible activity of the new creation. If God simply populated the new creation with fully formed selves, the chance to participate with God in forming new life by giving birth would be removed.

So often it is assumed that efficiency and the perfection of the final outcome are primary considerations in God's work. Yet, approached from the motivations of love, it is the participation of the other that makes the work worthwhile. No one who has created an art project or done baking with a young child would say that the work was more efficient or more perfect because of the partnership. Yet, many would say that the sloppy lines in the painting and the lopsided cupcakes that emerged were more worthwhile than the perfect efficiency that they might have achieved on their own. In the same way, a focus on creative love would lead to the conclusion that while there may have been another less painful way to produce embodied creaturely selves, there was no way apart from evolution to produce them in partnership with the creatures themselves.[78]

What other values would be lost, or never be expressed, in the new creation? It is hard to know, but values like courageous self-sacrifice are hard to imagine there. Many creatures, such as sentinel vervet monkeys, voluntarily place themselves in harm's way in order to protect others. Part of the value of these acts is that they are performed in the face of fear and danger. I do not mean to say that expressions of self-sacrifice fully justify the suffering world God has created. If they did, we would have no use for a future world without their existence. Values such as bravery and patience are temporary values (that is, they won't necessarily be exercised in a world without fear and suffering), but perhaps they add one more small reason why God did not simply create the ideal new creation first. If God is creating a great mosaic, these temporary values may add colours, textures, and shades that will deepen and enrich that future existence.

The place of the Christ event

What place does the Christ event have in the development of this image? Robert Russell, reflecting on the importance of Christ's resurrection for non-human theodicy, writes:

> Hence I propose that the only possibility for an adequate response to natural theodicy is to relocate the problem of sin and evil beyond a theology of creation into a theology of redemption – the kenotic suffering of God with the world together with the eschatological transformation of the universe in the new creation beginning proleptically with God's new act at Easter in the bodily resurrection of Jesus.[79]

Russell points out that the suffering of Jesus on the cross and the event of the resurrection are turning points in the understanding of evil and of eschatology. Vernon White, in *Atonement and Incarnation*, struggles with the seeming impossibility of understanding the traditional belief of atonement: that a particular historical event affected the whole of universal history.[80] Trends in theology, he argues, move towards either a total historical particularisation of Christ's work on the cross, such as in the moral exemplar theory where Jesus's death provides little more than one revelation of a good example of a human life, or toward an individualisation where salvation is only effected for individual souls.[81] Instead, White argues for an atonement model that embraces both the necessity of the particularity of Christ's work on the cross as well as its universal significance. He writes:

> God in Christ takes into his own divine experience that which qualifies him to reconcile, redeem, and sanctify in his relationship with all people everywhere. To adapt one of Fiddes' pictures: it is something like a mountain guide who first crosses a difficult terrain himself, in order to equip himself to take across all who will follow him.[82]

White acknowledges, along with Paul Fiddes,[83] that for the atonement to be a historical event with universal significance, the cross and resurrection must allow for some sort of change in God: God is able to do something that God was unable to do before.[84] In White's argument, it is that now Christ can lead people through the path of salvation, as an explorer can become a guide once he has crossed the unknown terrain himself.

Can the fractal mosaic image of redemption I proposed earlier fit this same set of criteria, affirming both the necessity of the historical Christ event and its universal consequences of salvation? I believe it can. In the mosaic image, imagine the events of the life, death, and resurrection of Christ as the central pixel, the mosaic's organising point at the lowest level of personal narrative. It is the event around which all other events are arranged, like a cornerstone or foundation stone from which the greater image is built.[85] The Christ event also acts as the algorithm that arranges and aligns the pixels with one another: the same upside-down

Kingdom power and logic that brought Jesus to the cross and leads him out the other side of death is the power and logic that places each creature in redemptive relation to all others.

The Christ event is both the starting point and the organising principle of the photo mosaic. To borrow the language of Colossians 1:20, "through [Christ] God was pleased to reconcile to himself all things." In Christ, and because of Christ, all other events coordinate to create the upper levels of redemptive imagery. The Christ event is not only revelation in the sense of showing that evil can be defeated by enduring in sacrificial love beyond it; it is also the revelation that shows in microcosm the type of redemption that God will ultimately effect in macrocosm. Christ is the "firstborn" from the dead, the cornerstone of the new creation.

There emerges, with this mosaic image, almost a pun on both the Hebrew and Greek conceptions of sin as something that has "missed the mark." In the redemption picture I offer, the re-alignment of personal narratives around the narrative of Christ represents a true reconciliation of sin, since the narratives of fallen humans are now aligned in right relationship to Christ, other people, and all of creation. The broken relationships caused by sin are now healed and rebuilt. In the uppermost level of the new creation, all of creation will be transformed. For the non-human world, transformation will involve a rearrangement of narratives into a larger redemptive image. This is "justification." For humans, transformation will involve both justification and sanctification. To push the analogy, only human pixels will need the restoration of their true colour and essence – like a painting being cleaned and restored or a video being digitally remastered.

It is in the stage of sanctification that the other human atonement theories – propitiation, vicarious substitution, ransom, etc. – can be invoked. I am perhaps pushing the boundaries of imagery, but I find that this picture of alignment illustrates how Christ had to come for the whole cosmos since every narrative pattern requires a central focus and pattern around which to form. I do not, therefore, have to follow David Clough in his assumption that because Christ came to reconcile the entire cosmos, that the non-human world is somehow subject to sin.[86] It is possible to articulate an account of non-human eschatological justification that does not require redemption from sin, although it may indeed involve redemption from the secondary and tertiary effects of human sin.

Moreover, the idea of Christ's narrative forming the central pixel ensures the importance of the particularity of Christ's historical life. Since the lower level mosaics are formed of earthly events, something like the Incarnation is needed in order for God to be able to have a foundation in history from which to start building. Without the Incarnation, without God's true presence in history, God could not be part of the mosaic. God could only be the organising architect, rather than a participant. Without the Incarnation, the whole narrative structure of history would lose its central organising feature.

Gregory of Nazianzus famously claimed that, "only what is assumed by the Word in the Incarnation can be redeemed."[87] Niels Gregersen's concept of "deep incarnation" has emphasised that, in Elizabeth Johnson's words, the Incarnation was a "radical divine reach through human flesh all the way down into the very tissue of biological existence with its growth and decay."[88] Building upon this concept, Johnson suggests that the idea of "deep resurrection" similarly affiliates all of creation with Christ's resurrection. Christ is the firstborn from amongst the dead, and all of creation will form part of that final resurrection. Johnson writes:

> The reasoning runs like this. This person, Jesus of Nazareth, was composed of star stuff and earth stuff; his life formed a genuine part of the historical and biological community of Earth; his body existed in a network of relationships drawing from and extending to the whole physical universe. If in death this "piece of this world, real to the core," as Rahner phrases it, surrendered his life in love and is now forever with God in glory, then this signals embryonically the final beginning of redemptive glorification not just for other human beings but for all flesh, all material beings, every creature that passes through death. The evolving world of life, all of matter in its endless permutations, will not be left behind but will likewise be transfigured by the resurrection of the Creator Spirit.[89]

The act of the Incarnation makes God part of the material mosaic. The algorithm informing the organisation of the mosaic, however, was not created in the Christ event, but existed before in the attitude God held toward creation. Thus, the universal scope of the Christ event (the organising algorithm) finds its first expression and historical anchor in the particularity of the death and resurrection of Jesus.

The picture of Christ as the central position of creation's mosaic and the "organising algorithm" of redemption is reminiscent – a small echo – of the great scene in Revelation 5. John stands in the midst of the throne-room of heaven, looking for the one who is worthy to open the scroll and bring history to its final conclusion. No one in all of creation is found worthy. John weeps amidst the praise of heaven until he is told by one of the elders, "Do not weep. See, the Lion of the tribe of Judah, the Root of David, has conquered, so that he can open the scroll and its seven seals."[90] John turns to behold this great Lion, and sees instead "a Lamb standing as if it had been slaughtered. . . . He went and took the scroll from the right hand of the one who was seated on the throne."[91]

John imagines that at the centre of heaven stands the Lamb, who had been slaughtered, holding the scroll with the instructions for the final judgement of history. I imagine the central pixel of creation's mosaic as the crucified and risen Christ, and he is the algorithm of reconciliation. Both images emphasise the centrality of the Christ event in the whole scheme of world history. Both images recognise that the suffering taken into the heart of God at the cross is the central organising principle for the outworking of eschatological fulfilment. The creatures that once suffered are drawn into the work of the cross, and aligned with all other creatures into a dynamic mosaic of praise. All hurts are healed, all relationships mended, and all creatures – whether by direct expression, or by simply being what they are[92] – live out the praise of God.

> Then I looked, and I heard the voice of many angels surrounding the throne and the living creatures and the elders; they numbered myriads of myriads and thousands of thousands, singing with full voice,

'Worthy is the Lamb that was slaughtered to receive power and wealth and wisdom and might and honour and glory and blessing!'

Then I heard every creature in heaven and on earth and under the earth and in the sea, and all that is in them, singing,

'To the one seated on the throne and to the Lamb be blessing and honour and glory and might for ever and ever!'[93]

Conclusion

Redemption as the transformation of evil, harm, and disvalue into the love, harmony, and diversity of the kingdom of God remains one of the most important elements of an evolutionary theodicy. I began this chapter with an exploration of four different models of redemption: immanent, ecological, objective, and classical. I then introduced how a fractal mosaic image could help picture the interrelations between the immanent and ecological models of redemption and the classical model. Each individual narrative holds meaning in itself (immanent), but also contributes to a greater picture in world history (ecological). Both of these together constitute the building blocks of God's eschatological redemption in Christ (classical). The glory of the overall narrative is returned upon the good of the individual through the care and attention of God. Finally, I explored the place of the Christ event in the picture of redemption, showing how Jesus's narrative constitutes the central organising focal point and the organising algorithm for the whole structure of redemption. Insofar as the world is redeemed, it is redeemed in, through, and around Christ.

Notes

1 Romans 8:19–22, Colossians 1:17–19, Isaiah 11, 35, 65, and Revelation 21–22 are examples of such "hints."
2 Paul Griffiths, "What Remains in the Resurrection? A (Broadly) Thomist Argument for the Presence of Nonrational Animals in Heaven," delivered at Blackfriars, Cambridge, 31 January 2013.
3 John Wesley, "The General Deliverance: Sermon 60," Accessed 18 October 2013. Online: http://new.gbgm-umc.org/umhistory/wesley/sermons/60/.
4 McDaniel, *Of God and Pelicans: A Theology of Reverence for Life* (Louisville, KY: Westminster John Knox, 1989), 42.
5 This is not to assert that non-human animals do not need to be redeemed from the ecological sins committed by humans, but that they do not need to be redeemed from their own sin, since I (unlike Clough and Hoggard Creegan) do not think non-human animals have the ability to sin.
6 Ruth Page, *God and the Web of Creation* (London: SCM Press, 1996), 63.
7 This is an analogy Page borrows from Peter Geach. Page, *Web of Creation*, 63.
8 Page, *Web of Creation*, 65.
9 Page, *Web of Creation*, 65. There is here an unacknowledged debt to process theism. Christopher Southgate points out the similarity in *The Groaning of Creation: God, Evolution, and the Problem of Evil* (Louisville: Westminster John Knox Press, 2008), 69.
10 Page, *Web of Creation*, 63.

11 Cf. Jürgen Moltmann, *God in Creation: A New Theology of Creation and The Spirit of God*, trans. Margaret Kohl (Minneapolis, MN: Fortress Press, 1993), 164–166.

12 Holmes Rolston III, "Does Nature Need to Be Redeemed?" *Zygon* 29:2 (June 1994): 205–229.

13 Rolston, "Does Nature Need to Be Redeemed?" 213.

14 Rolston, "Does Nature Need to Be Redeemed?" 227.

15 Rolston, "Does Nature Need to Be Redeemed?" 228. See also: Holmes Rolston III, "Naturalizing and Systematizing Evil," in *Is Nature Ever Evil? Religion, Science and Value*, ed. Willem B. Drees (London: Routledge, 2003), 67–86.

16 Southgate, *The Groaning of Creation*, 46; McDaniel, *Of God and Pelicans*, 43.

17 Lisa Sideris, "Writing Straight with Crooked Lines: Holmes Rolston's Ecological Theology and Theodicy," in *Nature, Value, Duty: Life on Earth with Holmes Rolston, III*, ed. Christopher J. Preston and Wayne Ouderkirk (Dordrecht, Netherlands: Springer, 2007), 77–101.

18 John F. Haught, *The Promise of Nature: Ecology and Cosmic Purpose* (Mahwah, NJ: Paulist Press, 1993), 131. Haught borrowed the term from Alfred North Whitehead.

19 Charles Hartshorne, *Omnipotence and Other Theological Mistakes* (Albany, NY: State University of New York, 1984), 117. John B. Cobb Jr. and David Ray Griffin, two of the most prominent process theists, have actually affirmed the possibility of the soul's survival of bodily death and the possibility of personal life after death (albeit temporarily). David Ray Griffin, "Process Theology and the Christian Good News: A Response to Classical Free Will Theism," in *Searching for an Adequate God: A Dialogue between Process and Free Will Theists*, eds. John B. Cobb Jr. and Clark H. Pinnock (Grand Rapids, MI: Eerdmans, 2000), 3. Cf. John B. Cobb Jr., *A Christian Natural Theology: Based on the Thought of Alfred North Whitehead* (London: Lutterworth, 1966), 63–79; John B. Cobb Jr., "The Resurrection of the Soul," *Harvard Theological Review* 80:2 (1987): 213–227; John B. Cobb and David Ray Griffin, *Process Theology: An Introductory Exposition* (Belfast: Christian Journals Ltd.,/Westminster, 1976), 124–125; Granville C. Henry, "Does Process Thought Allow Personal Immortality?" *Religious Studies* 31:3 (September 1995): 311–321.

20 John F. Haught, *God after Darwin: A Theology of Evolution* (Boulder, CO: Westview, 2000), 43. See also 114ff.

21 John F. Haught, *Deeper Than Darwin: The Prospect for Religion in the Age of Evolution* (Boulder, CO: Westview, 2003), 152.

22 Haught, *Deeper Than Darwin*, 154.

23 Haught, *Deeper Than Darwin*, 159.

24 Haught, *Deeper Than Darwin*, 150.

25 Ernst Conradie, "Resurrection, Finitude, and Ecology," in *Resurrection: Theological and Scientific Assessments*, eds. Ted Peters, Robert John Russell, and Michael Welker (Grand Rapids, MI: Eerdmans, 2002), 292.

26 Conradie explains that in the same way that a square both encapsulates and transcends a line, and a cube contains and transcends a square, so God's dimension of eternity contains and transcends our four-dimensional existence. Eternity is not the negation of our existence, but is its transcendence. Conradie, "Resurrection, Finitude, and Ecology," 288–290.

27 Conradie, "Resurrection, Finitude, and Ecology," 295.

28 Conradie, "Resurrection, Finitude, and Ecology," 294.

29 I am indebted to one of my students in the class "Evolution, God, and Gaia" 2013 at the University of Exeter for this apt phrase.

30 McDaniel, *Of God and Pelicans*, 44–47; Southgate, *Groaning of Creation*, 78–91; Trent Dougherty, *The Problem of Animal Pain: A Theodicy for All Creatures Great and Small* (London: Palgrave Macmillan, 2014), 134–153. The work of other proponents

of this view will be explored below, including Paul Griffiths, C. S. Lewis, John Polkinghorne, and Denis Edwards.

31 Paul Griffiths, "What Remains in the Resurrection?"

32 C. S. Lewis, *The Problem of Pain* (New York, NY: HarperCollins, 1940, 1996), 143–147; John Polkinghorne, *The God of Hope and the End of the World* (New Haven, CT: Yale University Press, 2002), 123.

33 *The Velveteen Rabbit: Or, How Toys Become Real* (New York, NY: George H. Doran, 1922) is a children's story by Margery Williams in which a toy rabbit is turned by a fairy into a living rabbit because a little boy loved it. Toys that are not truly loved by humans do not become real in the story.

34 Polkinghorne, *The God of Hope,* 123.

35 John Polkinghorne, *Science and the Trinity: The Christian Encounter with Reality* (New Haven, CT: Yale University Press, 2004), 152. In another place he writes: "What are we to expect will be the destiny of non-human creatures? They must have their share in cosmic hope, but we scarcely need suppose that every dinosaur that ever lived, let alone all of the vast multitude of bacteria that have constituted so large a fraction of biomass throughout the history of terrestrial life, will each have its own individual eschatological future." *The God of Hope,* 122.

36 Southgate, *Groaning of Creation,* 89.

37 Southgate, *Groaning of Creation,* 84.

38 This is a view Southgate shares with McDaniel. McDaniel, *Of God and Pelicans,* 46.

39 Southgate, *Groaning of Creation,* 85.

40 Dougherty, *The Problem of Animal Pain,* 142.

41 Jürgen Moltmann, *The Coming of God: Christian Eschatology,* trans. Margaret Kohl (London: SCM Press, 1996), 132. The one exception to this might be creatures with significant moral freewill, such as humans and, possibly, demons. The nature of love demands significant freedom, and therefore if one were to knowingly, intentionally, and persistently reject the gift of life, I believe that God would respect that choice. However, it may be that the gentle, creative, loving, and enduring call of God may eventually convince all to receive the gift of life freely.

42 John Wesley, "The General Deliverance: Sermon 60," Accessed 18 October 2013. Online: http://new.gbgm-umc.org/umhistory/wesley/sermons/60/.

43 The tens of millions of species alive today only represent about 1–2% of all species that ever lived, meaning an estimate of billions of species throughout all history.

44 Southgate, *Groaning of Creation,* 85.

45 Southgate, *Groaning of Creation,* 82–85.

46 Southgate, *Groaning of Creation,* 85. Southgate actually makes a critique of conceiving future life as compensation in Christopher Southgate and Andrew Robinson, "Varieties of Theodicy: An Exploration of Responses to the Problem of Evil Based on a Typology of Good-Harm Analyses," in *Physics and Cosmology: Scientific Perspectives on the Problem of Natural Evil,* eds. Nancey Murphy, Robert J. Russell, William R. Stoeger, S. J. (Vatican City and Berkeley, CA: Vatican Observatory, CTNS, 2007), 82–84.

47 McDaniel, *Of God and Pelicans,* 46.

48 Dougherty, *The Problem of Animal Pain,* 146–147.

49 Denis Edwards, "Every Sparrow that Falls to the Ground: The Cost of Evolution and the Christ-Event," *Ecotheology* 11:1 (2006): 117.

50 Edwards, "Every Sparrow That Falls," 118.

51 Edwards, "Every Sparrow That Falls," 118. Capitalisation in the title of this section is original to Edwards.

52 Edwards, "Every Sparrow That Falls," 119.

53 Edwards, "Every Sparrow That Falls," 119.

54 The concept of fractal narratives is explored in Eleonore Stump, *Wandering in Darkness: Narrative and the Problem of Suffering* (Oxford: Clarendon Press, 2010),

219–226, 466–467. She explores how a fractal narrative of redemption works out in various biblical narratives, particularly in the book of Job.

55 Image created by Bethany Sollereder through www.easymoza.com.

56 This imagery is found in Markus Mühling-Schlapkohl, "Why Does the Risen Christ Have Scars? Why God Did Not Immediately Create the Eschaton: Goodness, Truth and Beauty," *International Journal of Systematic Theology* 6:2 (April 2004): 185–193.

57 Ted Peters and Martinez Hewlett, *Evolution from Creation to New Creation: Conflict, Conversation, and Convergence* (Nashville, TN: Abingdon, 2003), 160.

58 Eleonore Stump also employs the idea of fractals of redemption. *Wandering in Darkness*, 219–221.

59 Southgate, *Groaning of Creation*, 89.

60 David Clough, *On Animals*, Vol. 1 of *Systematic Theology* (Edinburgh: T & T Clark, 2012), 158–159.

61 Dougherty, *The Problem of Animal Pain*, 148–153.

62 Dougherty, *The Problem of Animal Pain*, 150.

63 There are computer programmers working to develop video mosaics. One example is the video mosaic developed by Allison Klein, Tyler Grant, Adam Finkelstein, and Michael F. Cohen, "Video Mosaics," *NPAR 2002: Second International Symposium on Non Photorealistic Rendering* (June 2002): 21–28. An example of a video mosaic they produced by the method described in the paper can be viewed online: http://research.microsoft.com/en-us/um/people/cohen/npar2002.m1v. Accessed 16 May 2014.

64 In all the multiple ways explored in Chapter 5, 133ff.

65 God's final narrative may include the history of other worlds, other universes, and other non-physical beings (such as angels and demons).

66 Conradie, "Resurrection, Finitude, and Ecology," 283–284.

67 Revelation 5:9–10, 12, NRSV.

68 Holmes Rolston III, "Kenosis and Nature," in *The Work of Love: Creation as Kenosis*, ed. John Polkinghorne (Grand Rapids, MI: Eerdmans, 2001), 58–61.

69 New research continues to confirm this theory. See Paul R. Renne, et al., "Time Scales of Critical Events Around the Cretaceous-Paleogene Boundary," *Science* 339 (February 2013): 684–687.

70 Hebrews 11:39–40, NRSV.

71 Hebrews 12:1a, NRSV.

72 Hebrews 12:1b, NRSV.

73 John 8:56.

74 McDaniel, *Of God and Pelicans*, 45. The point is also insisted upon by Edwards, "Every Sparrow That Falls," 119.

75 Wesley J. Wildman, "Incongruous Goodness, Perilous Beauty, Disconcerting Truth: Ultimate Reality and Suffering in Nature," in *Physics and Cosmology: Scientific Perspectives on the Problem of Natural Evil*, eds. Nancey Murphy, Robert Russell, and William R. Stoeger, S. J. (Vatican City and Berkeley, CA: Vatican Observatory, CTNS, 2007), 292.

76 Southgate, *Groaning of Creation*, 90.

77 Southgate, *Groaning of Creation*, 87–90.

78 I have written a light-hearted article called "Toward a Theology of Astronaut Beavers" on the theme of God's sharing, which can be found at http://biologos.org/blogs/jim-stump-faith-and-science-seeking-understanding/toward-a-theology-of-astronaut-beavers.

79 Robert John Russell, "Natural Theodicy in Evolutionary Context: The Need for an Eschatology of New Creation," in *Theodicy and Eschatology*, eds. Bruce Barber and David Neville (Hindmarsh, Australia: ATF, 2005), 121–152, 152.

80 Vernon White, *Atonement and Incarnation: An Essay in Universalism and Particularity* (Cambridge: Cambridge University Press, 1991).

81 White, *Atonement and Incarnation*, 2–3.

82 White, *Atonement and Incarnation*, 53.

83 Paul S. Fiddes, *Past Event and Present Salvation: The Christian Idea of Atonement* (London: Darton, Longman and Todd, 1989), 110.

84 White, *Atonement and Incarnation*, 53.

85 The cornerstone, or foundation stone, was the first stone laid down in ancient stone architecture. Every other stone would, therefore, be set in reference to this first stone. Every other stone derived its place in the building because of the positioning of the cornerstone, and the entire structure was positioned in reference to this first stone.

86 Clough, *On Animals*, 125.

87 Alister E. McGrath, *Historical Theology: An Introduction to the History of Christian Thought*, 2nd ed. (Oxford: John Wiley & Sons, 2013), 48.

88 Elizabeth Johnson, *Ask the Beasts: Darwin and the God of Love* (London: Bloomsbury, 2014), 196. Gregersen coined the phrase in Niels H. Gregersen, "The Cross of Christ in an Evolutionary World," *dialog* 40:3 (Fall 2001): 192–207.

89 Johnson, *Ask the Beasts*, 209.

90 Revelation 5:5, NRSV.

91 Revelation 5:6–7, NRSV.

92 See the possibilities of creaturely praise in Mark Harris, " 'Let the floods clap their hands; let the hills sing together for joy' (Ps.98:8): Is joy the theological and emotional shaper of the inanimate world?" Accessed 22 August 2017. Online: www.academia. edu/6981351/_Let_the_floods_clap_their_hands_let_the_hills_sing_together_for_ joy_Ps.98_8_Is_joy_the_theological_and_emotional_shaper_of_the_inanimate_ world.

93 Revelation 5:11–13, NRSV.

7 Conclusion

The process of evolution has created the conditions for vast amounts of suffering, untimely death, and extinction for countless non-human sentient beings. The traditional Christian solutions for suffering cannot be applied in these cases: these creatures could not be benefited morally by this suffering, nor could their suffering be blamed on the corruption of the natural order by humanity, Satan, or any other kind of primordial defect or evil. In light of natural suffering and the abundance of disvalues in the world, how can Christians affirm with the Christian tradition that the world is the creation of a good, loving, and powerful God? The evidence from the natural sciences makes the picture more complicated when it insists that it is particularly the harms and disvalues – the suffering and death of individuals – that drives the development of skill, complexity, and new forms of life through evolution.

I have traced, in this book, one exploration amongst many through the realm of theodicy. First, I maintain the natural world, apart from human sin, is not fallen. By this I mean that the natural world is fit for the purposes of God's love. I do not mean that it is the best of all possible worlds, or that every instance of suffering is justified by this consideration alone, but that the disvalues in the natural world do not originate from a corruption of the world. The world is God's "very good" world, inclusive of pain and suffering. The curse laid on the earth in Genesis 3 is lifted after the flood, and does not reappear. The second step began with an investigation of the nature and practice of love. The central question was: "What does a creation made in love look like?" Drawing on Aquinas, Eleonore Stump, and W. H. Vanstone, I argued that a creation made in love would necessarily involve allowing creatures to "selve" with significant freedom. Creatures would selve without micromanagement into lions and lettuce, dinosaurs and diphtheria. Life was not drawn inexorably along fortuitous lines of descent, but was allowed to develop according to each creature's own needs and agency, sustained by the unflinching generosity of God to all life. But the project of creation, though unfallen, does not always reflect God's love. One eschatological day, it will. But until then, it must proceed without guarantees. Vanstone describes love's work:

> Love may be "frustrated": its most earnest aspirations may "come to nothing":
> the greatness of what is offered in love may be wholly disproportionate to the

smallness of that, if anything, which is received. . . . The activity of love contains no assurance or certainty of completion: much may be expended and little achieved. The progress of love must always be by tentative and precarious steps: and each step that is taken, whether it "succeeds" or "fails," becomes the basis for the next, and equally precarious, step which must follow.[1]

Creation through evolution is not efficient. Rather, love's generosity provides a superabundance of the gift of being that "wastes" resources on all sorts of unlikely and unproductive sorts of beings. From this perspective, evolution is deeply consistent with a world created in love.

Love's twin desires, the desire for the good of the beloved and for union with the beloved, set the conditions for God's creative work. God's work begins with kenosis, the choice not to control, which allows creatures the freedom to develop features that harm one another. God's work continues with presence, not to forsake the work of life, but to act within the world in empowering and meaning-making ways. God's work finishes in redemption, the healing and fulfilment of the suffering and lack of flourishing that characterises, to some extent, every creature's life.

The exploration of love also illuminated one anthropocentric trail: the goal of creating creatures that could return God's love. Although evolution is not an efficient process, it does create living beings that have strong desires. Drawing on Andrew Elphinstone's work,[2] I argued that these evolutionary desires, both selfish and altruistic, can be transformed within cooperative human individuals into the proper desires of love through the work of God. That the world did not initially develop by creating love (love is a latecomer in creation) is not a sign that things went wrong in God's plan, but simply shows that love was not something that could be fashioned *de novo*. It had to emerge out of the refining and transforming of passions, themselves developed through the competition and strife of evolution.[3]

In the chapter on divine action I explored how the character and nature of God's work is more important than how God's work happens. In light of God's love, I depicted four main avenues of special divine action: the gift of being, co-presence, divine lure, and participation. The superabundance of the gift of being I have already mentioned. Co-presence – or co-suffering – is the compassionate attention given to each creature, so that no creature suffers or dies alone. God's presence with the suffering creatures of creation does not necessarily alleviate the pain they go through, but it recasts the story of creation. Instead of God as the Lord of Creation who allows creatures to suffer and die alone in order to accomplish God's purposes,[4] God is present in the blood and struggle, experiencing the full effects of God's creative intent. The divine lure draws creatures towards the good, and thus towards God. It is the invitation to self-transcendence that persuades creation into redemptive forms, creating value out of disvalue, and good out of suffering. God's participation in the world through embodiment and meaning-making are further instances of God paying attention to individuals, of acting in their lives and creatively redeeming their suffering.

I have proposed that the final ontological meaning of events is not determined at the time they take place. Instead, meaning can change in light of new events. The meaning, and therefore the value, of a life is only determined eschatologically. Therefore, God works to redeem every life in such a way that the creature itself participates in the full redemptive meaning of its life.

Redemption for non-human creatures is multi-faceted. It involves the redemption of meaning when there has been little observable value. It involves contribution to the ongoing evolutionary development of life at the level of ecological systems. It involves personal transformation and fulfilment in the new creation. I have suggested that this redemption is completely universal amongst non-human life because of the particularity of divine love. I have also suggested that the redemption that is offered to all creatures is not simply compensation, but is a new form of life altogether. Such a reality may involve an increase in non-human capacities so that they can understand the meaning of their lives more fully, or it may simply exist on a pre-conscious level in the form of experienced peace, joy, and love.

Though violence and competition in the natural world are not evil, I affirm with the biblical tradition, that in the new creation violence will either not exist or will be so transformed that it will hold none of the disvalues it holds here. There is a helpful parallel in the now-and-*not*-then between violence in the non-human realm and our current limited physical embodiment. Christian orthodoxy has long affirmed that our physical embodiment is good, not evil. It is good that we have (or, better, *are*) bodies. Yet, the tradition has also affirmed that in the new creation, human bodies will be changed dramatically, and that this transformation is also good.[5] Affirming the present state of affairs as God's good creation does not mean that it is perfect, or that it is the desired end. Nor is affirming the goodness of the future state a quiet admission that God could not quite get things right the first time around.

Evolution is God's process for creating, and it is full of suffering, extinction, untimely death, and disvalue. In addressing the theological problems associated with this problem, I have tried to show that there are multiple helpful approaches, both in terms of setting up the problem and in exploring it. I argued in the first chapter that the task of a theodicist is not to stand in a courtroom and argue with the sceptics, but to explore the rich texture of reality. I have tried to do all this in the form of what Thomas Tracy calls a "thick defense," which, "attempts to weave a narrative that explains how suffering is consistent with beliefs held about God."[6] I have explored the narrative of a God of love who creates, sustains, suffers with, and redeems a most beloved creation.

Christopher Southgate has written that all real theodicies "arise out of protest and end in mystery."[7] I did not set out to "solve" the problem of suffering, but to explore and describe the world in realistic ways and to reflect theologically on how that affects our understanding of the mystery of God. And so, this theodicy ends with two mysteries: the mystery of the tragedy of suffering and the mystery of hope in an ever-present and ever-redeeming Creator.

Notes

1 W. H. Vanstone, *Love's Endeavour, Love's Expense: The Response of Being to the Love of God* (London: Darton, Longman and Todd, 1977), 46.
2 Andrew Elphinstone, *Freedom, Suffering & Love* (London: SCM Press, 1976).
3 See the discussion of Elphinstone in Chapter 4, 113–116.
4 Contrast with Holmes Rolston III's statement "If God Watches the Sparrow Fall, God Must Do So from a Great Distance," *Science and Religion: A Critical Survey*, 2nd ed. (West Conschohocken, PA: Templeton Foundation Press, 2006), 140.
5 1 Corinthians 15:35–44 is a particularly strong articulation of this theme.
6 Thomas F. Tracy, "The Lawfulness of Nature and the Problem of Evil," in *Physics and Cosmology: Scientific Perspectives on the Problem of Natural Evil*, eds. Nancey Murphy, Robert Russell, and William R. Stoeger, S. J. (Vatican City: Vatican Observatory Foundation, 2007), 152.
7 Christopher Southgate, *The Groaning of Creation: God, Evolution, and the Problem of Evil* (Louisville, KY: Westminster John Knox Press, 2008), 132.

Bibliography

Alexander, Denis. *Creation or Evolution: Do We Have to Choose?* Oxford: Monarch, 2008.

Allen, Diogenes. "Natural Evil and the Love of God." *Religious Studies* 16:4 (December 1980): 439–456.

Angel, Andrew R. *Chaos and the Son of Man: The Hebrew Chaoskampf Tradition in the Period 515 BCE to 200 CE*. London: T & T Clark, 2006.

Aquinas, Thomas. *Summa Theologica*. Translated by Fathers of the English Dominican Province. New York: Bazinger Bros, 1947.

———. *Summa Contra Gentiles*, Vol. 4. Translated by Vernon J. Bourke. Notre Dame, IN: University of Notre Dame Press, 1975.

Athanasius. *On the Incarnation of the Word*. Grand Rapids, MI: CCEL, 2005.

Attfield, Robin. *Creation, Evolution and Meaning*. Aldershot: Ashgate, 2006.

Augustine. *The Literal Meaning of Genesis*. Translated by J. H. Taylor. Mahwah, NJ: Paulist Press, 1982.

Bamberger, Bernard J. *Fallen Angels: Soldiers of Satan's Realm*. Philadelphia, PA: Jewish Publication Society, 1952.

Barbour, Ian. *Religion in an Age of Science: The Gifford Lectures 1989–1991*. London: SCM Press, 1990.

———. *Religion and Science: Historical and Contemporary Issues*. San Francisco, CA: HarperCollins, 1997.

Barrett, Lee C. *Eros and Self-Emptying: The Intersections of Augustine and Kierkegaard*. Grand Rapids, MI: Eerdmans, 2013.

Barrow, John D. *The Constants of Nature: The Numbers that Encode the Deepest Secrets of the Universe*. London: Random House, 2002.

Bateson, Patrick and Elizabeth L. Bradshaw. "Physiological Effects of Hunting Red Deer." *Proceedings of the Royal Society B* 264 (1997): 1707–1714.

Bauckham, Richard. *Bible and Ecology: Rediscovering the Community of Creation*. London: Darton, Longman & Todd, 2010.

———. *Living with Other Creatures: Green Exegesis and Theology*. Milton Keynes, UK: Paternoster, 2012.

Bauman, Christopher W., A. Peter McGraw, Daniel M. Bartels, and Caleb Warren. "Revisiting External Validity: Concerns about Trolley Problems and Other Sacrificial Dilemmas in Moral Psychology." *Social and Personality Psychology Compass* 8:9 (September 2014): 536–554.

Bennett, Gaymon, Martinez J. Hewlett, Ted Peters, and Robert John Russell, eds. *The Evolution of Evil*. Göttingen: Vanderhoeck & Ruprecht, 2008.

Bergmann, Martin. "Skeptical Theism and Rowe's New Evidential Argument from Evil." *Noûs* 35:2 (2001): 278–296.

Berry, R. J. "This Cursed Earth: Is 'the Fall' Credible?" *Science & Christian Belief* 11:1 (1999): 29–49.

Bimson, John J. "Reconsidering a 'Cosmic Fall'." *Science & Christian Belief* 18 (2006): 63–81.

Blenkinsopp, Joseph. *Creation, Un-Creation, Re-Creation: A Discursive Commentary on Genesis 1–11*. London: T & T Clark, 2011.

Bonting, Sjoerd L. "Chaos Theology: A New Approach to the Science-Theology Dialogue." *Zygon* 34:2 (June 1999): 323–332.

Boyd, Gregory A. *God at War: The Bible & Spiritual Conflict*. Downers Grove, IL: InterVarsity, 1997.

———. *God of the Possible: A Biblical Introduction to the Open View of God*. Grand Rapids, MI: Baker Books, 2000.

———. *Satan and the Problem of Evil: Constructing a Trinitarian Warfare Theodicy*. Downers Grove, IL: InterVarsity, 2001.

———. "Evolution as Cosmic Warfare: A Biblical Perspective on Satan and 'Natural Evil'." In *Creation Made Free: Open Theology Engaging Science*. Edited by Thomas Oord, 125–145. Eugene, OR: Wipf & Stock, 2009.

Braaten, Laurie J. "All Creation Groans: Romans 8:22 in Light of the Biblical Sources." *Horizons in Biblical Theology* 28 (2006): 131–159.

Bracken, Joseph. *Christianity and Process Thought: Spirituality for a Changing World*. Philadelphia, PA and London: Templeton Foundation Press, 2006.

Brotton, Melissa J., ed. *Ecotheology in the Humanities: An Interdisciplinary Approach to Understanding the Divine and Nature*. Lanham, MD: Lexington Books, 2016.

Brooke, John Hedley. " 'Darwin, Design, and the Unification of Nature'." In *Science, Religion and the Human Experience*. Edited by James D. Proctor, 165–184. Oxford: Oxford University Press, 2005.

Brown, William P. *The Seven Pillars of Creation: The Bible, Science, and the Ecology of Wonder*. Oxford: Oxford University Press, 2010.

Brunner, Emil. *The Christian Doctrine of Creation and Redemption, Dogmatics*, Vol. 2. Translated by Olive Wyon. London: Lutterworth, 1952.

Burrell, C. S. C., David B. *Knowing the Unknowable God*. Notre Dame, IN: University of Notre Dame Press, 1986.

———. "Incarnation and Creation: The Hidden Dimension." *Modern Theology* 12:2 (April 1996): 211–220.

———. "Creation, Metaphysics, and Ethics." *Faith and Philosophy* 18:2 (April 2001): 204–221.

———. "The Act of Creation: Theological Consequences." In *Creation and the God of Abraham*. Edited by David B. Burrell, Carlo Cogliati, Janet M. Soskice, and William R. Stoeger, S. J., 40–52. Cambridge: Cambridge University Press, 2010.

Burrell, C. S. C., David B. and Isabelle Moulin. "Albert, Aquinas and Dionysius." *Modern Theology* 24:4 (October 2008): 633–649.

Byrne, Brendan. "An Ecological Reading of Rom. 8.19–22: Possibilities and Hesitations." In *Ecological Hermeneutics: Biblical, Historical and Theological Perspectives*. Edited by David G. Horrell, Cherryl Hunt, Christopher Southgate, and Francesca Stavrakopoulou, 83–93. London: T & T Clark, 2010.

Calvin, John. "Commentaries upon the First Book of Moses called Genesis (1554)." In *Calvin's Bible Commentaries: Genesis, Part I*. Translated by J. King. London: Forgotten Books, 1847, 2007.

Capon, Robert Farrar. "The Third Peacock: The Problem of God and Evil." In *The Romance of the Word*. Grand Rapids, MI: Eerdmans, 1995.

Clark, W. M. "The Flood and the Structure of the Pre-Patriarchal History." *Zeitschrift für die alttestamentliche Wissenschaft* 83:2 (1971): 184–211.

Clayton, Philip. "Tracing the Lines: Constraint and Freedom in the Movement from Quantum Physics to Theology." In *Quantum Mechanics: Scientific Perspectives on Divine Action*. Edited by Robert Russell, Philip Clayton, Kirk Wegter-McNelly, and John Polkinghorne, 211–234. Vatican City and Berkeley, CA: Vatican Observatory, CTNS, 2001.

Clayton, Philip and Steven Knapp. "Divine Action and the 'Argument from Neglect'." In *Physics and Cosmology: Scientific Perspectives on the Problem of Natural Evil*. Edited by Nancey Murphy, Robert J. Russell, and William R. Stoeger, S. J., 179–194. Vatican City and Berkeley, CA: Vatican Observatory, CTNS, 2007.

———. *The Predicament of Belief: Science, Philosophy, Faith*. Oxford: Oxford University Press, 2011.

Clines, David J. A. *The Theme of the Pentateuch*. 2nd Edition. Sheffield: Sheffield Academic, 1997.

Clough, David. *On Animals*. Vol. 1. of *Systematic Theology*. Edinburgh: T & T Clark, 2012.

Coakley, Sarah. "Kenosis: Theological Meanings and Gender Connotations." In *The Work of Love: Creation as Kenosis*. Edited by John Polkinghorne, 192–210. Grand Rapids, MI: Eerdmans, 2001.

———. "God and Evolution: A New Solution." *Harvard Divinity Bulletin* 35:2–3 (Spring/ Summer 2007): 8–13.

———. "Evolution, Cooperation, and Divine Providence." In *Evolution, Games, and God: Principles of Cooperation*. Edited by Martin A. Nowak and Sarah Coakley, 375–385. Cambridge, MA: Harvard University Press, 2013.

Cobb, Jr., John B. *A Christian Natural Theology: Based on the Thought of Alfred North Whitehead*. London: Lutterworth, 1966.

———. *God and the World*. Philadelphia, PA: Westminster John Knox Press, 1969.

———. "The Resurrection of the Soul." *Harvard Theological Review* 80:2 (1987): 213–227.

Cobb Jr., John B. and Clark H. Pinnock, eds. *Searching for an Adequate God: A Dialogue between Process and Free Will Theists*. Grand Rapids, MI: Eerdmans, 2000.

Cobb Jr., John B. and David Ray Griffin. *Process Theology: An Introductory Exposition*. Louisville, KY: Westminster John Knox Press, 1976.

Conradie, Ernst. "Resurrection, Finitude, and Ecology." In *Resurrection: Theological and Scientific Assessments*. Edited by Ted Peters, Robert John Russell, and Michael Welker, 277–296. Grand Rapids, MI: Eerdmans, 2002.

Conway Morris, Simon. *The Crucible of Creation: The Burgess Shale and the Rise of Animals*. Oxford: Oxford University Press, 1998.

Conway Morris, Simon and Stefan Bengtson. "Cambrian Predators: Possible Evidence from Boreholes." *Journal of Paleontology* 68:1 (January 1994): 1–23.

Corey, Michael A. *Evolution and the Problem of Natural Evil*. Lanham, MD: University Press of America, 2000.

Cranfield, C. E. B. "Some Observations on Romans 8:19–21." In *Reconciliation and Hope: New Testament Essays on Atonement and Eschatology Presented to L. L. Morris on His 60th Birthday*. Edited by Robert Banks, 224–230. Exeter: Paternoster, 1974.

———. *The Epistle to the Romans*. Vol 1. of *International Critical Commentary*. Edinburgh: T & T Clark, 1975.

Cunningham, Conor. *Darwin's Pious Idea: Why the Ultra-Darwinists and Creationists Both Get It Wrong*. Grand Rapids, MI: Eerdmans, 2010.

Darwin, Charles. *On the Origin of Species*. London: John Murray, 1859.

Darwin, Charles R. to Asa Gray. "Letter 2814." 22 May 1860. The Darwin Correspondence Project. Online: www.darwinproject.ac.uk/letter/entry-2814.

———. "Letter 1924." 12 July 1860. The Darwin Correspondence Project. Accessed 19 October 2013. Online: www.darwinproject.ac.uk/letter/entry-1924.

Davies, Paul. "Teleology Without Teleology: Purpose Through Emergent Complexity." In *Evolutionary and Molecular Biology: Scientific Perspective on Divine Action*. Edited by Robert J. Russell, William R. Stoeger, S. J., and Francisco J. Ayala, 151–162. Vatican City and Berkeley, CA: Vatican Observatory, CTNS, 1998.

Dawkins, Richard. *River Out of Eden: A Darwinian View of Life*. New York, NY: Basic Books, 1995.

Day, John. *God's Conflict with the Dragon and the Sea: Echoes of a Canaanite Myth in the Old Testament*. Cambridge: Cambridge University Press, 1985.

de Nooijer, Silvester, Barbara R. Holland, David Penny. "The Emergence of Predators in Early Life: There Was No Garden of Eden." *PLoS ONE* 4:6 (2009). Open Access. Online: http://journals.plos.org/plosone/article?id=10.1371/journal.pone.0005507.

Deane-Drummond, Celia. *Wonder and Wisdom: Conversations in Science, Spirituality and Theology*. London: Darton, Longman & Todd, 2006.

———. "Shadow Sophia in Christological Perspective: The Evolution of Sin and the Redemption of Nature." *Theology and Science* 6:1 (2008): 13–32.

———. "Who on Earth Is Jesus Christ? Plumbing the Depths of Deep Incarnation." In *Christian Faith and the Earth: Current Paths and Emerging Horizons in Ecotheology*. Edited by Ernst M. Conradie, Sigurd Bergmann, Celia Deane-Drummond, and Denis Edwards, 31–50. London: Bloomsbury, 2014.

Deane-Drummond, Celia and David Clough, eds. *Creaturely Theology: On God, Humans and Other Animals*. London: SCM Press, 2009.

DeGrazia, David and Andrew Rowan, "Pain, Suffering, and Anxiety in Animals and Humans." *Theoretical Medicine* 12:3 (September 1991): 193–211.

Dembski, William. *The End of Christianity: Finding a Good God in an Evil World*. Nashville, TN: B&H, 2009.

Domjan, Michael and James W. Grau. *The Principles of Learning and Behaviour*. Belmont, CA: Cengage Learning, 2006.

Domning, Daryl and Monika Hellwig. *Original Selfishness: Original Sin and Evil in Light of Evolution*. Burlington, VT: Ashgate, 2006.

Dostoevsky, Fyodor. *The Brothers Karamazov*. New York, NY: Bantam, 1970.

Dougherty, Trent. *The Problem of Animal Pain: A Theodicy for All Creatures Great and Small*. New York, NY: Palgrave Macmillan, 2014.

Drees, Willem B. *Is Nature Ever Evil? Religion, Science and Value*. London: Routledge, 2003.

Dunn, James D. G. *Romans 1–8*. Word Biblical Commentary 38a. Dallas, TX: Word Books, 1988.

Edwards, Denis. "Every Sparrow That Falls to the Ground: The Cost of Evolution and the Christ-Event." *Ecotheology* 11:1 (2006): 103–123.

———. "Why Is God Doing This? Suffering, The Universe, and Christian Eschatology." In *Physics and Cosmology: Scientific Perspectives on the Problem of Natural Evil*. Edited by Nancey Murphy, Robert J. Russell, and William R. Stoeger, S. J., 247–266. Vatican City and Berkeley, CA: Vatican Observatory, CTNS, 2007.

————. *How God Acts: Creation, Redemption, and Special Divine Action*. Minneapolis, MN: Fortress Press, 2010.

Ellis, George F. R. "Quantum Theory and the Macroscopic World." In *Quantum Mechanics: Scientific Perspectives on Divine Action*. Edited by Robert Russell, Philip Clayton, Kirk Wegter-McNelly, and John Polkinghorne, 259–291. Vatican City and Berkeley, CA: Vatican Observatory, CTNS, 2001.

Elphinstone, Andrew. *Freedom, Suffering & Love*. London: SCM Press, 1976.

Emery, Gilles. "The Immutability of the God of Love and the Problem of Language Concerning the 'Suffering of God'." In *Divine Impassibility and the Mystery of Human Suffering*. Translated by Thomas J. White. Edited by James F. Keating and Thomas J. White, O. P., 27–76. Grand Rapids, MI: Eerdmans, 2009.

Farley, Wendy. *The Wounding and Healing of Desire: Weaving Heaven and Earth*. Louisville, KY: Westminster John Knox Press, 2005.

Farrer, Austin. *Love Almighty and Ills Unlimited*. London: HarperCollins, 1966.

————. *Faith and Speculation: An Essay in Philosophical Theology*. London: Adam & Charles Black, 1967.

Fiddes, Paul S. *The Creative Suffering of God*. Oxford: Clarendon Press, 1988.

————. *Past Event and Present Salvation: The Christian Idea of Atonement*. London: Darton, Longman & Todd, 1989.

————. "Creation Out of Love." In *The Work of Love: Creation as Kenosis*. Edited by John Polkinghorne, 167–191. Grand Rapids, MI: Eerdmans, 2001.

Fitzmyer, Joseph A. *Romans*. Anchor Bible 33. New York, NY: Doubleday, 1993.

Frankfurt, Harry G. *The Reasons of Love*. Princeton, NJ: Princeton University Press, 2004.

Fretheim, Terence E. "The God Who Acts: An Old Testament Perspective." *Theology Today* 54:1 (1997): 6–18.

————. *God and World in the Old Testament: A Relational Theology of Creation*. Nashville, TN: Abingdon, 2005.

————. *Creation Untamed: The Bible, God, and Natural Disasters*. Grand Rapids, MI: Baker Academic, 2010.

Gandolfo, Elizabeth O' Donnell. *The Power and Vulnerability of Love: A Theological Anthropology*. Minneapolis, MN: Fortress Press, 2015.

Garte, Sy. "New Ideas in Evolutionary Biology: From NDMS to EES." *Perspectives on Science and Christian Faith* 68:1 (March 2016): 3–11.

Geach, Peter. "The Future." *New Blackfriars* 54:636 (May 1973): 208–218.

————. *Providence and Evil*. Cambridge: Cambridge University Press, 1977.

Gempf, Conrad. "The Imagery of Birth Pangs in the New Testament." *Tyndale Bulletin* 45:1 (1994): 119–135.

Gobush, K., B. M. Mutayoba, and S. K. Wasser, "Long-Term Impacts of Poaching on Relatedness, Stress Physiology, and Reproductive Output of Adult Female African Elephants." *Conservation Biology* 22:6 (December 2008): 1590–1599.

Goldsmith, Timothy. *Biological Roots of Human Nature*. New York, NY: Oxford University Press, 1991.

Grau, Christopher. "Love and History." *The Southern Journal of Philosophy* 48:3 (September 2010): 246–271.

Graupner, A. "āsāb." *Theological Dictionary of the Old Testament*. Vol. 11. Edited by G. Johannes Botterweck, Helmer Ringgren, and Heinz-Josef Fabry. Grand Rapids, MI: Eerdmans, 2001.

Gregersen, Niels H. "The Cross of Christ in an Evolutionary World." *dialog* 40:3 (Fall 2001): 192–207.

————. "Special Divine Action and the Quilt of Laws: Why the Distinction between Special and General Divine Action Cannot Be Maintained." In *Scientific Perspectives on Divine Action: Twenty Years of Challenge and Progress*. Edited by Robert J. Russell, Nancey Murphy, and William R. Stoeger, S. J., 179–199. Vatican City and Berkeley, CA: Vatican Observatory, CTNS, 2008.

Griffin, David R. "Creation Out of Chaos and the Problem of Evil." In *Encountering Evil: Live Options in Theodicy*. Edited by Stephen T. Davis, 101–136. Edinburgh: T & T Clark, 1981.

————. "Process Theology and the Christian Good News: A Response to Classical Free Will Theism." In *Searching for an Adequate God: A Dialogue between Process and Free Will Theists*. Edited by John B. Cobb Jr. and Clark H. Pinnock, 1–38. Grand Rapids, MI: Eerdmans, 2000.

Griffiths, Paul J. "What Remains in the Resurrection? A (Broadly) Thomist Argument for the Presence of Nonrational Animals in Heaven." Delivered at Blackfriars, Cambridge, 31 January 2013.

———— "Impossible Pluralism." *First Things* (June/July 2013): 44–48.

————. "Goods from Evils." *First Things* (October 2013): 14.

Gunkel, Hermann. *Genesis*. Translated by Mark E. Biddle. Macon, GA: Mercer University, 1997.

Gunton, Colin E. *The Triune Creator: A Historical and Systematic Study*. Grand Rapids, MI: Eerdmans, 1998.

Habel, Norman. *The Birth, the Curse and the Greening of the Earth: An Ecological Reading of Genesis 1–11*. Sheffield: Sheffield Phoenix, 2011.

Hahne, Harry A. "The Birth Pangs of Creation, The Eschatological Transformation of the Natural World in Romans 8:19–22." Paper presented at the annual meeting of the Evangelical Theological Society, November 1999. Accessed 18 September 2013. Online: www.balboa-software.com/hahne/ BirthPangs.pdf.

———— *The Corruption and Redemption of Creation: Nature in Romans 8:19–22 and Jewish Apocalyptic Literature*. London: T & T Clark, 2006.

Harris, Mark. " 'Let the floods clap their hands; let the hills sing together for joy' (Ps.98:8): Is Joy the Theological and Emotional Shaper of the Inanimate World?" Accessed 22 August 2017. Online: www.academia.edu/6981351/_Let_the_floods_clap_their_hands_let_the_hills_sing_together_for_joy_Ps.98_8_Is_joy_the_theological_and_emotional_shaper_of_the_inanimate_world.

Hart, David Bentley. "No Shadow of Turning: On Divine Impassibility." *Ecclesia* 11:2 (Spring 2002): 184–206.

————. *The Beauty of the Infinite: The Aesthetics of Christian Truth*. Grand Rapids, MI: Eerdmans, 2003.

————. *The Doors of the Sea: Where Was God in the Tsunami?* Grand Rapids, MI: Eerdmans, 2005.

Hartshorne, Charles. *Omnipotence and Other Theological Mistakes*. Albany, NY: State University of New York, 1984.

Hasker, William. "An Adequate God." In *Searching for an Adequate God: A Dialogue between Process and Free Will Theists*. Edited by John B. Cobb Jr. and Clark H. Pinnock, 215–245. Grand Rapids, MI: Eerdmans, 2000.

————. *Providence, Evil and the Openness of God*. London: Routledge, 2004.

Hasker, William, Thomas Jay Oord, and Dean Zimmerman, eds. *God in an Open Universe: Science, Metaphysics, and Open Theism*. Eugene, OR: Pickwick, 2011.

Haught, John F. *The Promise of Nature: Ecology and Cosmic Purpose*. Mahwah, NJ: Paulist Press, 1993.

————. *God After Darwin: A Theology of Evolution.* Boulder, CO: Westview, 2000.

————. *Deeper Than Darwin: The Prospect for Religion in the Age of Evolution.* Boulder, CO: Westview, 2003.

————. "The Boyle Lecture 2003: Darwin, Design and the Promise of Nature." *Science and Christian Belief* 17 (2005): 5–20.

Hayes, Katherine M. *"The Earth Mourns": Prophetic Metaphor and Oral Aesthetic.* Academia Biblica 8. Leidin: Koninklijke Brill, 2002.

Hebblethwaite, Brian L. "Providence and Divine Action." *Religious Studies* 14:2 (June 1978): 223–236.

————. *The Incarnation: Collected Essays in Christology.* Cambridge: Cambridge University Press, 1987.

Hefner, Philip. "Biological Perspectives on Fall and Original Sin." *Zygon* 28:1 (March 1993): 77–101.

Henry, Granville C. "Does Process Thought Allow Personal Immortality?" *Religious Studies* 31:3 (September 1995): 311–321.

Hick, John. *Evil and the God of Love.* London: HarperCollins, 1966.

————. ed. *The Myth of God Incarnate.* 2nd Edition. London: SCM Press, 2012.

Hill, Jonathan. "Introduction." In *The Metaphysics of the Incarnation.* Edited by Anna Marmodoro and Jonathan Hill, 1–19. Oxford: Oxford University Press, 2011.

Hoggard Creegan, Nicola. *Animal Suffering and the Problem of Evil.* Oxford: Oxford University Press, 2013.

Hopkins, Gerard Manley. *Poems and Prose.* London: Penguin, 1953, 1963.

Horrell, David G. *The Bible and Environment: Towards a Critical Ecological Biblical Theology.* London: Equinox, 2010.

Horrell, David G., Cherryl Hunt, and Christopher Southgate. *Greening Paul: Rereading the Apostle in a Time of Ecological Crisis.* Waco, TX: Baylor University, 2010.

Howard-Snyder, Daniel. "The Argument from Inscrutable Evil." In *The Evidential Argument from Evil.* Edited by Daniel Howard-Snyder, 286–310. Bloomington, IN: Indiana University Press, 1996.

Hunt, Cherryl, David F. Horrell, and Christopher Southgate. "An Environmental Mantra? Ecological Interest in Romans 8:19–23 and a Modest Proposal for Its Narrative Interpretation." *Journal of Theological Studies* 59:2 (October 2008): 546–579.

Jablonka, Eva, Marion J. Lamb, and Anna Zeligowski. *Evolution in Four Dimensions: Genetic, Epigenetic, Behavioral, and Symbolic Variation in the History of Life.* Revised Edition. Cambridge, MA: MIT Press, 2014.

Jantzen, Grace M. *God's World, God's Body.* London: Darton, Longman & Todd, 1984.

Jeanrond, Werner. *A Theology of Love.* London: T & T Clark, 2010.

Jenson, Robert W. *Systematic Theology.* Vol. 1 of *The Triune God.* Oxford: Oxford University Press, 1997.

Johnson, Elizabeth. *Ask the Beasts: Darwin and the God of Love.* London: Bloomsbury, 2014.

Jordan, Jeff. "Divine Love and Human Suffering." *International Journal for Philosophy of Religion* 56 (2004): 169–178.

Kaiser, Otto. *Isaiah 13–39: A Commentary.* Translated by R. A. Wilson. Philadelphia, PA: Westminster, 1974.

Käsemann, Ernst. *Commentary on Romans.* Translated by Geoffrey W. Bromiley. Grand Rapids, MI: Eerdmans, 1980.

Kasper, Walter. *The God of Jesus Christ: New Edition.* New York, NY: Continuum, 2012.

Kaufman, Gordon D. "On the Meaning of 'Act of God'." *Harvard Theological Review* 61 (1968): 175–201.

Kennett, Jeanette. "True and Proper Selves: Velleman on Love." *Ethics* 118:2 (January 200): 213–227.

Klein, Allison, Tyler Grant, Adam Finkelstein, and Michael F. Cohen. "Video Mosaics." *NPAR 2002: Second International Symposium on Non Photorealistic Rendering* (June 2002): 21–28.

Knight, Christopher. "Divine Action: A Neo-Byzantine Model." *International Journal for Philosophy of Religion* 58 (2005): 181–199.

Kolodny, Niko. "Love as Valuing a Relationship." *The Philosophical Review* 112:2 (April 2003): 135–189.

Koperski, Jeffrey. "God, Chaos, and the Quantum Dice." *Zygon* 35:3 (September 2000): 545–559.

Kramer, Kenneth. *World Scriptures: An Introduction to Comparative Religions.* Mahwah, NJ: Paulist Press, 1986.

Kraut, Robert. "Love *De Re.*" *Midwest Studies in Philosophy* 10 (1986): 413–430.

Lamoureux, Denis. *Evolutionary Creation: A Christian Approach to Evolution.* Eugene, OR: Wipf & Stock, 2008.

Lane, Anthony N. S. "Lust: The Human Person as Affected by Disordered Desires." *Evangelical Quarterly* 78:1 (2006): 21-35.

Leslie, John. *Universes.* New York, NY: Routledge, 1989.

Levenson, Jon D. *Creation and the Persistence of Evil: The Jewish Drama of Omnipotence.* Princeton, NJ: Princeton University, 1994.

Lewis, Clive S. *The Problem of Pain.* New York, NY: HarperCollins, 1940, 1996.

Linzey, Andrew. *Animal Theology.* London: SCM Press, 1994.

———. "Good News for the World?" *Third Way* 26:6 (2000): 23–25.

Lloyd, Michael. "The Cosmic Fall and the Free Will Defence." Ph.D. Dissertation. Worcester College, University of Oxford, 1996.

———. "Are Animals Fallen?" In *Animals on the Agenda.* Edited by Andrew Linzey and Dorothy Yamamoto, 147–160. London: SCM Press, 1998.

London, Jack. *Call of the Wild.* London: Macmillan, 1903.

Margulis, Lynn and Dorion Sagan. "The Role of Symbiogenesis in Evolution." In *Back to Darwin: A Richer Account of Evolution.* Edited by John B. Cobb Jr., 176–184. Grand Rapids, MI: Eerdmans, 2008.

McCarthy, Dennis. " 'Creation' Motifs in Ancient Hebrew Poetry." *Catholic Biblical Quarterly* 29 (1967): 393–406.

McDaniel, Jay B. *Of God and Pelicans: A Theology of Reverence for Life.* Louisville, KY: Westminster John Knox Press, 1989.

McFague, Sallie. *The Body of God: An Ecological Theology.* London: SCM Press, 1993.

McGrath, Alister E. *Science & Religion: A New Introduction.* 2nd Edition. Oxford: Wiley-Blackwell, 2010.

———. *Historical Theology: An Introduction to the History of Christian Thought.* 2nd Edition. Oxford: John Wiley & Sons, 2013.

Merricks, Trenton. "The Word Made Flesh: Dualism, Physicalism, and the Incarnation." In *Persons Human and Divine.* Edited by Peter van Inwagen and Dean Zimmerman, 281–300. Oxford: Oxford University Press, 2007.

Merton, Thomas. *No Man Is an Island.* Tunbridge Wells: Burns & Oats, 1955.

Messer, Neil. "Natural Evil after Darwin." In *Theology after Darwin.* Edited by Michael S. Northcott and R. J. Berry, 139–154. Milton Keynes, UK: Paternoster, 2009.

Meyers, C. "asab." *Theological Dictionary of the Old Testament.* Vol. 11. Edited by G. Johannes Botterweck, Helmer Ringgren, and Heinz-Josef Fabry. Grand Rapids, MI: Eerdmans, 2001.

Midgely, Mary. *Beast and Man*. New York, NY: Routledge, 1978.

Miles, Sara Joan. "Charles Darwin and Asa Gray Discuss Teleology and Design." *Perspectives on Science and Christian Faith* 53:3 (2001): 196–201.

Miller, Kenneth. *Finding Darwin's God: A Scientist's Search for Common Ground Between God and Evolution*. New York, NY: HarperCollins, 1999.

Moltmann, Jürgen. *God in Creation: A New Theology of Creation and the Spirit of God*. Translated by Margaret Kohl. Minneapolis, MN: Fortress Press, 1993.

———. *The Coming of God: Christian Eschatology*. Translated by Margaret Kohl. London: SCM Press, 1996.

———. "God's Kenosis in the Creation and Consummation of the World." In *The Work of Love: Creation as Kenosis*. Edited by John Polkinghorne, 137–151. Grand Rapids, MI: Eerdmans, 2001.

Moo, Douglas J. *Epistle to the Romans*. Grand Rapids, MI: Eerdmans, 1996.

Moo, Jonathan. "Romans 8:19–22 and Isaiah's Cosmic Covenant." *New Testament Studies* 54:1 (2008): 74–89.

Moritz, Joshua. "Evolution, the End of Human Uniqueness, and the Election of the Imago Dei." *Theology & Science* 9:3 (2011): 307–339.

Mühling-Schlapkohl, Markus. "Why Does the Risen Christ Have Scars? Why God Did Not Immediately Create the Eschaton: Goodness, Truth and Beauty." *International Journal of Systematic Theology* 6:2 (April 2004): 185–193.

Murphy, Nancey. "Divine Action in the Natural Order: Buridan's Ass and Schrödinger's Cat." In *Chaos and Complexity: Scientific Perspectives on Divine Action*. Edited by Robert Russell, Nancey Murphy, and Arthur Peacocke, 325–358. Vatican City and Berkeley, CA: Vatican Observatory, CTNS, 1995.

———. "Science and the Problem of Evil: Suffering as a By-Product of a Finely Turned Cosmos." In *Physics and Cosmology: Scientific Perspectives on the Problem of Natural Evil*. Edited by Robert John Russell, and William R. Stoeger, S. J., 131–152. Vatican City and Berkeley, CA: Vatican Observatory, CTNS, 2007.

Murphy, Nancey, Robert John Russell, and William R. Stoeger, S. J., eds. *Physics and Cosmology: Scientific Perspectives on the Problem of Natural Evil*. Vatican City and Berkeley, CA: Vatican Observatory, CTNS, 2007.

Murray, Michael J. *Nature Red in Tooth and Claw: Theism and the Problem of Animal Suffering*. Oxford: Oxford University Press, 2008.

National Research Council Committee on Recognition and Alleviation of Pain in Laboratory Animals. *Recognition and Alleviation of Pain in Laboratory Animals*. Washington, DC: National Academies Press, 2009. Online: www.ncbi.nlm.nih.gov/books/NBK32655/.

Niditch, Susan. *Chaos to Cosmos: Studies in Biblical Patterns of Creation*. Chico, CA: Scholars Press, 1985.

Nowak, Martin A. "Evolving Cooperation." *Journal of Theoretical Biology* 299 (2012): 1–8.

Nowak, Martin A. and Roger Highfield. *Supercooperators: Altruism, Evolution, and Why We Need Each Other to Succeed*. New York, NY: Free Press, 2011.

Nowak, Martin A. and Sarah Coakley. *Evolution, Games, and God: The Principle of Cooperation*. Cambridge, MA: Harvard University Press, 2013.

Nygren, Anders. *Agape and Eros*. Translated by Philip S. Watson. New York, NY: Harper & Row, 1953.

Oord, Thomas Jay. "An Open Theology Doctrine of Creation and Solution to the Problem of Evil." In *Creation Made Free: Open Theology Engaging Science*. Edited by Thomas J. Oord, 28–52. Eugene, OR: Wipf & Stock, 2009.

———. *The Nature of Love: A Theology*. Atlanta, GA: Chalice Press, 2010a.

———. *Defining Love: A Philosophical, Scientific, and Theological Engagement*. Grand Rapids, MI: Brazos, 2010b.

———. *The Uncontrolling Love of God: An Open and Relational Account of Providence*. Downers Grove, IL: IVP Academic, 2015.

Padgett, Alan G. "God and Miracle in an Age of Science." In *The Blackwell Companion to Science and Christianity*. Edited by J. B. Stump and Alan G. Padgett, 533–542. Oxford: Wiley-Blackwell, 2012.

Page, Ruth. *God and the Web of Creation*. London: SCM Press, 1996.

Pannenberg, Wolfhart. *Systematic Theology*. Vol. 2. Translated by Geoffrey W. Bromiley. Edinburgh: T & T Clark, 1994.

Parmelee, David F. *Bird Island in Antarctic Waters*. Minneapolis, MN: University of Minnesota Press, 1980.

Peacocke, Arthur. *Creation and the World of Science: The Bampton Lectures, 1978*. Oxford: Clarendon Press, 1979.

———. *Theology for a Scientific Age: Being and Becoming – Natural, Divine, and Human*. Enlarged Edition. London: SCM Press, 1990, 1993.

———. *Paths from Science Towards God*. Oxford: Oneworld, 2001a.

———. "The Cost of a New Life." In *The Work of Love: Creation as Kenosis*. Edited by John Polkinghorne, 21–42. Grand Rapids, MI: Eerdmans, 2001b.

———. "Some Reflections on 'Scientific Perspectives on Divine Action'." In *Scientific Perspectives on Divine Action: Twenty Years of Challenge and Progress*. Edited by Robert J. Russell, Nancey Murphy, and William R. Stoeger, S. J., 201–223. Vatican City and Berkeley, CA: Vatican Observatory, CTNS, 2008.

Peters, Ted and Martinez Hewlett. *Evolution from Creation to New Creation: Conflict, Conversation, and Convergence*. Nashville, TN: Abingdon, 2003.

Pinnock, Clark. "Systematic Theology." In *The Openness of God: A Biblical Challenge to the Traditional Understanding of God*. Edited by Clark Pinnock, Richard Rice, John Sanders, William Hasker, and David Bassinger, 101–125. Downer's Grove, IL: InterVarsity, 1994.

———. *Most Moved Mover: A Theology of God's Openness*. Grand Rapids, MI: Baker Academic, 2001.

Pinnock, Clark, Richard Rice, John Sanders, William Hasker and David Bassinger, eds. *The Openness of God: A Biblical Challenge to the Traditional Understanding of God*. Downers Grove, IL: InterVarsity, 1994.

Planet Earth. "Jungles." episode 8, originally aired 19 November 2006.

Plantinga, Alvin. *God, Freedom and Evil*. Grand Rapids, MI: Eerdmans, 1977.

Polkinghorne, John. *Science and Providence: God's Interaction with the World*. London: SPCK, 1989, 2005.

———. *Science and Christian Belief: Theological Reflections of a Bottom-Up Thinker*. London: SPCK, 1994.

———. *Science & Theology: An Introduction*. London: SPCK, 1998.

———. "Physical Process, Quantum Events, and Divine Agency." In *Quantum Mechanics: Scientific Perspectives on Divine Action*. Edited by Robert Russell, Philip Clayton, Kirk Wegter-McNelly, and John Polkinghorne, 181–190. Vatican City and Berkeley, CA: Vatican Observatory, CTNS, 2001a.

———. ed. *The Work of Love: Creation as Kenosis*. Grand Rapids, MI: Eerdmans, 2001b.

———. "Kenotic Creation and Divine Action." In *The Work of Love: Creation as Kenosis*. Edited by John Polkinghorne, 90–106. Grand Rapids, MI: Eerdmans, 2001c.

————. *The God of Hope and the End of the World*. New Haven, CT: Yale University Press, 2002.

————. *Science and the Trinity: The Christian Encounter with Reality*. New Haven, CT: Yale University Press, 2004.

Pribram, Karl. "A Review of Theory in Physiological Psychology." *Annual Review of Psychology* 111:1 (1960): 1–40.

Provan, Iain. "Pain in Childbirth? Further Thoughts on 'An Attractive Fragment' (1 Chronicles 4:9–10)." In *Let Us Go Up to Zion: Essays in Honour of H.G.M. Williamson on the Occasion of His Sixty-Fifth Birthday*. Supplements to *Vetus Testamentum 153*. Edited by Iain Provan and Mark Boda, 285–296. Leiden: Brill, 2012.

Quinn, Thomas P. *The Behavior and Ecology of Pacific Salmon and Trout*. Seattle, WA: University of Washington Press, 2005.

Ratzinger, Cardinal Joseph. *'In The Beginning. . . ': a Catholic Understanding of the Story of Creation and the Fall*. Translated by Boniface Ramsey, O. P. Grand Rapids, MI: Eerdmans, 1990.

Rees, Martin. *Just Six Numbers: The Deep Forces That Shape the Universe*. London: Weidenfeld & Nicolson, 1999.

Regan, Tom. *The Case for Animal Rights*. Berkeley, CA: University of California Press, 2004.

Renne, Paul R., Alan L. Deino, Frederik J. Hilgen, Klaudia F. Kuiper, Darren F. Mark, William S. Mitchell III, Leah E. Morgan, Roland Mundil, and Jan Smit. "Time Scales of Critical Events Around the Cretaceous-Paleogene Boundary." *Science* 339 (February 2013): 684–687.

Rissler, James D. "Open Theism: Does God Risk or Hope?" *Religious Studies* 42 (2006): 63–74.

Ritchie, Sarah Lane. "Dancing Around the Causal Joint: Challenging the Theological Turn in Divine Action Theories." *Zygon* 53:2 (June 2017): 361–379.

Roedell, Christopher. "The Beasts That Perish: The Problem of Evil and the Contemplation of the Animal Kingdom in English Thought, c. 1660–1839." Ph.D. Dissertation. Georgetown University, 2005. UMI Number: 3193309.

Rolston III, Holmes. "Does Nature Need to Be Redeemed?" *Zygon* 29:2 (June 1994): 205–229.

————. "Kenosis and Nature." In *The Work of Love: Creation as Kenosis*. Edited by John Polkinghorne, 43–65. Grand Rapids, MI: Eerdmans, 2001.

————. "Naturalizing and Systematizing Evil." In *Is Nature Ever Evil? Religion, Science and Value*. Edited by Willem B. Drees, 67–86. London: Routledge, 2003.

————. *Science and Religion: A Critical Survey*. 2nd Edition. West Conschohocken, PA: Templeton Foundation Press, 2006.

————. *A New Environmental Ethics: The Next Millennium for Life on Earth*. New York, NY: Routledge, 2012.

Rowe, William. "The Problem of Evil and Some Varieties of Atheism." *American Philosophical Quarterly* 16:4 (October 1979): 335–341.

Rupke, Nicolaas A. *Vivisection in Historical Perspective*. London: Francis & Taylor, 1987.

Ruse, Michael. "The Relationship between Science and Religion in Britain, 1830–1870." *Church History* 44:4 (December 1975): 505–522.

Russell, Robert J. "Does 'The God Who Acts' Really Act? New Approaches to Divine Action in Light of Science." *Theology Today* 54:1 (April 1997): 43–65.

————. "Divine Action and Quantum Mechanics: A Fresh Assessment." In *Quantum Mechanics: Scientific Perspectives on Divine Action*. Edited by Robert Russell, Philip

Clayton, Kirk Wegter-McNelly, and John Polkinghorne, 293–328. Vatican City and Berkeley, CA: Vatican Observatory, CTNS, 2001.

———. "Natural Theodicy in Evolutionary Context: The Need for an Eschatology of New Creation." In *Theodicy and Eschatology*. Edited by Bruce Barber and David Neville, 121–152. Hindmarsh, Australia: ATF, 2005.

———. "Physics, Cosmology, and the Challenge to Consequentialist Natural Theodicy." In *Physics and Cosmology: Scientific Perspectives on the Problem of Natural Evil*. Edited by Nancey Murphy, Robert Russell, and William R. Stoeger, S. J., 109–130. Vatican City and Berkeley, CA: Vatican Observatory, CTNS, 2007.

———. "The Groaning of Creation: Does God Suffer with All Life?" In *The Evolution of Evil*. Edited by Gaymon Bennett, Martinez J. Hewlett, Ted Peters, and Robert John Russell, 120-140. Göttingen: Vandenhoeck & Ruprecht, 2008).

Russell, Robert J., Philip Clayton, Kirk Wegter-McNelly, and John Polkinghorne, eds. *Quantum Mechanics: Scientific Perspectives on Divine Action*. Vol. 5. Vatican City and Berkeley, CA: Vatican Observatory, CTNS, 2001.

Russell, Robert J., Nancey Murphy, and William R. Stoeger, S. J., eds. *Scientific Perspectives on Divine Action: Twenty Years of Challenge and Progress*. Vatican City and Berkeley, CA: Vatican Observatory, CTNS, 2008.

Russell, Robert J., William R. Stoeger, S. J., and Francisco J. Ayala, eds. *Evolutionary and Molecular Biology: Scientific Perspectives on Divine Action*. Vol. 3. Vatican City and Berkeley, CA: Vatican Observatory, CTNS, 1998.

Sagan (Margulis), Lynn. "On the Origin of Mitosing Cells." *Journal of Theoretical Biology* 14 (1967): 225–274.

Sanders, John. *The God Who Risks: A Theology of Divine Providence*. 2nd Edition. Downers Grove, IL: IVP Academic, 2007.

Sansbury, Timothy. "The False Promise of Quantum Mechanics." *Zygon* 42:1 (March 2007): 111–121.

Saunders, Nicholas. *Divine Action & Modern Science*. Cambridge: Cambridge University Press, 2002.

Scharbert, J. "qll." *Theological Dictionary of the Old Testament*. Vol. 13. Edited by G. Johannes Botterweck, Helmer Ringgren, and Heinz-Josef Fabry. Grand Rapids, MI: Eerdmans, 2001.

Schreiner, Thomas R. *Romans*. Baker Exegetical Commentary on the New Testament 6. Grand Rapids, MI: Baker Academic, 1998.

Settle, Tom. "The Dressage Ring and the Ballroom: Loci of Double Agency." In *Facets of Faith and Science*. Vol. 4. *Interpreting God's Action in the World*. Edited by Jitse van der Meer, 17–40. Lanham, MD: University Press of America, 1996.

Sideris, Lisa. "Writing Straight with Crooked Lines: Holmes Rolston's Ecological Theology and Theodicy." In *Nature, Value, Duty: Life on Earth with Holmes Rolston, III*. Edited by Christopher J. Preston and Wayne Ouderkirk, 77–101. Dordrecht, Netherlands: Springer, 2007.

Siebert, Charles. "Orphans No More." *National Geographic* 220:3 (2011): 40–65.

Smith, James K. A. "Is the Universe Open for Surprise? Pentecostal Ontology and the Spirit of Naturalism." *Zygon* 43 (2008): 879–896.

Sollereder, Bethany. "Evolutionary Theodicy: Towards an Evangelical Perspective." MCS Thesis. Regent College, 2007.

———. "The Darwin-Gray Exchange." *Theology and Science* 8:4 (2010): 417–432.

———. "The Purpose of Dinosaurs: Extinction and the Goodness of God." *The Christian Century* 130:20 (October 2013). Online: www.christiancentury.org/article/2013-09/purpose-dinosaurs.

————. "From Suffering to Love: Evolution and the Problem of Suffering." *The Christian Century* 131:19 (September 2014). Online: www.christiancentury.org/article/2014-08/survival-love.

————. "When Humans Are Not Unique: Perspectives on Suffering and Redemption." *The Expository Times* 127:1 (2015a): 17–22.

————. "A Modest Objection: Neo-Thomism and God as a Cause Among Causes." *Theology & Science* 13:3 (2015b): 345–353.

Solomon, Andrew. *Far from the Tree: A Dozen Kinds of Love*. London: Chatto & Windus, 2013.

Sommer, Benjamin D. *The Bodies of God and the World of Ancient Israel*. Cambridge: Cambridge University Press, 2009.

Southgate, Christopher. *The Groaning of Creation: God, Evolution, and the Problem of Evil*. Louisville, KY: Westminster John Knox Press, 2008.

————*God, Humanity and the Cosmos: A Textbook in Science and Religion*. 3rd Edition. London: T & T Clark, 2011a.

————. "A Test Case: Divine Action." In *God, Humanity and the Cosmos: A Textbook in Science and Religion*. 3rd Edition. Edited by Christopher Southgate, 274–312. London: T & T Clark, 2011b.

————. "Re-Reading Genesis, John, and Job: A Christian Response to Darwinism." *Zygon* 46:2 (June 2011c): 370–395.

————. "Review of *The End of Christianity* by William A. Dembski." *Reviews in Science and Religion* 60 (November 2012): 43.

————. "Review of *The Predicament of Belief* by Philip Clayton and Steven Knapp." *Religious Studies* 49:1 (March 2013): 125–130.

————. "Does God's Care Make Any Difference? Theological Reflections on the Suffering of God's Creatures." In *Christian Faith and the Earth: Current Paths and Emerging Horizons in Ecotheology*. Edited by Ernst M. Conradie, Sigurd Bermann, Celia Deane-Drummond, and Denis Edwards, 97–114. London: T & T Clark, 2014.

————. *New Thought on Humans Created in the Image and Likeness of God*. ISSR Conference presentation, Vienna 27–29 August 2015.

————. "Cosmic Evolution and Evil." In *The Cambridge Companion to the Problem of Evil*. Edited by Chad Meister and Paul K. Moser, 147-164. Cambridge: Cambridge University Press, 2017.

Southgate, Christopher and Andrew Robinson. "Varieties of Theodicy: An Exploration of Responses to the Problem of Evil Based on a Typology of Good-Harm Analyses." In *Physics and Cosmology: Scientific Perspectives on the Problem of Natural Evil*. Edited by Nancey Murphy, Robert J. Russell, and William R. Stoeger, S. J., 67–90. Vatican City and Berkeley, CA: Vatican Observatory, CTNS, 2007.

Stoeger, S. J., William R. "Conceiving Divine Action in a Dynamic Universe." In *Scientific Perspectives on Divine Action: Twenty Years of Challenge and Progress*. Edited by Robert J. Russell, Nancey Murphy, and William R. Stoeger, S. J., 225–247. Vatican City and Berkeley, CA: Vatican Observatory, CTNS, 2008.

————. "The Big Bang, Quantum Cosmology and *creatio ex nihilo*." In *Creation and the God of Abraham*. Edited by David B. Burrell, Carlo Cogliati, Janet M. Soskice, and William R. Stoeger, S. J., 152–175. Cambridge: Cambridge University Press, 2010.

Stump, Eleonore. "The Mirror of Evil." In *God and the Philosophers*. Edited by Thomas Morris, 235–247. Oxford: Oxford University Press, 1994.

————. "Love by All Accounts." *Proceedings and Addresses of the American Philosophical Association* 80:2 (November 2006): 25–43.

————. *Wandering in Darkness: Narrative and the Problem of Suffering*. Oxford: Clarendon Press, 2010.

Surin, Kenneth. *Theology and the Problem of Evil*. Oxford: Basil Blackwell, 1986.

Swinburne, Richard. *Providence and the Problem of Evil*. Oxford: Clarendon Press, 1996.

Swinton, John. *Dementia: Living in the Memories of God*. Grand Rapids, MI: Eerdmans, 2012.

Taylor, Gabriele. "Love." *Proceedings of the Aristotelian Society* 76 (1975–76): 147–164.

Tegmark, Max. "Is 'the theory of everything' Merely the Ultimate Ensemble Theory?" *Annals of Physics* 270 (1998): 1–51.

Toner, Jules J. *The Experience of Love*. Washington, DC: Corpus Book, 1968.

Torrance, Alan. "Is There a Distinctive Human Nature? Approaching the Question from a Christian Epistemic Base." *Zygon* 47:4 (December 2012): 903–917.

Tracy, Thomas F. "Particular Providence and the God of the Gaps." In *Chaos and Complexity: Scientific Perspectives on Divine Action*. Edited by Robert Russell, Nancey Murphy, and Arthur Peacocke, 289–324. Vatican City and Berkeley, CA: Vatican Observatory, CTNS, 1995.

———. "Creation, Providence, and Quantum Chance." In *Quantum Mechanics: Scientific Perspectives on Divine Action*. Edited by Robert Russell, Philip Clayton, Kirk Wegter-McNelly, and John Polkinghorne, 235–258. Vatican City and Berkeley, CA: Vatican Observatory, CTNS, 2001.

———. "The Lawfulness of Nature and the Problem of Evil." In *Physics and Cosmology: Scientific Perspectives on the Problem of Natural Evil*. Edited by Nancey Murphy, Robert Russell, and William R. Stoeger, S. J., 153–178. Vatican City and Berkeley, CA: Vatican Observatory, CTNS, 2007.

Tsumura, David. *Creation and Destruction: A reappraisal of the Chaoskampf Theory in the Old Testament*. Winona Lake, IN: Eisenbrauns, 2005.

van Inwagen, Peter, ed. *Christian Faith and the Problem of Evil*. Grand Rapids, MI: Eerdmans, 2004.

———. *The Problem of Evil: The Gifford Lectures Delivered in the University of St. Andrews in 2003*. Oxford: Clarendon Press, 2006.

Van Slyke, James A. "Cognitive and Evolutionary Factors in the Emergence of Human Altruism." *Zygon* 45:4 (December 2010): 841–859.

Vanstone, W. H. *Love's Endeavour, Love's Expense: The Response of Being to the Love of God*. London: Darton, Longman & Todd, 1977.

van Wolde, Ellen. *Stories of the Beginning: Genesis 1–11 and Other Creation Stories*. Translated by John Bowden. London: SCM Press, 1996.

———. "Facing the Earth: Primaeval History in a New Perspective." In *The World of Genesis: Persons, Places, Perspectives*. Edited by Philip R. Davies. Sheffield: Sheffield Academic, 1998.

Velleman, J. David. "Love as a Moral Emotion." *Ethics* 109:2 (January 1999): 338–378.

von Rad, Gerhard. *Genesis: A Commentary*. London: SCM Press, 1961.

Walton, John H. *The Lost World of Genesis One: Ancient Cosmology and the Origins Debate*. Downer's Grove, IL: InterVarsity, 2009.

Ward, Keith. *Divine Action*. London: HarperCollins, 1990.

———. *Religion and Creation*. Oxford: Oxford University Press, 1996.

Ward, Peter and Donald Brownlee. *Rare Earth: Why Complex Life Is Uncommon in the Universe*. New York, NY: Copernicus, 2004.

Watson, Rebecca S. *Chaos Uncreated: A Reassessment of the Themes of "Chaos" in the Hebrew Bible*. New York, NY: Walter de Gruyter, 2005.

Webb, Clement C. J. *Problems in the Relations of God and Man*. London: James Nisbet & Co, 1911.

Webb, Stephen H. *The Dome of Eden: A New Solution to the Problem of Creation and Evolution.* Eugene, OR: Cascade, 2010.

Wegter-McNelly, Kirk. "Does God Need Room to Act? Theo-Physical in/Compatibilism in Noninterventionist Theories of Objectively Special Divine Action." In *Scientific Perspectives on Divine Action: Twenty Years of Challenge and Progress.* Edited by Robert J. Russell, Nancey Murphy, and William R. Stoeger, S. J., 299–314. Vatican City and Berkeley, CA: Vatican Observatory, CTNS, 2008.

Weinandy, Thomas G. "God and Human Suffering: His Act of Creation and His Acts in History." In *Divine Impassibility and the Mystery of Human Suffering.* Edited by James F. Keating and Thomas J. White, O. P., 99–116. Grand Rapids, MI: Eerdmans, 2009.

Wenham, Gordon J. *Genesis 1–15.* Word Biblical Commentary 1. Nashville, TN: Thomas Nelson, 1987.

Wesley, John. "The General Deliverance: Sermon 60." Accessed 18 October 2013. Online: http://wesley.nnu.edu/john-wesley/the-sermons-of-john-wesley-1872-edition/sermon-60-the-general-deliverance/.

White, Vernon. *The Fall of a Sparrow: The Concept of Special Divine Action.* Exeter: Paternoster, 1985.

———. *Atonement and Incarnation: An Essay in Universalism and Particularity.* Cambridge: Cambridge University Press, 1991.

Whitney, Barry L. *Theodicy: An Annotated Bibliography on the Problem of Evil 1960–1991.* Bowling Green, OH: Bowling Green State University Philosophy, 1998.

Wildman, Wesley J. "The Divine Action Project, 1998–2003." *Theology and Science* 2:1 (2004): 31–75.

———. "Incongruous Goodness, Perilous Beauty, Disconcerting Truth: Ultimate Reality and Suffering in Nature." In *Physics and Cosmology: Scientific Perspectives on the Problem of Natural Evil.* Edited by Nancey Murphy, Robert Russell, and William R. Stoeger S. J., 267–294. Vatican City and Berkeley, CA: Vatican Observatory, CTNS, 2007.

Wiles, Maurice. *God's Action in the World.* London: SCM Press, 1986.

Wilkinson, Loren. "A Christian Ecology of Death: Biblical Imagery and the 'Ecologic Crisis'." *Christian Scholar's Review* 5:4 (1976): 319–338.

Williams, Margery. *The Velveteen Rabbit: Or, How Toys Become Real.* New York, NY: George H. Doran, 1922.

Williams, N. P. *The Idea of the Fall and of Original Sin.* London: Longmans, Green and Co., 1927.

Williams, Patricia A. "Sociobiology and Original Sin." *Zygon* 35:4 (December 2000): 783–812.

Williams, Sarah C. *The Shaming of the Strong: The Challenge of an Unborn Life.* Vancouver, BC: Regent College, 2007.

Wilson, Jonathan R. *God's Good World: Reclaiming the Doctrine of Creation.* Grand Rapids, MI: Baker Academic, 2013.

Witherington III, Ben. *Paul's Letter to the Romans: A Socio-Rhetorical Commentary.* Grand Rapids, MI: Eerdmans, 2004.

Woodruff, David M. "Presentism and the Problem of Special Relativity." In *God in an Open Universe: Science, Metaphysics, and Open Theism.* Edited by William Hasker, Thomas Jay Oord, and Dean Zimmerman, 94–124. Eugene, OR: Pickwick, 2011.

Wright, Chris. "Theology and Ethics in the Old Testament." *Transformation* 16:3 (1999): 81–86.

Wright, George Frederick. *Studies in Science and Religion*. Andover: Warren F. Draper, 1882.

Yancey, Philip and Paul Brand. *The Gift of Pain*. Grand Rapids, MI: Zondervan, 1997.

Yong, Amos. *The Spirit of Creation: Modern Science and Divine Action in the Pentecostal-Charismatic Imagination*. Grand Rapids, MI: Eerdmans, 2011.

Young, Frances M. *Face to Face: A Narrative Essay in the Theology of Suffering*. Edinburgh: T & T Clark, 1990.

Zhu, M-Y., J. Vannier, H. V. Iten, and Y-L. Zhao. "Direct Evidence for Predation on Trilobites in the Cambrian." *Proceedings of the Royal Society B* 271:5 (August 2004): S277–S289.

Index